Updating Planetary Consciousness

a pathway of hope

Ann Surya

KUMARA PRESS

Text copyright © 2023 by Ann Surya

All rights reserved. No part of this publication may be reproduced, distributed or transmitted in any form or by any means, including photocopying, recording, or other electronic or mechanical methods, without the prior written permission of the publisher, except in the case of brief quotations embodied in critical reviews and certain other noncommercial uses permitted by copyright law. For permission requests, contact the publisher.

Published by Kumara Press, South Australia

www.calloftheheart.net/books

Additional copies of this book are available through the website, together with a searchable library of hundreds of teachings, podcasts, and guided practices (free mp3 downloads) to help you take a conscious journey of heart.

Updating Planetary Consciousness / Ann Surya -- 1st ed.
December 2023, minor revisions February 2024
ISBN 978-0-9751801-2-9

for Ananda

Contents

Preface	ix
Introduction	xiii
Evolution	**1**
The Intent of Evolution	1
Evolutionary Streams on Earth	3
Human Choice & Angels' Flow	6
The Ocean of Love	9
Evolution, Love & Conscious Choice	12
Evolutionary Life on Earth	14
Cosmic Love & Earthly Evolution	17
Love's Drive & Matter's Pull	19
Building Form & Change	22
The Three Stimuli of Conscious Evolution	26
Your Note of Consciousness	29
The Living Evolution of Earth & Angels	32
Our Relationship with Earth	36
Loving Flow with Angels	38
Love's Intent	**43**
Loving Intent in Your Heart	43
The Flow of Cosmic Intent	46
Living Light & Your Choice	49
Love's Touch in Your Heart	52
Doubt & Certainty	55
Our Evolutionary Choice	58
The Three Forces Creating Heart	62

Consciousness — 67

- True Consciousness — 67
- Heart in Your Daily Journey — 70
- The Difference You Make — 74
- The Search for Meaning — 78
- Awakening Consciousness of Your Path — 82
- Heart Intuition & Discernment — 85
- Discerning Emotions — 89
- Certainty, Change & Choosing Light — 93
- Emotions & the Heart Path — 98
- Mind & Wisdom — 101

Earth Consciousness — 107

- The Last Kumara — 107
- Meeting Global Crises with Heart — 112
- The Blood of Humanity & Earth — 116
- Love the Earth — 119
- The Trap of the Absolute — 123
- Discerning Higher Truth — 126
- Creating Change through Heart — 130

Soul — 135

- Expressing Soul on Earth — 135
- Journey of Soul on Earth — 138
- Differentiating Darkness & Evil — 142
- Justice & Sticky Guilt — 147
- Incarnating as Soul — 151
- Involution to Evolution — 154
- Living a Soul Life — 159
- Soul's Loving Embrace — 163
- Our Soul's Flow to Nature & Earth — 167
- Nature's Song & Your Purpose — 172
- Why Loving the Earth Matters — 175
- Conscience through Heart Consciousness — 180
- Love, Care & Peace — 185
- The Full Moon's Grace — 189
- The Soul's Journey — 194

The Human Journey — 199

- Your Heart & Soul Consciousness — 199
- The Human Journey — 203
- The Conscious Journey — 208
- The Great Choice — 212
- The Worlds of Souls & Humans — 217
- Soul & Greater Hearts — 222
- Love & Will in Your Heart — 226
- Christ, Buddha, Greater Hearts & Your Path — 230

Call of the Heart — 235

- Wake to the Call of Your Heart — 235
- The Call of Evolution — 239
- Your Evolutionary Role — 243
- The Resonance of Your Heart — 247
- Aligning Our Conscious Evolutionary Flow — 250
- Angelic Flow & Divine Mother — 254
- The Great Change: Form to Flow — 257

Become Living Light — 262

Responding to the Call of the Heart — 264

- Practices — 264
- Continue Your Journey — 267

Glossary — 268

Index — 279

Preface

I am deeply affected by the adversities we face on Earth today, from the global challenges of climate change, war, environmental destruction and economic inequity, to the social and physical repression, distortion of truth and disadvantage experienced by so many. At the same time, I believe there are reasons for these challenges that go deeper than the superficial splash of news headlines, political debates, social norms and corporate pronouncements. Reasons that give insight into how we can collectively create the positive change we so urgently need. But we can't find and respond to those reasons if we don't understand the system we live within.

We know our world is made up of complex systems ecologically, socially, economically and politically, but where is our understanding of our whole Earth as a living, evolving system in which we have a vital role? We need to update our consciousness and understanding of our purpose and relationship with this beautiful planet.

Most religions and spiritual pathways are human-centric, and certainly the economic world view is. We need a new perspective and a new moral framework to lift humanity out of Earth-ignorance and the destructive actions that come with that, into the consciousness where we understand our role within Earth as a living system. With that understanding, we can become conscious contributors to the great change unfolding around us. That's what this book is about.

I have long sought a deeper perspective in my own life. As a young child I would sink into the embracing branches of a nearby jacaranda tree, seeking insight into my challenges from the vibrant life-force of nature I could see and feel around me. I have always loved and intuitively known the Earth as a beautiful, living being.

My search has continued throughout my life, and I have researched, taught and practiced the ageless wisdom for over 40 years. This wisdom is a non-doctrinal expression of truth that guides spiritual evolution, brought into focus through Helena Blavatsky and Alice Bailey over the last 150 years.

My journey was deeply nourished and inspired by my spiritual teacher Ananda, who taught a new heart-centred approach to this esoteric knowledge, and how to apply it in a life of practical service of Earth healing and personal transformation. She was my dearest friend and I was privileged to work closely with her for 20 years until her passing in 2002. She has remained my deep inner heart teacher, and continually inspires my work and my hopes. She gave me the spiritual name Surya, which brings her love around me.

I have been writing for over 20 years. The way I write has evolved over these years, but always involves my deep inner attunement to the great wealth of wisdom in the inner worlds, and with the great and wise hearts who guide and inspire conscious evolution from there. I tune in deeply through my heart and write what I can access through my consciousness. Sometimes it comes as an ethereal concept, sometimes as a direct dictation, usually somewhere in between. Much of it is new to me. I ask questions and strive to write it in everyday language, because it is so important that the spirituality of the heart can reach everyone. Our global transition will not be a product of the illuminated few, but of the heart-centred many that care and want a better world for all.

The information always comes to me as a spoken flow of words and, if you imagine receiving a stream of words just a few at a time, you will understand that including the right punctuation mid-stream is quite the challenge! I am forever grateful to my beloved husband

Preface

Brenton, who tirelessly edits my work to make it as clear as possible as a written document, while holding true to the intent given in the energy flow of the words. Because of this, however, you will still find quirky expressions in the text. Sometimes you will read 'I' and 'we', which does not refer to me, but to the inner being or beings with whom I am in contact.

I continually check my attunement while writing, and do my best to accurately represent the loving truth I perceive. That said, every spiritual teaching comes through a human being and is necessarily a product of that person's life experience and consciousness, and I am no different. Every spiritual teaching is also contextual, given to meet the needs of the time. Ultimately, you have to be the judge of what resonates in truth for you, and what nourishes your journey.

The teachings in this book are written as short pieces, because they are to stimulate your consciousness, not fill your mind; and also because I can only maintain the intense concentration required for the one to two hours they take to write. There is no intention from where I access this wisdom to write a long treatise, as there is already plenty of knowledge written in this world. It is what we do with the knowledge that matters now: how we let it stir our consciousness, and awaken us to purpose, soul and our living Earth.

Each teaching explores the possibilities and opportunities for conscious development around a particular concept, while not dictating a dogma of knowledge and absolutes. The wisdom of the heart is not a prescriptive doctrine, but a pathway of choices to help you deepen and enrich your consciousness, increase your radiance, and create positive change in our world.

This collection was written over eight months in 2022, and although presented in the order received, they can be read in whatever order your intuition guides. They offer a framework for understanding our conscious journey and responsibilities in this world, including Earth's evolution as a living spiritual system, and new ways of understanding soul, heart and our human experience. Throughout, there are many touch points to help you hear and respond to the call of your own heart, and be nourished by Earth's love.

My greatest hope is that this book will give you hope. Not the emotional hope of wishful thinking, but the undimmable light of hope born in the conscious understanding of life, purpose and community on this beautiful planet. The more we love Earth and this shared journey, the more our hearts shine and hasten our collective awakening and healing. This is how we create a world of love, respect and peace for all.

In love and kindness,

Ann ♡

December 2023

Introduction

Many of us strive to understand how humanity's current crisis has come about and how we must respond to get out of it. This revolutionary collection of inspired notes offers a deeper understanding of the energetic and evolutionary underpinnings of these changing times. It relates the root causes of humanity's current challenges to our evolving personal consciousness, which is embedded within the Earth's consciousness and the purposeful field of the Cosmos.

Based on our understanding gained from this higher and broader perspective, we can choose to respond to the Call of the Heart! Responding to the Call of the Heart requires us to understand consciousness beyond most of society's mainstream thinking, and then to act upon our understanding to connect with our heart and soul, and through them to gain a higher consciousness.

Consciousness

There are no totally agreed theories about consciousness in current science or philosophy – which is where it is discussed, if at all. Nonetheless, in their far-reaching pursuits, some scientists and philosophers have proposed theories about a conscious and purposeful Cosmos that are consistent with the ageless wisdom of more esoteric sages and spiritual traditions.

Consciousness is mostly considered in neuroscience to be some kind of by-product of the functioning of our physical brain: a result of the evolving complexity and accumulation of neurons and their connections – this view is often called 'emergentism'. As yet, there is no accepted explanation of how this happens: how the objective, material brain and subjective, experiential consciousness relate, or even what consciousness is exactly! That is, how do electrical and chemical processes in the physical brain produce our subjective, private and personal feelings, memories, dreams, thoughts, meaning, purpose, etc., which cannot be observed by others? That is not to mention near-death experiences, verified knowledge of past lives, and intuition of events remote in time and space – all of which seem to have no correlation with brain states! In philosophy, this gap of explanation is called 'the hard problem'.

Consciousness has ever been the subject of speculation in philosophy, with 'materialism' or 'identity theory' remaining the frontrunner of possible explanations in a little over 50 percent of relevant academics. As this is the same theory as in neuroscience, philosophers of mind (as the subject is traditionally called) have also had to contend with 'the hard problem' of reconciling the gap between verifiable brain activity and the subjective experience of consciousness.

These material and mental approaches contrast with the less well-known ageless wisdom, as expressed in the more esoteric aspects of many religions (e.g., Buddhism, Islam, and Hinduism, among many others). These tackle consciousness on its own terms, as a given experiential dimension of life, about which much is known and has been taught over millennia. Developing certain qualities of personal consciousness is often a central goal of their more contemplative, spiritual practices. Over the last 50 years, many of these spiritual practices have become popular in Western culture, along with their perspectives on the Cosmos.

Even more revolutionary to our consciousness have been the exponential developments in physics over the last 100 years, which have led to a profound characterisation of the universe as a single expanding entity to which some scientists attribute purposeful consciousness. The previously-assumed mechanistic randomness of the universe has been refuted in quantum theory, astrophysics and cosmology, which have encountered dark matter and black holes in the fabric of the universe that have led to ever more intentional explanations. These concepts challenge our minds because we have been taught to think and speak of reality as consisting of material things made up of solid atoms; whereas this non-

Introduction

visible realm is now known to be extremely powerful and causative in the unfoldment of the universe and of our lives.

Our knowledge and consciousness have been expanded further in the 21st century by the images of deep space by the James Web and Hubble telescopes, revealing literally billions of galaxies and trillions of stars and planets in an incomprehensively vast Cosmos. These images challenge many conventional creation stories and religious cosmologies, at the same time as requiring us to consider more deeply our understanding of humanity's place on Earth and in the Cosmos.

Evolution

Rather than being a by-product of physical evolution by survival of the fittest – as proposed by Charles Darwin in the 19th century – consciousness is increasingly being acknowledged in science as inherent in the energy (or quantum) field in which matter emerges and vanishes as it forms expressions of the evolution of this one underlying, purposeful consciousness. In short, matter emerges as an expression of an evolving consciousness (rather than vice versa) and there is continuous development (or evolution) of this matter towards a particular inherent purpose. The rationale of this approach in quantum theory requires a deep dive into the mathematical basis of physics that is beyond my scope here.

The ageless wisdom has a similar approach, explaining how humanity has emerged from the physical manifestation of the one life out of cosmic night, where there was only un-manifested consciousness. Sparks of consciousness were manifested in order to develop greater consciousness through taking forms in denser levels of being as vehicles for this development. On a physical level, we can imagine atomic particles emerging from waves or higher vibration to amass into viable forms to achieve this development – in humans, animals, planets and stars!

From this perspective, the Earth is a manifested form of consciousness, held and fostered by the Planetary Logos, the being on a higher level of vibration (and consciousness) who holds and guides its development. Then there is the Solar Logos, a being of higher consciousness embodied in the physical Sun, who guides the development of the whole Solar system, receiving energetic and intentful impulses from the central sun of our Cosmos, Sirius. Beyond that, we can assume the manifestation continues in a similar fashion throughout the universe, which is beyond our immediate consideration and comprehension.

Earth

Coming down to Earth, humanity is a form of consciousness developed over millions of years – much longer than everyday history teaches us – that has gone through many phases of development. Originating, as it does, in the one consciousness, it is easy to understand that humanity has an interdependent role with all other forms of the one consciousness on Earth, and with the Earth itself, out of which it was specifically formed.

These revelations stimulate our everyday consciousness to encompass a moral and loving identification with life, nature, and all that exists; they require us to embrace our responsibilities towards all life and Earth itself. However, it has got to be asked: what has happened through this arc of evolutionary development that humanity currently faces an existential crisis greater than any in the past?

It is noteworthy that humanity is a relative late comer to this evolutionary process of Earth and the Cosmos. Even the ageless wisdom assigns only a few million years to humanity's evolution on Earth, which we believe to be some four to six to ten billion years old (depending on who you ask!). A reasonable conclusion from this broader perspective is that Earth did not form and develop just for humanity's sake, with us as some form of overlord, but that we are part of a grander scheme with many other participants of equal significance!

The narcissistic belief of humanity, that we are the crowning purpose of creation, is intertwined with our attachment, exploitation and wish to control the material world – in response to our fears of suffering, misery and death! That we are so self-centred and relatively un-evolved in consciousness in this way underlies our current planetary crisis.

Introduction

Through our arrogant and self-centred attachments, we are directly responsible for the greatest change in the planet since the extinction of the dinosaurs some 65 million years ago (after their living here for some 165 million years!). So it is not just a small change that we face, but a serious threat to our existence and the future of life on Earth as we know it.

Humanity is changing planet Earth at a macro level, depleting irreplaceable resources of minerals, timber, top soil, gas, oil and freshwater, while poisoning all life with its wastes. To make matters worse, unsustainable food production and consumption are significant contributors to greenhouse gas emissions that are causing atmospheric temperatures to rise, wreaking havoc across the globe. The climate crisis is causing everything from severe droughts to more frequent and intense storms. It also exacerbates the challenges associated with food production that stress species, while creating conditions that make their habitats inhospitable.

The interdependent relationships between the food system, climate change, and loss of biodiversity are placing immense pressure on our planet. In short, human activity is driving a mass extinction of species that is estimated at between 1,000 and 10,000 times what would occur if humanity did not exist. While extinctions are a normal and expected part of the evolutionary process, the current rates of decline and extinction of species populations threaten many critical ecological functions that support human life on Earth.

The Human Journey

The irony is that this threat is a direct result of humanity's development of our mental consciousness with its application of science and technology to all aspects of life, producing irreversible changes. This relatively recent phenomenon can be tracked back, perhaps, to the systemisation of science from the 16th century onwards, as humanity sought to improve its physical environment and mitigate the impacts of disease and famine. This material focus had a decided upturn through the industrial age and, more recently, since the Second World War, a mere 80 years ago. For a telling example, now there are well over 150,000 man-made chemicals being produced, increasing at 2,000 per year, with some 700 present in the human body, of which some 400 are known carcinogens.

I am not denying the value of the many scientific and technological inventions that have increased both human life span and its quality – for a small proportion of Earth's population, at least. That was an original application of our evolutionary development of mind, and it has been very successful – to a point. Rather, I am pointing to humanity's lack of balance in evaluating their usage against greater, more inclusive perspectives. Our political, governmental, legal, social, religious, corporate, commercial, economic and education systems do not value, reflect on or consider our presence on planet Earth; nor foster an appropriate moral, spiritual and responsible relationship with its myriad other-than-human aspects. We seek to control every aspect of life by skills and cunning, taking over everything else, and abusing the planet to support an extravagant, greedy and unbalanced human population.

Through this behaviour, we show how humanity is still in the adolescence of its evolution of consciousness, where self-fascination, absorption and gratification blind it to its own greater good and its responsibility to the Earth as a whole. Humanity acts as if we have an unquestionable right to exploit the non-human limitlessly – while blindly believing we will somehow find a way out of the enormous and potentially catastrophic changes we are facing on the total structure of life on Earth.

Our civilisation considers itself the possessor of great wisdom, the pinnacle of human achievement, and allows itself to be dazzled by its own achievements, believing they will continue endlessly into the future. This world view is in contrast to that of many indigenous cultures that have understood how all participants in this Earth's life have rights and dignity, as well as having complex interdependent relationships. They know that humanity is only one form of being, and that we need all others to thrive and to complete the fullness of Earth's life and development. They understand and acknowledge that the ultimate value is the order and purpose of the universe – the totality of creation; and that human exceptionalism is not the right reference point for evaluating our behaviour!

Introduction

While humanity has a particular role in Earth's evolution, it is clear that we have overplayed that role. As a species destined for self-awareness, we seem to have gotten side-tracked, and entered a developmental cul-de-sac: a crisis that will necessarily (and hopefully) bring us back into greater alignment with Earth's evolutionary purpose. By any view of the current world, this correction is likely to be one of massive, uncontrollable change and suffering. Many peoples have already entered this phase, while many people in the world are stressed and anxious because they feel it coming in their lives, but do not know what to do about it.

The developmental crisis facing humanity requires us to take the next step in developing our consciousness within the evolution of Earth: to become more aware and to open our hearts to soul and to our relationship with the Earth and all life on it. Through the application of this consciousness, humanity might well be able to re-balance and heal itself, and save the planet. This is the Call of the Heart, the move to the higher, more inclusive consciousness that is our inevitable evolutionary goal.

Soul

What we know from the ageless wisdom is that the one consciousness has sent individual sparks of itself to lower, denser levels of being, there to be sheathed in the distilled knowledge of existence forming the soul. The soul gains the experience, knowledge and, ultimately, wisdom being sought in this evolutionary process by animating a series of incarnations in human form at even denser levels. When our series of incarnations has developed our human consciousness and its worldly skill sets sufficiently, we are prompted to seek higher and broader consciousness – that is, we seek direct connection with our soul. As a guiding light through our heart, our soul has a more inclusive awareness of our purpose and of our relationships with life on Earth both in each life and in our series of incarnations.

It is not possible to over-emphasise the significance of how humanity as a whole has reached this phase of its development of consciousness over the last few hundred years. In itself, that time period is insignificant compared with the last 5,000 years of urban, literate civilization, which in turn is insignificant compared with (at least) some hundreds of thousands of years of humanity's physical incarnation on Earth. These timeframes all point to the criticality of where humanity is in its evolution within the larger picture. If we consider humanity's daily life and its relationship to nature, animals, food and our living circumstances on Earth over these relatively short development periods, we can begin to gain a fuller perspective on the macro phases of planetary evolution and the nature of this great change that humanity has entered now.

Call of the Heart

It is not just our own heart calling, it is the heart of the Earth, the heart of the Solar system, the greater beings of consciousness within which we have our lives. We have entered a critical time for the development of heart consciousness, and we need to evolve within this larger process and with these greater hearts by responding to the call.

If humanity does not choose consciously to participate in this evolutionary step, to optimise our path forward and to mitigate the situation on Earth, then it is difficult to consider how this inevitable development will take place. At the very least, we will become out-of-step with the Cosmos, and somehow obsolete by our own doing – with potentially severe consequences for all life on Earth.

It is through our heart that we feel in tune with life, with our purpose, with a higher vision and knowledge – qualities humanity needs desperately. In our heart lies our accumulated experience, knowledge and wisdom that can guide our minds to better paths and better relationships, and that can feel and express the love that pervades our Earth and Solar system – and ultimately update our total planetary consciousness.

Brenton Phillis
Balaklava, South Australia,
December 2023

Evolution

The Intent of Evolution

In the living Cosmos there is life force, the living breath, the pulse of Cosmic Heart, the embrace of loving intent. All have a reason for living, all have a purpose in their manifestation.

Cosmic Heart beats in the silent intention of will, love and purpose. Life cannot exist without these. Will brings life to a point of focus, whether inner or outer. Love is what attracts and builds substance around that focus, and reaches out to create relationships to other expressions of life. Love is the drive to initiate and sustain connection and networks of loving flow and nourishment. Purpose enacts the focus of will and the building, connecting capacity of love. It is the inner driving force of any life form to understand itself, to find its home in the world in which it lives, to act in that world to achieve fulfilment of that inner drive.

If life's intent is to incarnate into the depths of un-illumined matter, then the will provides the force to engage with those depths upon that journey. This is the path for all who incarnate upon Earth, for that is her choice, her dharma. She said 'yes' to being a home to physical consciousness: that interweaving of cosmic intent in life force, will, love and purpose; the anchor in our Solar embrace of Cosmic Will, to bring love to matter, and the deepest enactment of cosmic purpose to fulfil love's embrace on all levels of existence.

You are a part of this great cascade! Every human can become a conscious beacon of loving light in this descending journey of expression. Every human has a choice to be so – for every human has a soul, and soul is the vehicle of apprehension of Cosmic Love, intention, will and purpose. Soul is that part of our being that bathes in the Ocean of Love, Earth's emotional body infused with the intention of Cosmos.

You may be a young soul, and simply know that you are in and of that flow; or you may be an older soul, and start to align with knowledge and awareness, with the currents and movements of cosmic flow. No matter where you are in conscious development, your soul is of this loving, focussed, purposeful Ocean of Love, and your journey it is to seek that awareness in your human self. While soul may bathe in this ocean, in your human self you must take a conscious journey to bring that will, love and purpose into the substance of your being upon Earth.

This is the great duality of evolution upon Earth. Because of how long it can take to evolve consciousness in human form – so that it may apprehend and engage with cosmic embrace – soul was evolved as an intermediary. Soul takes its own journey of learning and evolving; increasing awareness and consciousness in the sphere of cosmic flows.

This is not the same as the soul's learning to engage with, and flow into the depths of matter, through human incarnation. This is another journey of learning, and many souls do not take their journey that far. Rather, they stay on their path of learning within the ocean of cosmic love, will and purpose.

It is important to know this, so that we realise the preciousness of this most remarkable of places in our universe, in which we can come into such deep physical existence. It helps us to understand the depth and fullness of the resources available, as we come to know our soul, and find ways to allow that portion of love, will and purpose that is within our soul to flow to our physical, human self.

It is all enabled by heart. Heart is the source point of life within every conscious being. Heart is a vehicle of intense will, to beat and flow love into the world in which it is anchored, yet hold its own integrity, purposefully, intentfully and individuated.

It is a unique expression of life's force, enabling the cascade of all the richness and fullness of that life force all the way from Cosmic Heart, down through all the embracing, holding hearts of Solar systems, planetary systems, to you, the human system.

Within our planetary system there are also many hearts that temper, soften, and make real that cosmic-solar flow into the deeper layers. Otherwise it would be too much for your soul, a tiny speck within the great ocean, to absorb into itself all the intention and love of that ocean. Like any and every path of evolution, it is developed into smaller journeys, so that the fullness and greatness of the whole does not overwhelm.

Great Angels hold the intent and meaning of the great ocean's flows, and step that intensity down through the myriad of smaller angels who form that flow, so you can experience this flow in a gentle touch without being swept away.

Great, evolved hearts from the human family (or who have come to assist the human family), hold certain aspects of the ocean's intent, so you may learn the qualities one by one, and perfect them in your being. This is the journey of your soul, and – as you are seeking – your journey of conscious growth.

As you become aware, then your soul may infuse more of these subtleties into your human self. Confusing at first, for these forces come from within, when the growing human has mostly focussed upon understanding and dealing with the stimuli and impacts of the outer world.

But such joy awaits you! For how can life not be filled with joy, when the ocean of living love touches your being? With all its loving intent, clarity of focussed will, and richness of fulfilling purpose regenerating you from within. This is life, in fullness.

Evolutionary Streams on Earth

Stand on the bridge of your soul. The bridge of love, light, hope, knowing. The bridge on which flows all that you know you are as a being of light, all that you are able to be as a being of love, all that you are able to do as a human agent, here, on loving beautiful Earth.

The bridge of souls traverses time and space, time and meaning, to awaken the traveller to vistas beyond, while also sustaining the connection to Earth's loving embrace.

Too many are seeking that bridge, to rush across and never look back, even though Earth then weeps that another heart has withdrawn from her loving embrace.

Too many yearn for escape, when it is not Earth they seek escape from, but their own memories held within their personal sphere. Memories that gift learning, karma release, awakening, redemption. They can be so overwhelming, especially in times like these, of such rapid transition to a new and higher awareness and, ultimately, greater consciousness.

The goal of evolution is consciousness, but you cannot be conscious of that of which you have no awareness. How can you grasp the need for forgiveness if you have never felt guilt? For illumination, if you have never experienced the lack of answers for your life questions? Or for hope, if you have never felt despair? Or compassion, if you have never experienced suffering? Or generosity, if you have never experienced loss? So it goes.

Awareness is the first step, to prod and stimulate your inner and human self to seek, learn, change and become someone you would like to be. Someone with more skills to navigate life upon Earth, then to become someone with more heart to give in your life upon Earth.

That is why Earth weeps a tear, or many, when her souls withdraw, due to their human self saying 'no' to the learning journey – for then there is one less bridge of light into her being. One less pathway of heart love into her heart. One less point of light to enlighten the body of humanity, which as a whole grapples with the same journey.

We are not just individuals upon this beautiful Earth. We are members of families, groups, races, nations and humanity, even if we do not always feel this. Part of the awareness journey is to gain this realisation. Humanity is the body of consciousness that has responsibility for incarnating a certain level of light and love upon and within the body of Earth.

Planetary beings are curious entities, to our comprehension of livingness and consciousness. They can choose a path of self-development, slowly evolving to become carriers of the light of the universe that is theirs to hold. Or they may choose a more rapid path, to absorb other conscious beings and evolve in the journey together, in interaction.

That has been Earth's choice, many millennia ago. When Sun called for the evolution of deeper heart in her Solar being, Earth responded, and opened her ring-pass-not for those souls and incarnational forces that could more rapidly help her evolve into a planet of heart. In turn, she gives those souls a chance for rapid growth into beings of heart, who can then continue to travel the universe, empowering the unfoldment of heart throughout this wondrous living, breathing Cosmos of which we are a part.

The souls that Earth welcomed are of two streams: human, and angel. Souls are those units of light that may travel freely, guided by the call and response of the great and benevolent teacher, karma.

Earth welcomed many souls of humans, of course, including those already enlightened from journeys undertaken elsewhere in our universe – hence reference is often made to those enlightened ones from Sirius, and Venus – plus souls of animals and plants in that stream.

Plants have an interesting soul development, for although they have their own path of development, they co-habit their path on the journey of evolution with the body of the Earth herself – for they are so much a part of her substance in the most physical way – and with angels, who embody streams of light and cosmic, solar or earthly intent into the body of plants and Earth.

Animals have group souls, sharing the journey of conscious development amongst many expressions. Many humans have more than one concurrent incarnation too, a valued way of speeding up the journey.

Angels are another stream of souls sought and welcomed by Earth in her quest for greater heart evolution. Angels have a different soul expression than humans, as their being is of flow, whereas the human being is of form.

Angels flow in co-habitation with plants, but also of the physical evolution of Earth's elements themselves – water, fire, minerals, air. They hold the soul and earthly evolutionary intent of mountains, streams, oceans, forests – all of Earth's features – and thus the special vibration of many of these expressions of Earth's body is felt. That is because there is a presence there: all to stimulate and align matter and the substance of consciousness with heart and soul, and cosmic-solar intent.

In this great evolutionary expression upon Earth, we also have angel and human streams merging, to maximise opportunity for conscious growth. The stimulus of angel flow is greatly challenging, and thus awakening, to human consciousness. While the physicality of human incarnation – something angels do not have within their pure form of evolutionary expression – is greatly challenging to their consciousness, it is also how much growth can occur.

Suffice it to say, evolution of consciousness has meaning, intent, and utmost love behind it, driving, guiding, shaping the unfoldment through so many spheres of expression within our cosmic and solar spheres.

Find your journey and take it with loving acceptance and joy in your heart, for to be here upon Earth is a miracle and blessing in its opportunity, to become a presence and guide of the utmost heart, wherever you go in the wondrous world of Cosmos.

Human Choice & Angels' Flow

Angels and humans co-habit this Earth, at Earth's request. However, it is humans who control the most physical expression of consciousness, as they are the beings of form, expressing as they do within the matter of Earth's physical, emotional and mental energy bodies.

Humans are key in the success of the expression of light. If carelessness and degrading pollution of Earth's physical and inner bodies continues by the many humans who brook no conscience in their actions (these are the people in roles of leadership who know better), angels will leave. They cannot function in such an environment.

Angels will flow endlessly into places of darkness, and into matter that is as yet un-illumined or un-qualified into love, light or creativity. But the darkness created by a seemingly endless attachment of some humans to the materiality of their greed for wealth, control and/or power is a self-perpetuating darkness, and unresponsive to angelic infusion of light.

Choice. It comes down to choice within the human family. Angels have a form of choice, but not in the same way. As beings of flow, angels go with the flow. Their choice lies in how to nuance that flow, through timing, strength, tone, colour, vibration. They will never say no to the flow.

Humans, however, do. They are not beings of flow, and have the task before them (evolutionarily speaking) of learning how to discern between the drivers from within that come from the infusion of soul, and those that arise from the physical-emotional-mental personality self. This is the crucial test for every human!

You must first build your personal self from experience, learning, knowing, because as a young incarnate you come with little or none – depending upon any previous training and development upon inner levels or other planetary spheres. You learn to recognise the messages you receive from your life's experiences, and to work from them to make choices for safety, nourishment and wellbeing.

As evolution proceeds, then you receive more input from soul and the increased global consciousness of light. How to discern? How to discern if the powerful drivers of a well thought-out mental reasoning or the compelling emotional reactions, are energised by heart and soul, or by mind and emotions only?

1. Make mistakes and acknowledge them, and use that to instigate personal change.
2. Realise you have a global responsibility to Earth, humanity and all life. You are part of the Earth, not a separate being. You cannot make choices outside the Earth sphere, and therefore they influence the Earth sphere. This comes down to simply choosing from goodness, in the simplest decisions, to accepting global responsibility by leaders in political, corporate or other influential positions.

You are not here to plunder, repress, be greedy or self-centred. No conscious evolution is achieved that way – except when those imbalances are recognised and lessons learned. However, now Earth has little room for erroneous ways, for greed-filled actions and choices.

Angels cannot function in many of the needed flows, because too much hard matter has been built from human greed and selfishness, and those barriers stop the flow. This is like stopping the blood flow in a human being: where the blood does not flow, life declines. Our planet relies upon a certain flow of loving, gracious light, infused from cosmic and solar love through angels into her body, for her health and wellbeing.

Choice really matters. Even if you are not in a position of global influence, it is the actions of every heart that create the pathways for loving light to flow, and break the solidity of darkened aggregates of human greed and selfishness so the greater flows may resume, for the health of our planet and all life. When you make your choices, out of a wish for goodness to prevail, in the light of your heart, you become a mini beacon of light.

There is one beautiful thing that happens when one heart lights up from a choice and action of goodness – it sets up a vibration that awakens other hearts. Unless totally closed, and very, very few humans are, for it is only those who have immersed so totally in their own desires and mental constructs that they have forged an impenetrable door over their heart. Virtually every heart is *not* like this. The heart is the vehicle of light and love, and will *always* respond when in the presence of that vibration.

Yes, it takes time for the human consciousness to recognise and deepen that resonance within, but always there is a response. Which means that every little, or greater, choice of goodness that awakens your heart, will stimulate other hearts, and in turn open you to the light and love of other hearts.

No aggregate of darkness can withstand the network of a million, million hearts aflame with hope and care. Awaken yours, and ensure the flow of living light brought by the angels, awakened by humans, magnified by choice, can nourish all.

The Ocean of Love

Within Cosmos there is a pulse, a life force, a breath; for Cosmos is alive, just as you are alive. Cosmos is a living, breathing entity of consciousness, like you, like planets, like stars, like Solar systems and galaxies.

The mysterious emptiness humans perceive within the Cosmos is none other than the substance of consciousness unworked out, the milieu of expression yet to take form within substance. Ultimately all life force comes to inhabit and consciously express through matter within this cosmic expression, for that is the nature of evolution at this time. Do not mistake this as meaning all life must look human as, in the conscious diversity of our universe, that is absurd. Nor make the mistake of assuming an expression through matter means a physical life form of mobility, thought and expression in the way humans perceive – for this is also not the truth.

Matter within Cosmos encompasses everything of the human consciousness – from body to soul to spirit. This is cosmic matter, the densest level of conscious expression there is, manifest in planets, stars, humans and angels alike, not to mention in the vast number of other expressions of evolving life.

Sirius is one such focus of life within our known (to humanity) expressions of consciousness in the physical realm of Cosmos. She is full of life and holds so many life streams, expressing divinity and love, for that is the dharma of this beautiful being of our skies.

Sirius is vastly more evolved than we are upon Earth, yet she sends love our way, and stimulus via stunningly enlightened beings. As a perfected planet on her conscious journey, beings within her embrace have not only become conscious on the cosmic physical level, but from that wholeness they can touch into and resonate with the consciousness of cosmic flow, the loving pulse and wave of life force that moves through the flowing substance of our universe. Physics is the same throughout our Cosmos: as above, so below; what you see where you are gifts you with insight as to where you go, in consciousness.

The densest matter coalesces into firm shapes bound together to fulfil conscious intention – humans, animals, trees, mountains, planets and Solar systems. Then there is the liquid that moves in and around these aggregates of matter, wherein there is the birth of flow, and wherein the pulse of life, no matter how faint, is born.

Thus, on Earth, within the physical expression of Cosmos, we have earthly physicality, and oceans and rivers and water of all expressions, as the life-resonating liquid within and around which we live.

In Cosmos, we have the same, and all of the physical expressions of Cosmos bathe in what we call the Ocean of Love. So all-pervading with life force and loving intent is this ocean, it feels like nothing other than the highest divinity.

Those enlightened beings of Sirius touch this ocean, and bring that evolutionary, loving resonance down into the physical world we live within, to create the resonance and stimulus to love. To love, both cosmologically and personally speaking, is to see outside oneself and to seek to connect to another; whether to another being of like expression such as another human, whether to Earth and nature, our loving home, or whether to that which is so far beyond our physical senses that we call it divine.

This cosmic, loving ocean carries the heartbeat of Cosmos itself, and thus the fullness of the loving life force within which we are born and evolve.

Every great moment upon Earth, evolutionarily speaking, has been stimulated and nourished by this ocean of divinity, this loving resonance of Cosmos. Whether the incarnation of an enlightened one, like the great teachers we have seen in history, who stimulate the awakening of human and earthly consciousness; or the incarnation of an impulse that must then express through the many, like the many great world events that have changed the course of history, and thus, of evolution, and thus, of the evolving heart. Those world events, unfortunately, are mostly remembered as the shattering side of love – that love that brooks no evil expression, that is invoked when human greed, lust for power, cruelty or utter lack of Earth-care becomes too all-pervasive in its reach, corrupting the expression of love and the evolution of consciousness in all her expressions. Think of the demise of Atlantis or, more recently, the second world war. Beware, for the lack of Earth-care reaches strongly into the unconscious of many, who blindly follow the pull of materiality (matter without life force), and ignore the pull of divinity, the Ocean of Love with all its intention for evolution of consciousness contained therein.

Regarding great teachers, who can bring that resonance of Cosmic Love, that true vibration that evolves consciousness, there are none incarnate upon this Earth at this time. So do not prostrate yourself at the feet of anyone believing them to be God's expression. Show respect to great teachers who stimulate consciousness and guide your evolutionary journey, but beware of the ones who claim to be more than a fellow human traveller.

Do not read anything uttered as if it is from a great deity of the inner realms, for there are very few true expressions of absolute divinity reaching into the minds and hearts of humanity directly. Most express through that great body of Greater Hearts who know the path of embodiment upon Earth, and who have evolved consciousness such that they can bridge this flowing ocean of cosmic intent into the worlds of human and earthly unfoldment. However, at this time there is neither a physically incarnate expression of divinity at work in this way, nor is there any great teacher incarnate claiming such, who can actually embody such divinity of the Ocean of Love into words and teachings.

The truth can be found via your heart. Beware the pull of emotional needs, for they can blind you to that truth.

The Ocean of Love is resonant throughout our Cosmos, awash through our Solar system, and bathes little Earth in her embrace. It is brought into a resonance that we can perceive by those Greater Hearts who bridge such spans of consciousness, and show us the way to truth and knowing, within the heart. This leads us another step forward on the great evolutionary unfoldment into this great Ocean of Love, while we are also beings of, and resonating love into, our beautiful Earth.

Evolution, Love & Conscious Choice

In the cosmic embrace we call love – or the divine, or God – there is a flow that enables both life, and evolution.

These are not the same, for there can be life without much evolution occurring – where the intent is simply to be what is first created, rather than to start in one form and evolve to another. Many planets hold this path, for now. They live, in quiet stillness, but may in time come to a dharma of evolving into new and differently awakened spheres.

Evolution, however, cannot occur without life. Evolution can be fast or slow, all depending upon the intent of the loving, life-giving flow from Cosmos. Cosmos is the loving, living being within which we all come into existence, and journey as part of her journey, just as planets, stars and galaxies do in the great unfolding. Thus, the big bang, so often spoken of in astronomical circles, is the start of cosmic outflow for this period of life-giving and life-evolving embrace!

In this descent of the loving flow of Cosmos to our planet, we have now a strong evolutionary intent. This presents in two ways: the complexity of the organisation of beings in the inner worlds, tasked with incarnating that evolutionary intent into our earthly sphere so we can perceive and respond; and the rapidity of the current presentation of opportunities here upon Earth in our physical sphere, also known as the 'Great Change'!

Loving, evolutionary intent always comes as a flow, for it is that life-giving pulse from Cosmic Heart. Thus it is always conveyed through those of the angelic family, for their whole beingness is one of flow. Anytime you feel flow, in the flow, infused with life force, that is the angelic family at work.

Humans, on the other hand, are builders of form, building in thought, feelings and in the physical world; building their own conscious and human selves, and building in the world around them.

When something is built that is in alignment with evolutionary flow, and not discordant from it, then not only will it be built of human intent and action, but it will be infused with the loving presence of angelic flows.

That is why some buildings, some organisations, touch you in a different way. They have been built with both human and angelic input. That is also why some things, perhaps many, can be called lifeless, for they have no intent other than to satisfy a human emotion or some locked-in thought about what creates beauty and joy. Even the simplest things can be created with love. Love is *always* a flow that invites angelic presence, for love comes from heart, and all hearts are nourished by other hearts and higher hearts; ultimately from the great cascading flow from Cosmic Heart, gently softening in intensity as it flows down into our human world.

That which evolves is ever infused with this loving flow, brought by angels, held and then manifested by humans into life upon Earth. Angels are always evolving, as they are perpetually of the loving flow of Cosmos. Humans, however, are of matter, building form, and it is possible for humans to stay stagnant, if you like, or to evolve ever so slowly, when left to their own unfoldment alone. This is the difference between just being alive, and evolving. Evolutionary pressure does not come from within the form itself. As our human family is of the substance of Earth, and Earth has chosen to awaken and open to the angelic flow of Cosmic Love, then the very substance of our beings is infused with that intention to evolve. Thus the search begins, ever the characteristic of the human self when touched and blessed by this loving, evolutionary intent.

As Earth accepts more and more loving flow into her being, so too do we become infused with more and more of this love. It is not the love that invites the staidness of contentment. No, this love holds within it that which lies beyond, that which is of magic, of wonder, yet of undeniable truth and purpose. You know this, because you are made of this substance and flow! So when weird coincidences happen in your life that prompt you to seek, to ask questions, to open doors within your inner landscape and explore beyond what you already know in your mind, you realise that you know in your very being too. You know the substance of our world is alive, and that you are a part of that. You know that you contribute to the great unfoldment of evolution in your smaller or greater sphere of influence, through your loving alignment with that life force within you.

Then, once realised, you can create it. Easy? Not usually, for what consciousness can grow without choice, and what choice is ever made without a tussle between influences, whether emotional, mental or of heart? And without conscious choice, you are not a life-giving being playing your part in evolution's joyous unfolding; you go back to being alive, but not evolving. It is rarely this black and white, for we evolve on many trajectories of consciousness, but you get the idea.

Your choices matter, as does your willingness to open to that quality of livingness we call flow: that which infuses your heart with certainty, that which fills your mind with hopeful visions, that which uplifts your emotions to stillness and alignment.

When you take these steps, then can Cosmic Love descend, filtered down, down, down in intensity and vibration, through angel after angel, into your heart, and you become a co-creator of loving unfoldment in your own life, and as part of beloved Earth's journey of evolving heart and joyful consciousness, and the angels of flow sing their song of perfect, loving evolution.

Evolutionary Life on Earth

Love is the meaning, the force, the magnetism, the intent, that brings matter together into form. Matter has no inherent need or consciousness through which to aggregate or connect. Love is the ultimate expression of livingness in our universe that does this. It is at the core of the expression of cosmic livingness, and from there, all unfolds.

Even before Cosmic Heart came into being, there was love. For a heart, on any level of consciousness, needs a flame, a spark, to create the force field within which it can function, let alone the forces of attraction that builds the heart in the substance of the life force it is to energise.

Before anything comes to life, there is love. Cosmic Love is what flows and energises matter and light on every level, infusing it with intent, from where the force of evolution becomes manifest.

Evolution

Love is this force of evolution in intention. Then it is up to the evolving medium to take the path laid out by that intent, to make choices – remember, you can't evolve without consciousness, and consciousness comes about through choice – to learn, to understand and to act. Thus it becomes an incarnated expression of that loving intention, and thus a living presence that magnifies and extends the presence of that Cosmic Love.

This is the story of planets and stars, galaxies and all that lies between. Where form is present, it is Cosmic Love that has instigated that gathering, infused that matter with the force of attraction that joins molecules and atoms, that electrified their constituents so that they became bound in the force field of that charge. This is the start of the descending cosmic intention called love.

As a planet forms, such as Earth, it faces choices just as all life does. The fundamental proposition is simple: as love infuses matter and matter gathers and binds together to become an entity, then what? To be a gathering of matter infused with love at the most basic level of electrical and atomic force is just the beginning. Cosmic Love holds so much more intention, but to open to, and flow with that intention is a choice.

We do not need hundreds, thousands, millions of Earths in our Cosmos, because the evolutionary intention of love does not need so much expression in consciousness.

Think upon your own beingness. You may become a highly conscious being, radiant and resplendent in the loving presence you have evolved into, but does that mean you are at all times conscious of the atoms and cells throughout your being? No, it does not, for as consciousness evolves, you align the substances that make up your being with the intent and magnetism of the loving force you embody, and all those smaller elements fulfil their function based on that alignment and the resulting flow of life-giving love. They do not need conscious direction, or to be conscious in and of themselves for the greater whole to become an illuminated and evolved, conscious being. So it is in Cosmos, in Solar deities, in planets, in humans – in all evolving life. As you aggregate matter within the loving flow of evolution's intention, it is the evolution of the whole that is the point.

It all comes back to love, the living breath and blood of our universe, the creator of life. Love is the force that binds matter into forms that can hold life. Life is the expression of love that enables our universe to infuse the whole of its being, in conscious, evolving creation.

The substance of the being is not important, except that it is coherent enough to be gathered harmoniously by the force of love, to create that curious entity we call conscious life: matter, infused with love, holding intention, and able to make choices to evolve.

Earth chose to become a physical embodiment of love's great expression in matter, a pulsing, beating heart radiant with living light. Our Solar deity chose to hold that physical expression of loving, living light for our part of the galaxy. That is enough.

Other planets and stars hold love's intent through different expressions, sometimes just at its simplest, as a being formed of matter in Cosmos. Others hold loving intent in very powerful ways, yet not on the physical realm, such as Venus, whose great embodiment of consciousness and love reached the astral levels. And Sirius, who embodies Cosmic Love to the extent that her being pulses as the heart of the expression of cosmic life we live within – but not on the physical level. She sends out wave upon wave of consciously directed heartbeats, flowing throughout the Cosmos on angels' wings, touching, blessing, infusing, showering that love where it may nourish life's journey and evolution's intent.

That is what our Solar deity embodies, and both Solar and Cosmic Love (that is, qualified by both) nurtures, embraces, and when time is right, infuses beloved little Earth on her journey of becoming a heartbeat of Cosmic Love in the substance of physical matter. A difficult journey, for heart creates life by sending out life force and loving nourishment through flow – and not all physical matter flows easily. That is the journey of consciousness we are on, here on Earth.

Our journey is to gather in harmonised intent all of who we are, so that we can resonate with this brilliance of life itself: the living light of the heart. This living light cascades from cosmic intent, through the heartbeat of Sirius and the pulse of Solar deity, to the living, beating heart of our Mother Earth. Then it flows to us, humans of heart, aligning in love and cooperating with the angels of flow, so that we illuminate and shine in that brilliant spectrum of life's very essence, the living light that is love, born of heart in matter.

Cosmic Love & Earthly Evolution

As love unfolds, so too does life. As love expresses, so too does the evolutionary impulse.

Think about it: what stimulates the ever evolving progression of life? It is not DNA, it is not human wish or prayer. These play a part in unfolding that evolutionary expression, but what stimulates it in the first place? What makes the difference between matter and life? What creates the spark that moves molecules, atoms, beingness, to seek – and thus to evolve?

It is always that touch within, which every life form has even if very veiled: that touch that is other. That touch that is luminous, that is perpetual, that is embracing, and in all its unfamiliarity in the world of matter, it is something we know.

Because every life form – planets, stars, humans and all creatures of nature – all come into being because the force and intention of love have entered the world of matter, and aggregated around it those molecules and atoms that resonate with that intention.

Intention is key, and is often overlooked in understanding love. Love is pure intention, of the highest spheres of consciousness. Love only exists in movement, from one level of consciousness to another, from one being to another. Movement only occurs when there is direction and expression, and they are created by intention.

We come back to the one great heartbeat of our universe, that spreads love all throughout our universe, to become manifest in expression, then to become that expression. Then there will be another great cosmic heartbeat, that again floods our universe, awakening and stimulating the next wave of love's expression, from the highest conscious beingness of Cosmos, to the most dense expression in matter.

This is life in the big picture, within the universe in which we live, are nourished, and evolve. The point of explaining this reality, even if it seems so distant to our human and earthly lives, is that it is the blueprint for how our planet is evolving, and how we are all evolving.

In our planetary sphere there is a great gathering of illumined, lovingly conscious beings of the angel and human families, who together have formed the heart of conscious intent for our Earth's evolution. She has her own heart deep within her body, which you can feel through your bare feet and hands when you touch her in certain locations where that loving heart vibrates into your being. If more people would seek this, then we, humanity, would love her more and cease the senseless plundering, destruction and pollution of her being.

Her heart is just like your heart. It contains the spark of loving intent that awakens life, but it is not of that intent in its fullness. For humans, we have souls that hold our earthly learning yet that are also bathed in the loving ocean of intent. For Earth, she has this group of beings, most of whom have evolved with her, and who have become the conscious loving heart that opens to and receives the cosmic inflow, and brings that resonance into both the human family and Earth's own consciousness as a physical being, including all the families of nature she embraces in her being.

This spiritual heart of Earth has evolved because Earth's intent, and plea, was to take the rapid path to being a physical embodiment of heart. Had she, like many other planets, chosen to evolve more slowly and through her own means, then she would have gently evolved her own soul and spirit self, through which the loving grace of the cosmic heartbeat would have come to infuse her being.

However, that is not her chosen path, so neither can it be yours; for you are made of the matter and substance of this beautiful being we call Earth. You cannot take any path but the path stimulated by her choice, and openness to the cosmic impulse infused through her being, and thus your being, by this great family of heart beings upon the inner levels, who bring this cosmic intent to us all.

What about the Solar deity? The Solar deity is an evolutionary being within whom all her encircling planets live and are nourished. She is like the soul of our Solar system, for she has evolved to the point of becoming one with the flame of spirit's expression, the cosmic intent that is the spark of life. She is the life force that nourishes all within her living reach. She has taken that path. Not to become a place upon which consciousness itself becomes manifest in physicality, but to be the living force field in which love flows as the fire of heaven, the living spark of Cosmic Love.

Her role is to be that living force, and as such she radiates and circulates that love into all beings in her care, and this is the nourishment of heart that she provides. However, she is not providing the force of evolutionary intent. Rather, she is nourishing it.

Love takes many forms in its expression from Cosmos to us! The great spiritual family of Earth who open to Cosmic Love's intent, also opens to and receives Solar love and nourishment, but so too does Earth. The spiritual family of Earth does not need to infuse Earth and her beings, including us, with Solar love, because that comes about naturally through Earth's absorption of Solar radiance. Rather, they absorb it as nourishment for their own work, the work of guiding evolution.

Thus you begin to see the map of evolving life of which you are a part, so that you may awaken in wonder and trust to the loving light in which you are immersed; and within which you are evolving to become a great being of heart, where Cosmos shines through your eyes, yet Earth's heartbeat pulses and radiates through your being, to infuse that love so deeply into our world that all matter, and our whole universe, shall shine in luminosity, born of Cosmic Love!

Love's Drive & Matter's Pull

When a human loves, it is to connect. Love is the driving push to do this in all life, whether that connection is to aggregate like-with-like vibrationally (as the elements of Earth do to create gems and minerals), or it is an aspect of consciousness seeking connection. Always, it is the seeking of that which is familiar, is similar, in vibration.

That which drives you to seek, and that which you seek, change as the substance of your being evolves, which happens through the simple reality of being built of the substance of Earth, and she is evolving, or through your own soul stimulus.

This is not about seeking the connection between partners, which is not just a connection of like-with-like. In fact, often it is not a lot to do with this. The truth is that our relationships upon Earth are very largely guided by our karma. Karma is the patterning you have built in your personal being, through lives of learning and trials, of experience and challenge, of growth and exploration. These patterns are like the fabric of our being, through which we see, feel and think, and thus connect with others. Of course, our patterns invariably involve others, from connections made and unmade, explored and abandoned. We have journeyed in so many ways in different lives with our close soul mates upon this Earth and this has more bearing, for most, in the formation of connections and relationships in our current life.

Ultimately, love is behind the working out of all karma, and thus the evolution, creation, development and healing of all relationships on all levels.

Love drives karma because karma cannot exist without love. If we have no drive to explore, to seek, to connect to that which is outside our personal sphere, we are inert, and the gracious presence of the great teacher that karma is, goes unexpressed in our presence. Love is the driver that comes from within us, and through which we seek, evolve, learn, and establish opportunities for future learning, all of which is held by the Law of Karma.

The driver of evolution is love, the guide and teacher and record keeper is provided and governed by the Law of Karma.

If you have a discordant relationship with another, born out of the past, karma guides how and when you shall meet and have opportunity to resolve that discord. It is all done under the evolutionary driver of love. To evolve is to learn, to learn requires experience. Experience always

Evolution

includes failures, otherwise you know not what the value is in the learning; so on the evolutionary journey, you gather both the learning and the memory of failures. This means failures in the most general and energetic sense, defined purely as those instances when the presence of your higher consciousness does not reverberate through your actions, thoughts or feelings. That can be anything from the simple check provided by emotional conscience, to the illumined soul vibration guiding your choices. It matters not what level, just that it is the highest vibration of your consciousness for where you are today on your evolutionary journey.

We make connections in every sphere, so this is not just about human to human relationships. Love is in all expressions of life upon Earth. Depending upon where we are at and what our journey gifts us, we can explore and build many connections, to Earth herself, to nature, to animals, oceans, places, experiences, etc.

The journey of evolution is to understand that all true seeking and connecting is stimulated by love. However, there is another pull upon our consciousness that is not of love. It is the pull of matter itself; a type of magnetism, if you like. Ultimately, it is a force created to enable evolution, for without it we would not be able to descend so deeply into matter; but in and of itself its focus is to become matter, deeper and denser in vibration, not to become light, of finer and finer vibration.

This is the paradox of evolution: the creator of both love, and that which makes physical consciousness possible.

Love exists to drive connection – but that is only possible if there is differentiation between where love arises, and what love seeks. Otherwise there is but one presence, and no need to seek the other, therefore no need to have the driving force of love. There is a presence of consciousness in the oneness, but that is not the journey of our universe. The pull of matter was created to draw consciousness to a place of otherness, to experience separation, then to seek connection, and thus to evolve.

The pull of matter, however, creates its own force field, and the human consciousness begins its journey immersed in this. As we evolve, and our souls, which are not pulled by the force of matter (but reside in the

Ocean of Love), begin to resonate more purposefully in our hearts, then we begin to discern and differentiate. The pull of matter, through which we make many earthly connections in life after life, becomes something other than the milieu in which we exist and perceive love. Much of the human journey is to discern this, and then disentangle that inherent pull of matter, that feels like a connection, from the real connector which is love.

This is the difference between existing in matter, and evolving. As Earth is evolving, and has long ago differentiated the pull of the material forces from that of the driver that is love, so must we.

Choice! One of the most powerful opportunities for growth of consciousness, and evolution of love. When you feel needs, wants or yearnings, your choice is to discern and determine if it is the pull of matter, or the drive of love.

You can find this truth in your heart. You most certainly will not find it in matter, or in the material things formed from that pull. Much of our world is filled with things created by this material pull, energised by the lower emotions that coalesce around perceived needs and expectations. But such things can never be infused with love, and thus enable an uplifting and joyful connection of love, unless created with that intention in the first place. I am sure you will agree that most things in our material world are not created with love.

This is a significant step on our evolutionary journey: to discern the pull of materiality, of matter itself, from the force of love that drives us to seek. One comes from within, one pulls from without. Learn the difference and your binds will loosen, and your consciousness shall soar!

This is the evolutionary journey of love.

Building Form & Change

True love, the love that emanates from Cosmos, the love that enables evolution, the love you can find in your heart – this love expresses in many ways upon Earth, in our physical world.

Earth herself absorbs it to some extent, and it is her path to be able to absorb it more fully, so that she is a heart pulse herself of this great, loving force. The spiritual family of Greater Hearts of the inner worlds absorb much too, and mediate it into a multitude of streams through which all life can perceive that love, and thus evolve.

One of those great streams is expressed through spirituality itself, that stimulus of human and earthly life (including all families of nature) that is direct and to the point concerning the unfolding path ahead. Religion is one such expression of this stream of spiritual stimulus. But does it hold love? The challenge with any spiritual stimulus reaching into and incarnating, if you like, into the physical world is that in order to do so, it must become expressed in matter, else it remains only in the inner realm of the heart.

This incarnation into matter requires the building of form in the dense substance of consciousness, which, spiritually and evolutionarily speaking, is the substance of physical matter, but also the substance of human mind and emotions. The mind and emotions are included because, from an evolutionary point of view, they are builders and holders of form, thus behaving more like matter than the gently responsive and flexible substance of the higher worlds, where a type of form may be assembled to achieve certain ends, but then can be easily disassembled should that form no longer be required or serve its purpose.

The challenge ever for the evolving human consciousness is that to exist, it must build form. That is the means by which the incarnating soul impulse can come into existence and live in matter. The pull of matter enables this, showing how to do this via the expressions already here, around us, in nature.

As an evolving human, we build forms for body, then emotions, then thoughts, then our whole human expression. Necessary, but then the form must also be able to disassemble when the spiritual, evolutionary impulse requires a more nuanced, or even a quite different response.

How many people do you know who have experienced a crisis of some sort, inner or outer that has led to a complete reworking of the structure and certainty of their being, such that something completely other has awoken in their awareness, in their actions, in their choices – and thus they experience and demonstrate a significant shift in consciousness? Perhaps you have been upon this path yourself. Many are these days, as the relentless evolutionary and loving stimulus expresses more and more via the spiritual family of Greater Hearts, and via Earth herself, as the cosmic need, and Solar and Earth choice must make manifest.

Sorry if you do not like this situation. You can go elsewhere in Cosmos if you deeply choose it, for Earth's choice has been made and you simply cannot take an alternative pathway, or you become a cancer within her being. How would that rest in your consciousness? Or be allowed karmically, for as Earth has chosen, the range of choices possible to all living here has to fit within the energy parameters of her embrace.

This evolution does not require an instant choice and switch in consciousness, or the dissolution of the personal self so that the soul-aligned presence can express. This is a process of change that occurs over centuries, even millennia for some, depending on how developed they are. The more developed a personality is, the more cancerous are the negative (that is, anti-evolutionary) choices within Earth's and their own being.

Change is inevitable within our own consciousness, and the forms of our being that it dwells within, built of our physical, emotional and mind beingness. However, this is not the only change needed. Change must also be able to occur in the forms of consciousness built around great spiritual stimuli. To date, such change is always initiated by a great teacher from the family of Greater Hearts, incarnating in order to pierce the veils of ignorance and express that stimulus in the world of human awareness.

This stimulus, manifest as a religion, or doctrinised spiritual practice, becomes a form in order to reach and touch humanity. But it is a form that can also be built over, strengthened in its concrete expression by human attachment, need or belief; and, as we know from history, also by human desires for power, authority, control, dominance in the global milieu. How many ways have we seen, and continue to see to this day, the expression of a spiritual impulse no longer express that, but instead become a rationale for violence, hatred, destruction, intolerance?

Other expressions of spiritual stimuli face the same challenge. Spiritual stimuli express through all fields of human endeavour to enable positive development of human consciousness, not just through religion or spirituality. Any stimulus that is brought into earthly and human conscious apprehension to awaken an evolutionary step can become solidified by layers of human self-interest, whatever expression that takes.

These forms must change! This does not mean destruction and dissolution, if the initial spiritual impulse still shines within, and can still hold relevance for the spiritual and conscious development of the human family.

Any form thus solidified can no longer flex and evolve to express the nuances of change as evolution proceeds – let alone if major shifts are required.

We are now in a period of very rapid change, over these last 50 years, and continuing for some time until a certain amount of change is achieved. Forms in personal and global or societal consciousness that have puttered along for centuries, maybe even millennia as some spiritual stimuli have, must now choose to evolve, or be crushed by the force and weight of evolutionary change. For the new stimuli need free-flowing substance in which to build the new forms of consciousness that fit the times into which we are entering.

How does a global or societal form change? Through conscious intervention of those involved, and/or the sheer volume of awakened hearts dwelling within or that care about that form, whether a religion, an expression of science, a structure of politics, or something else.

Your choice matters! Not only do you awaken your own indwelling spirit and heart's expression, but you become an active blood cell within the body of Earth, circulating in the world of consciousness with vitality, love and nourishment, such that the great evolutionary step before us all can be taken with as little shattering as possible.

Stay grounded, but be of heart. That is the greatest, most illuminating contribution you can make. Avoid all fanciful thoughts of global or personal influence. Just be the best expression of heart you can be, and you have done yours, and love shall flow, and the Great Change unfold with joyful and sustaining embrace for all, including beautiful Earth herself.

Love, and be.

The Three Stimuli of Conscious Evolution

In the human world, that is, the physical, emotional and mind levels of our physical existence, we have several stimuli that awaken the indwelling light and vibration of soul (that resides in Earth's Ocean of Love), and thus move us on the evolutionary path of soul, heart and love.

These stimuli are: Earth herself; the angelic family; and the family of Greater Hearts.

Your soul can be a stimulus – but not until that awakening to soul has occurred within your human consciousness, and this almost never occurs through the soul's effort alone. This is because as a human incarnated within this physical realm, it is usual that your soul is new to this journey too. Very few souls incarnate with deep insight, understanding and knowledge of the journey of love's evolution deep into the world of matter. Even those Greater Hearts arriving with awakened souls, have had to rely on the angelic family to help them bring that awakening deep into their human selves so they could understand the journey, and bring their soul and spirit wisdom to bare upon the unfolding journey of all the other young souls in Earth's care.

In the beginning, it could only be the stimulus of the great sweeping flows of the angelic family to stimulate this physical awakening, because Earth herself had also not awakened and developed her substance of, and alignment with, the great Cosmic Love that was coming to bathe her and her incarnating souls.

We owe our evolutionary possibilities to the Great Angels, who know love because they are of that great milieu, they are birthed in that great cosmic outflow. All matter touched by love becomes a flow, and that flow is of angels. In Cosmos, the great presence of love became a flow when

Cosmic Heart awakened, and the pulse of intent began. That pulse could only move through time and space via substance.

As physics tells us, a wave of energy cannot travel though a vacuum. Angels are the embedded, intrinsically present consciousness that bridges what seems to be that vacuum, according to our human, scientific capacity to measure its properties. Consciousness is unmeasurable by the physical sciences.

Angels embody and are the substance that resonates with the pulse of love, a great gift to our Cosmos from a previous incarnation of cosmic life and learning, where flow was a significant evolutionary intention.

Now angels embody that flow all the way from Cosmic Heart to our planetary family of Greater Hearts, now also to Earth's heart, and soon, to many of humanity's hearts. They bridge the seeming chasm of consciousness created by the impulse to create life and love in matter. Matter cannot in and of itself begin with the consciousness of love, else it would never seek, never evolve, and therefore physical life could not become a conscious co-creator of a loving universe, as it is intended to be.

In bridging this vacuum in what can be consciously apprehended, angels bring to Earth that loving presence that both Earth and humans can sense, feel, and thus awaken to seek and create. Early in the Earth's evolutionary journey, this was via angelic embodiment within Earth herself, in mountains, forests, oceans, rivers – in fact any feature of our natural world. You can still find and seek these places, where you stand upon Earth and are transported somewhere else, awakened to something other, more beautiful, more loving, more stimulating of your own, deep inner self. It is the beginning of awakening your contact with, and seeking of your soul.

Now, as millennia have passed, and the human family has more individuals who are awakened to soul, angels can also work more directly through the human family when human intent is aligned and open; for example, in those great temples built to hold and sanctify a space for that which is higher. Here, angels will not only facilitate the flow to stimulate awakening of consciousness, and thus more enlightened choices to enable the light to be present in that building, but also at least one angel will engage with and hold that loving intent in that physical part of Earth until such time as it is no longer required or able to stay.

This is why we have sanctified spaces of human construction that can transport you into an awakened consciousness, or at least touch you with that grace so that you may continue to know the love of soul, and become awakened upon your journey.

This conveys some of how angels have and continue to stimulate our awakening.

Now let us consider Earth herself. Not only does she have places sanctified by angelic presence, but as her own evolution unfolds further (also, in part, stimulated by that great loving intentful presence brought by angels), the very substance of her being becomes imbued with more love. The matter of her consciousness has slowly differentiated into those aspects of consciousness that bring love into the vibrational level of physical matter itself, and into the substance from which we gather together the life force within which we incarnate. This means that the matter from which our physical, emotional and mind layers of beingness are created comes already imbued with this loving light, and thus we cannot avoid the stimulus of evolution. Even when we experience the pull of matter that draws us into physicality and thus pulls our consciousness into that depth of being, it cannot stop us evolving, but instead creates the ever present challenge of choice, as we journey in consciousness.

Now we come to the stimulus afforded by the family of Greater Hearts, who hold a great presence of heart within Earth's beingness. They are the great teachers, because they have walked this exact path of consciousness upon which we walk: to become a loving unit of awareness in the great unfolding journey of love's evolution upon Earth.

These Greater Hearts specialise in different streams upon which conscious awakening may occur, so to tap into the stimulus arising within the human self upon its journey of wonderment and curiosity, created by the two previously mentioned stimuli.

As the human consciousness wonders, there will be a pathway to explore that expression of light, stimulated and often held by a Greater

Heart, or those who work closely with them on the inner levels. There are great numbers of inner, enlightened beings on various levels of consciousness, but aligned and totally cooperative with the stimulating pathway of light held and nourished by those in the family of Greater Hearts. It is all organised to provide levels of conscious learning, opportunities for conscious choice, and healing for conscious awakening. Yet, there is no dogma, no enforcement.

For you, human upon this path, the journey you take is always of your choice. However, recognise that there is a greater picture of which you are a part, and if you choose again and again not to learn or implement the lessons of love – for ultimately, all evolution, no matter how it is qualified, is of love's expression – then you will simply need to go elsewhere. You are free to learn, but not free to destroy. That is the simple reality of learning, being, evolving, becoming here upon Earth, in her wondrous loving beingness, embraced by the angels and Greater Hearts dedicated to the deepening evolution of love into this body we call matter.

Your Note of Consciousness

When you become light in matter, you glow. Not a physical glow (although that may manifest for higher initiates), but a deep, inner glow of finely vibrating light.

Everything in our universe is vibrating, from very fine to very deep in resonance. A deep vibration will not harmonise with a finer vibration unless there is a harmonic relationship between them.

This is one way of looking at the evolution of consciousness, planets, stars, humans, all living beings.

If you resonate on a denser level, a higher vibration passes straight through you unhindered, for there is much space in the landscape of more densely vibrating substance through which the finer vibrating waves may pass, effectively both unhindered, but also un-perceived.

All vibrations of light and matter, and everything in between, carry the full wisdom of the note they sound in their vibration.

Take intuition, as a human example. This is the slight and gentle touch of a higher vibrating note, just registering in the soundscape of your consciousness. Or did it register? You are left wondering, did you hear or perceive that? What was its message? As your awareness ponders this, you become more attentive to that tiny sound, until in time you become more receptive, and can hear it better. This is a journey of refining and harmonising your vibrational constituents, such that there is enough silence, so you can hear it; and harmonious resonance, so that it can create that nudge of vibration within you in the first place. If your daily living creates a cacophony of challenge, emotional surges (desires), mental obtuseness (rigidity of thought), your soundscape has too much going on to be able to hear and resonate with a higher note.

We need to be able to hear these higher notes because they hold the promise of what lies ahead, as the unfoldment of consciousness occurs. They hold the note of love, to help you discern that which enables and empowers you to choose with love, and awaken to love, and become that love. They can hold the wisdom of the Greater Hearts, of Earth herself and of that which discerns the homeward bound journey of the soul, from the matter-bound journey of physical existence. As a human, you have both vibrational pulls at work.

Your task is to become your song, in which both the vibration of your physical nature, and the vibration of your soul, can sound and merge in harmony.

The journey of evolution is not to become the sound of light and soul alone, or else why be here as a human? It is not the evolutionary path to come here to Earth, just to rush off as soon as possible. Here I am talking to the awakening ones, who are in that process of perceiving their dense physical self vibration, as well as that note, that finely vibrating song of their soul.

There are many beings who incarnate here on Earth but do not stay. They have a small journey to take, a gift to both give and receive, and then, without (usually) having become aware of the great cosmic dance unfolding in consciousness around them, they leave.

However, if you have an awakening awareness of spirit, if your soul's love has sounded a note that you cannot un-hear – the note that urges you to seek, to understand, to resolve what at first seems dis-harmonious between your human self in vibration, and that soul note ringing throughout your consciousness – my friend, you are here to become a conscious heart, within Earth.

You are here to become a finely vibrating hum, a song of soul blended with your physicality, shining into the world with your presence, your harmonies at play, your wisdom and love resonating into that which is around you.

This is the journey of consciousness as a vibrating human self, full of love, resonant with soul, allowing the harmony of soul to sing through the song of your physical life. Then you can help others do the same. Then you are helping Earth become a planet of heart.

Heart is the part of our human selves that can resonate with soul. Heart is the part of Earth's self that can resonate with our physical hearts. In all mixes of sound vibrations, if there is a concerted effort to hold those vibrations within one space, then there is always a point at which the vibrations touch each other, no matter how diverse, and here is the start of awareness.

It is through the heart that this diversity of sounds, of soul, of human self, of Earth, mix. As you become more aware that all these resonances go through your heart, you can begin to sit with them, hear them, and harmonise them by turning down the volume of those vibrations that create discord, or that overwhelm other notes.

This is the journey with any truly spiritual practice, to dampen the sounds of past experiences that hinder awakening, and increase the resonance of those that bring love. You create the song of your being: physical, of light, of love, of Earth, full of the resonating vibrations of everything you have learned as a human, as a soul, and as a consciousness seeking oneness with love.

Then you shine, radiant in the inner, and perhaps physical worlds; harmonising your note with that of Earth and soul, helping the evolutionary resonance of love sound ever more deeply into our beautiful world.

This is your note to become. Start by making enough stillness in your consciousness that you can hear the note resonant in your heart, then you will hear the note trilling from your soul, the deep hum of Earth's livingness, and the all-embracing note of love's presence. As your consciousness awakens, these notes harmonise, and you become that harmony of human life, and light and love live in your radiant being.

The Living Evolution of Earth & Angels

In the living flow of angelic life, Earth is not a body of inert, lifeless matter, and neither is nature. Earth is a living being, evolving, expressing and becoming more refined and coherent in her vibrational presence, just as all evolving life must.

The interaction of Earth and angels is utterly life-giving, to both. Angels need Earth, for the very essence of their evolutionary journey is to be in the realm where substance can flow, for angels evolve through flow, not static presence within a fixed form.

In the evolutionary process through form, the learning comes from the stimulus afforded by external stimuli, and internal exploration meeting those stimuli at the edge of that form; and the stimulus from deep within via heart and soul, or enlightened inner teacher, when time is ready.

When you learn and evolve through flow, your experience and conscious development come from the discernment of all the differences available in flow: texture, density, speed, vibration (which we see as colour, or measure on other non-visible spectra of electromagnetic energy) – and through all these, the intent. Flow always comes from somewhere. In our Cosmos, it comes from the vehicle we know as heart, and heart always sends out pulses of life with intent.

Angels are imbued with this, from the broadest, fullest presence that the higher angels are both made of, and distribute; right down to the tiniest of angels who hold the smallest aspect of intent in the evolutionary flow of life's expression, for example, to aid in the building of a flower so that Earth's joy and nature's life force can continue to express in our world.

Evolution

For angels, Earth and nature are one of the rare places in our universe where living intent invites their participation in the physical expression of evolution, by blending spiritual flow with physical matter.

How does this happen?

All matter is gathered and conditioned by the internal forces embedded within its very structure, as all matter is fundamentally imbued with the blueprint of evolution that has enabled its creation in the first place.

There is a fundamental principle in the world of vibration, of which matter is a part, and that is that like seeks like. Matter of a certain vibration resonates with matter of the same vibration and they cohere in that resonance. As vibrational complexity increases, both resonance and harmony build between matter of different vibrational notes.

You can say exactly the same about the evolving human consciousness: we seek and connect with like-minded people, then in groups of people with nuanced perspectives but a like-minded purpose, and so on.

Angels work in the realm of vibration – for is not flow a vibration? This is an edge where the science of physics explores: when is an electron a wave of energy, when is it a physical point of matter? It can be both.

At this interface, on every level of form and of vibrational flow, is where angels can interact, and create positive influence on the vibrational intent being expressed.

The small angel that helps in the building of a flower receives vibrational guidance from the angel that works with the plant, or group of plants as a whole, and who holds the evolutionary intent for that plant. That guidance enables the smaller angel to bring a flow of vibrational influence on the matter created by the plant; so that the inner blueprint of life creates that stunning expression we call a flower. So it goes, on every level of physical expression, for all of nature.

Nature's evolution, and thus life-force, vitality, beauty and existence, is enabled by the angels that bring this refinement of vibrational stimuli into relationship with physical matter, by holding that matter in their flow of intent.

They will do the same for animals and humans, when that is permitted or required by evolution's progression. Remember, human evolution comes from the stimuli at the edge of consciousness in interaction with the world (driven by love, as previously detailed), and by the inner stimulus from soul, teacher, guide, through heart. Animals follow a similar path, just with a group soul (mostly), rather than an individuated one.

Angels can work at this edge of consciousness, and within the flow to and through heart.

To come back to the evolutionary flow in which angels touch, imbue and nurture Earth herself with the flow of love and light and cosmic intention: this is also a stimulus of Earth's evolutionary expression, and intent is felt.

As noted before, when you can feel a presence upon a great mountain, near a beautiful tree, amidst a field of flowers, within the healing balm of living waters, on the desert sands, or simply anywhere in nature upon the Earth herself, it is because there is a presence of angelic beings, holding that presence in interaction with Earth's loving, evolutionary intent.

However, Earth and angels do not evolve in isolation. Humanity has a significant evolutionary role upon and within Earth. Humans are of Earth's substance and of their own soul's intent, and the joint unfolding can only truly benefit both when human consciousness awakens to this reality. We are not here to learn what we want and then go, we are not here to learn only the human journey, for two reasons: there is no such thing as a human journey alone, for we incarnate and evolve within the substance of Earth and are thus part of her journey; and the very essence of our journey involves interaction with whatever is around us. This is love's driver.

Herein comes one of the major interactions we have with angels: through nature. That is why starving humans of an interaction with nature is so catastrophic for the evolution of consciousness. However, that interaction may come through simply being in the physical presence of nature with conscious awareness. Even in the barest and most barren of cities, where nature is banished, there will be some expression of nature somewhere that, with intent, you can use to ignite the presence of Earth's living, loving life-force within you. And thus open to angelic love of the Earth angels.

One thing to note is that this interaction goes both ways. Angels interact with nature to facilitate the loving and intentful flow of evolutionary expression, but that includes the evolution of humans too. If you acknowledge the beauty of a flower, the presence in a tree, the vitality anywhere you perceive it in nature, you open a flow of your love to those creating that presence. You open to create a relationship with these places and these beings, and that nourishes all.

In the urbanisation of so many of Earth's and humanity's places of evolutionary focus, we forget too easily that we still need to share our love with Earth, our evolutionary home.

The great and old trees, including some that remain in parks or gardens, usually have older and more developed angels, as they have journeyed long together. Peoples of the land, before urbanisation, would acknowledge and share love with these great beings, and loving flow would be reciprocated. Now these angels are in presence largely with nature alone, and are bereft of the key interaction with the human family, starving both of that mutual flow of love.

Where great and old trees are removed, the angels usually leave too, unless the human intent enables another focus in which the angel can bring its flow of conscious intent into interaction with Earth, and humans. This is rarely done, as human ignorance is great, but can be repaired, if human intention is applied.

Trees of the land in which they evolved have the closest relationship with the substance of the Earth at that place, and the strongest relationship may evolve that way.

What is your intent regarding nature?

See this as a two-way interaction and responsibility, and you will be blessed with nature's love, via the great embrace of angels, and you will help the gentle unfoldment of loving intent in our needy world, to nourish Earth, nature, and us all.

Our Relationship with Earth

In the flowing love that is life, evolution, nourishment, evocation of spirit – all things that we hope for and seek in human life – there is one further factor that is the enabler of all these expressions through us as humans, and that is our connection with Earth.

You are part of Earth because your being has been built of her substance. You may have brought some substance with you if you have developed different elements of consciousness in other spheres. However, what you are built of does not inherently connect you to it. It is like being in the embrace of mother: as a child you may welcome that, sink into that, feel the nourishment, heartbeat and love given through that embrace; or, you may squirm and wriggle to be free, because your attention is elsewhere.

Earth is the Mother that embraces us, but how often do you perceive this embrace that enables life, let alone sink into it and let love wash over you? As humans, we can connect with Earth in many ways, whether through awareness and consciousness, through physical touch or through spiritual understanding. But it is not just this connection that is needed. There is also a need to be in relationship with Earth for love to flow, whether yours to her, or hers to you. Without that love flowing, it is harder to live a sustained life of Earth and heart consciousness, which is where our evolution is leading.

We are here on Earth as part of an evolutionary journey with Earth, to create a planet of heart. This is not a mental exercise, or one achieved through emotional wishes, or physical actions. All these are good, but it is our relationship with Earth that truly enables spirit to flow, heart to prosper, life to unfold.

Indigenous peoples have understood their relationship with Earth, so much so that their personal selves have a more fluid boundary that enables them to be emotionally and mentally one with nature and Earth. They feel and think in concert with nature's expression, particularly in the place on Earth where they have connected for generations. This is also why they, and nature, have so easily been ravaged and dominated by humans who do not have this perception and whose consciousness is contained to the personal impulse, driven by self-interested mental or emotional motivations.

As our evolutionary journey continues, we do not need just one or the other, but a blend of both capacities of consciousness.

Much human evolution has been achieved by the tight containment of mental and emotional energy around the personal self, disconnecting from nature. It has allowed great development of mind in particular. But then what?

Mind can so often be like the squirming child that will not accept mother's embrace, thinking it knows better, knows all, is invincible. Look at the mind-driven exploitations of people, of nature, of animals, of our Earth, where, because we can, we do, without conscience – certainly without consciousness of the greater whole of which we are a part.

Development of mind has always been one of risk, from an evolutionary perspective, yet it is essential on the pathway of becoming conscious, and ultimately becoming a heart-centred being living in cooperative creativity within the greater flow of evolutionary love that enfolds all.

Mind develops by analysis, problem solving and breaking challenges down into simple choices so decisions can be made. Here is where mind and heart can agree: they both stimulate consciousness with the simple choices that are either yes or no, or that flow or do not flow.

The challenge is to merge these two levels of perception in our consciousness, so that they can align, and enable the flow of loving life force to infuse us, and what we do.

If mind has analysed, for example, a major life choice, and broken down all the reasons into the pros and cons, a certain decision can be reached, based on what mind can perceive. Let us say this was about a significant job or career change. Mind might evaluate factors such as money, time, further career opportunities, etc. Useful evaluations. However, your heart will evaluate as to whether you can evolve, whether you can be nourished, whether you can be in your heart's flow and contribute in that flow. In this age of unfolding heart consciousness, you need to listen to both.

Mind and mental analysis have been the pinnacles in much of human society for so long. This is a strong mould of our beingness, and it is challenging to take steps to break it. Yet it is so deeply dissatisfying if you hear the note of your heart sounding in your being, giving you that intuitive nudge, but you do not heed that, and exist only within the boundaries of known mind evaluations.

In the constructs of mind, you cannot feel Earth or be in relationship with her, because relationships need flow and connection, and mind does not do that. You may feel emotional connections to Earth, but being a fragmented human where a part of you lives in analytical mind, part in emotional flow, is challenging in this evolutionary moment.

Learning from the oneness that indigenous people have with nature is valuable: it is where you may change your mental and emotional awareness to be both in alignment with the living Earth and her presence, and with your own flows and needs. However, in the Age of the Heart we will need both the ability to use the separative, analytical mind, but also the deep connection that comes from being in relationship with Mother Earth. This gives the nourishment and boundaries for our personal expression. This gives us the ultimate presence of conscience, so that no matter how analytically justifiable an action may be, it will always be tempered by the conscience that comes from heart, that exists because we know we are not isolated, but part of this great being of Earth, and have her care in our awareness.

This is the path of heart, the evolution of consciousness that lies ahead, and the journey of love that invites all to open to, and connect with our beautiful Earth and her worlds of living expression through nature.

Loving Flow with Angels

In the gentle sweep of angels' wings, the softest touch is felt, whether by a human or a planet: receiving a healing touch, upliftment, the reminder of joy and hope, the clarity of love. It may be the gentlest touch, yet it is of utmost singularity and thus intention.

Evolution

Angels can be so singular in their work because they are of, and embody, flow. Flow is singular. It may be tempered in force, but not direction. It simply is, and all angels are in the gracious flow from higher realms to lower, for that is the only way flow can occur – so they have no need to doubt. Unlike humans, angels do not wonder, analyse, doubt, dissect the options, or fear the outcome of their flow. They can experience sadness though, when the flow is deflected, resisted or unwanted.

It is a tricky thing as a human, to discern and open to the flow of angelic intent, because we are not beings of flow. We are beings of form, we are builders of form, and our evolutionary journey is to build the form of our physical beingness (body, feelings and mind), and awaken consciousness throughout that form – thus building consciousness within the substance of Earth. This is the primary purpose of our opportunity to be here, incarnated upon Earth.

Angels work with flow, and are also here to aid in the development of consciousness upon Earth. We have touched upon how they embody and incarnate loving intent into and with the plant family, but, how, really, can they work with us, humanity?

Firstly, that comes with intent. If you care, truly care with your heart, then you shine from within and attract the input of both angelic and soul love. Like attracts like, so love (heart-felt care in manifestation) attracts love! Soul love comes as a stimulus of consciousness that awakens your journey within you: stimulating realisations, nourishing choices, stirring actions so you may step forward upon your path. Angel love comes as that gentle whisper, like a breeze, caressing your senses, awakening you to something outside yourself. Soul stimulus awakens you from within. Angelic stimulus awakens you from outside your conscious reach.

Angels are the vehicles through which we may perceive what is not within us, but also through which we can send out what is within us to Earth, to nature, to others.

Everything we do that shares caring and positive intention must flow through something in order to reach its intended recipient. We, as humans, have auric boundaries within which our consciousness is contained. With development (over lifetimes), we can learn to expand our energy presence both to hold greater light and to radiate greater love, but still, that radiance can only travel through a medium of similar vibration, and this is enabled by angels!

If left to time alone, more human consciousness could certainly achieve the capacity to expand and embody more light into the substance of Earth, and the evolutionary intention to create a planet of loving light could be achieved – but how long it would take! Too long, for cosmic, solar and Earth's intent.

The angels have come from the very beginning to be the medium through which the emerging intentions of light can sweep through the substance of earthly realms that is not yet illumined or light-infused. They span that space, reaching from human to human, nature and Earth; and from soul and Greater Hearts to humans, nature and Earth.

Thus their flows are essential for the evolutionary plan. Yet, as humans, we do not respect them very often, or even the idea of them. We, all powerful, individuated human beings, easily succumb to the idea that we control all in our space; that is a necessary motivator for conscious development. Without feeling like we have control over our place or our destiny, we would not be motivated to seek more control, and thus stretch our consciousness to achieve that, as life's and evolution's journey bumps us, inevitably, into situations where we experience not being in control of the outcome.

With increased awareness, we can awaken to the profound and beautiful presence of angels all around us, and recognise how they assist us to manifest positive intentions through care and love. Positive intentions are emphasised, because we do not always have those in our feelings, thoughts or actions. However, there is a difference between acting out of ignorance, and acting as if ignorant, when you have learned to choose more wisely. Basically, if you know better, you need to show it in your actions!

This is easier said than done. We have powerful programs that run much of our interactions, thoughts and feelings, created in past lives and often emphasised in this life's experiences. But that just makes what we can achieve more powerful, when the software of our being is updated to run a more loving, intentful program, more in keeping with the times in which we live, and where we are on our journey of heart.

Angels contribute this most essential of elements to our, and Earth's, awakening consciousness: they link the positive flows of love and care. As with all flows, when you feel it, you can be swept into it, and as others join, so the flow magnifies. Great loving intent can then manifest, awakening human consciousness through the experience, and nourishing the substance of Earth (and thus humanity) with the presence of the greater love and light brought through.

This is one way you can work with angels: let yourself perceive their flow, and allow yourself to simply lend your consciousness to that loving presence, so that it can magnify. However, be wary, for there are other enticing flows upon Earth, which are of human doing and built out of astral (emotional) matter that can also flow to some extent without angelic support. Flows of positivity always attract angelic participation, but flows can also be born out of the myriad of emotional programs in humanity; basically programs of anger and hatred, for these emotions are directional, and need a target, so to speak, and thus an emotional flow can be created. When these aggregate, usually led by one who is developed enough in consciousness to be able to wield such emotional charge, and therefore who knows better, these negative emotions gather and swirl amongst many participating humans (creating karma for all involved), and a tide of darkened astral waters may develop. It is with sadness in angels and Greater Hearts that these are created, for darkened waters harm Earth and the humans involved, and it is hard for angels and soul intentions alike to penetrate and enlighten this flow.

Beware, therefore, and discern deeply before entrusting yourself fully into the flows that awaken your feeling self. Go to your heart and seek truth. And never choose anything that invites and magnifies hatred of one to another, or anger in actions and thoughts. These separate human from human, and in encasing the human consciousness with the often self-righteous determination invited by these lower astral energies, these flows can solidify the personal self, creating such resistance to the true loving light that a shattering is often the only way the evolutionary journey can resume.

Unfortunately, we see these solidified emotional constructs of human creation in both organisational and national expressions, within which each participant will have their share.

Therefore, we also see now, and shall see more in the future, the shattering to release the energies bound by falsehoods, so that those energies can flow freely again, and be supported and nourished by angelic flow.

This describes a major way in which we take the conscious journey of evolution with angels: through our intent, qualified and carefully manifested by our conscious, heart-centred discernment and choice to be of loving and caring expression in our world.

The second way angelic flow touches us and our world is through nature. Angels not only guide the evolutionary expression that creates such beauty and wonder in nature, but they embody streams of loving light that flow into and out from Earth in special places. These are places where you can feel the presence of loving intent that is other to you, which does not come from within your heart and soul; yet it also stimulates your conscious awakening, and gifts to you the embrace of that loving presence that angelic flow creates.

Awaken your senses to this loving presence and gentle touch of angels, and let it sweep you into places of light where your heart sings and Earth's love embraces, and the pure singularity of hope's enlightenment nourishes your journey and those for whom you care.

Love's Intent

Loving Intent in Your Heart

In the pure white light of cosmic intent, every colour is found. In every colour is found every octave of existence, from human to planetary, to Solar and cosmic. The resonances on the octaves – or whatever musical system you know, for it is all the same in terms of harmonic resonance – enable development through such a myriad of pathways that the diversity we see in the evolution of consciousness is enabled.

In human terms, this is what energises the multiplicity of ways consciousness can develop – for this does not occur by a spiritual pathway alone or by a religious convergence of practice and insight (if not too concretised by dogma). It may occur through any field of human effort, exploration and service, as long as the light shines within it.

Even within the spiritual expression of light there is multiplicity, and here is the truth for every seeker of heart: all spiritual/religious pathways that hold light and teach harmlessness offer a pathway to greater oneness with soul, spirit, God – however that higher consciousness is expressed and is meaningful to you. Judgement and intolerance between religions, claiming one teacher is the one and only – this is human foible, and not based in reality.

The expression of loving intent is singular in its purity, but a multiplicity in its possible expressions. How would life evolve if there was only one expression? It would not. Thus, as replicated in our physical dimension, the singularity we call light from the Sun, our source of illumination both on the inner and outer, does in fact contain a great diversity of vibrations. On the visible spectrum this light can be refracted into the fullness of the colour palette we know in our world: the main colours of the rainbow, plus all the nuances of shades between them. In addition, there are the deeper vibrations extending from red through infrared and beyond, and of finer vibrations extending from violet through ultraviolet and beyond.

Just because we cannot see all these vibrations as colours does not mean they do not exist, and of course we know they exist through the capability to measure them scientifically. Now extend your understanding to the reality that vibrational waves have never ended at the point where we stop seeing, or hearing, or measuring. As measuring techniques evolve, so too will confirmation arrive, but do not wait.

Our universe is structured in the complexity, diversity and multiplicity of interactions between all the vibrations of cosmic intent. If you let yourself know this, you can let yourself believe in the finer vibrations of intuition, the nudges of consciousness, the calling of certain pathways, where perhaps in your human self, you cannot find fact or reason for this. When true light calls, there is always truth, even if not manifest in the physical realities you feel comfortable with.

In exploring the light and life of vibrations, we also have to understand that as they express in the physical world, there are blends of colours and sounds that do not hold a resonance with higher intent. This is possible because of the freedom to choose in the personal sphere of development, in mind, emotion and physical expression. This choice enables opportunity for more rapid evolution, but also for confounding mixes of intent from spiritual realms with human expression.

For example, the expression of love can be mixed with, and sometimes overruled by, sexual urges. The infusion of knowledge can lead to concretisation of ideas, arrogance and separatism. The presence of joy can become shrouded in astral glamours, such that things become the perceived source, not the actual presence vibrationally. And so it goes, through all the spectrum of loving intent's expression, in all vibrations of light.

One factor discerns all human generated confusions of light with matter (of mind, feelings and body), from that of the true light and intent, and that is how it resonates in your heart.

Your heart is the great truth-teller in your consciousness, when you give space for that gentle presence to be felt and heard within your being. It is not always easy or simple, but it is possible for every human to learn, for every human has a heart, and every heart is born out of the spiritual intent of soul and the gift of physical presence from Mother Earth. Inside you is that which vibrates in harmony (no matter what octave it is on), with the intentional note of spirit's love, and the harmonic of Earth as a living, loving being. Inside you is that note, that harmony, against which you can hold those vibrations given by life's circumstances and choices, and learn.

Still the voice of emotions, wherever they come from, and that of the fact-finding analysis of mind, and distil those vibrations until purity is reached. Do not dismiss them – purify them. Do not silence them, bring them into harmony, where the still note of truth may resonate, and inform your choice. In that harmony of mind and feelings, your heart shall either sing in that harmony, or be unheard. It is as simple as that, from a heart-centred vibrational point of view.

Of course, there are many situations when time does not allow deep consideration, or circumstances crush the opportunity to reflect. This is not a 'must do' in every experience to take an evolving path of heart. This is a guide, to nourish your thoughts, feelings, personal self: know there is a deep harmonic of love within you, a deep presence of truth and alignment with light, and you can find it. Seek it when you can, especially when making life-impacting choices, and choices that impact others or Earth in your care. Not all decisions carry the weight of major life importance, but listen to that small voice, that note, of your heart, for you may also be surprised at what choices do enable you to open the door to a greater presence of loving, living light to nourish you and those in your care.

Evolving consciousness is all about choice, else it is not consciousness you develop.

Understanding the reality of the vibrational milieu in which we exist is an essential component for making wise choices, for certainly in the extraordinarily diverse world of thought and feeling, theory and practice, dogma and opinion in which we live, there is no shortage of influences that seek to align us to their cause.

Your cause needs first and foremost to be that which sings in your heart, then you can work out the rest from there, and become more and more aligned and harmonised with the note of loving intent's expression that it is yours to sound into our world.

The Flow of Cosmic Intent

As light descends from cosmic intent down into denser substance, it will refract, or bounce off, or pass through unnoticed. This is the property of matter's interaction with waves of light on every level, whether cosmic, Solar, or earthly.

The greatest evolutionary unfoldment occurs when light can enter matter and interact, i.e., its waves can be felt and absorbed by that matter, because then the intentful stimulus within the light actually creates change in the matter. If the light passes through, then nothing changes, nothing can change, and – in human terms – ignorance remains. The same occurs if it bounces off. These two effects occur when the vibrational level of the matter has nothing at all that can resonate with the incoming light: no vibrations even on octaves lower in frequency that can feel in the tiniest way the passage of that energy through, or bumping into, its medium.

That is why throughout Cosmos there is a great cascade of beings of consciousness, who can hold the higher intent, and translate it into expression in denser matter with love. This is what happens upon and within Earth. The great waves of cosmic intent cannot be perceived by most, if any, living humans. The human body, its thoughts and feelings, are of a dense vibration, in order to exist here in the densest physical world of Earth. Through evolution, we refine and expand the vibrational substance we can perceive and respond to. This is why we often speak of the intuition as that fine, tiny sound – because it is! It comes, for most, from the note sounded by your soul, which is of a much finer vibration than thought, feeling or physical matter.

In order to perceive intuition, you need to firstly develop refinement in your human vibrations of feeling, thought and body, so it is possible for the vibration of soul to resonate within you; and secondly create enough stillness so your consciousness can perceive it. This has been the intent of all spiritual training for millennia; but it can also be developed on other pathways of human endeavour, because when the light of cosmic intent resonates in deeper vibrations, its refraction creates thousands of nuances of that vibrational impulse, and all hold the intent of the light. Just like a rainbow, in all its multitude of shades and tones.

As Earth engaged consciously with cosmic intent through her own evolutionary journey – and with Solar and planetary beings of consciousness assisting her – she created refinement and diversity within her own being, which enabled that cosmic intent to slowly and purposefully express in vibration and colour.

The conscious beings of Earth who assist this vibrational intent to be perceived and stepped down sufficiently to resonate within Earth are primarily twofold: those of the conscious human lineage, and those of angelic lineage.

Angels work with flow, so they absorb this loving cosmic intent and step it down through their own being, and then through the myriad of progressively smaller angels in their alignment; and flow it out into Earth and nature, and to the few of humanity who can cope with the particular type of intensity of angelic flow (although even then, that is usually only in small doses). The conscious beings of the human lineage also step down this cosmic intent, but do so by becoming that vibration, embodying it so that their being is of that light.

Think of this difference as between standing in a breeze, where you can feel it touch and flow over and through you; and standing in the radiance of a great light, where you can feel the light's vibration gently resonating into your being.

If you sit in inner stillness in the sunlight, you can feel its waves of energy penetrate your body. It is no different with the Greater Hearts of the human conscious lineage; they become like mini suns, radiating the vibration of cosmic intent into you via your soul, and into the Earth.

These beings of human lineage work together to create a whole, so that all resonances of cosmic intent have a landing place, a vehicle if you like, where that vibration can resonate. They work in the diversity of resonance that comes when light refracts into its constituent vibrations, and thus we have the many pathways of conscious evolution upon Earth, through every shade of the rainbow, guided by these greater beings.

All of these pathways are spiritual in their ultimate expression, but will manifest in a multitude of ways as they reach into the world of human expression. That is why we can see great scientists, for example, working deeply intuitively, or some may call it creatively, at the edge of known physical facts: the nudge of stimulus to explore in certain ways comes either from the perception of a higher resonance, in which the blueprint of life is held, or from a guiding expert on the inner levels of consciousness.

In every field of human endeavour, where the motivation is to understand and then enable improvement in our world, people reach deeply into the nourishment and epiphanies of higher consciousness, thus tapping into an expression of loving evolutionary intent as it cascades into our world through those of higher consciousness.

Musical and other similar creative expressions (but music especially) are a little different, as they primarily move the energy of emotion rather than illuminating the energy of thought and understanding. In the expression of music, we can often feel the flow of angels, who are attracted to support the creation and expression of music when the human endeavour is intentful on their vibration. Hence, you feel music which is loving, uplifting, deepening, awakening, joyful, etc., depending upon which angelic stream it evokes.

Music that moves you in a positive way, not just happy music, creates or evokes feelings that stimulate your consciousness. Music that does not do this is either not vibrationally simpatico with your conscious journey, or it simply has no angelic flow or higher intent.

It is the same in areas of human thought. Not all efforts of human intelligence are to create and stimulate insight into the human world.

Opportunity is there to open to and perceive that which comes from the worlds of finer vibration, because cosmic intent envelops our little

Earth, and is brought down into levels of resonance we can perceive by the greater beings of consciousness, whether angels or humans.

Then it is our choice: do we seek light and greater good for all? Or are we not yet ready?

Choice is ever the start of the journey of consciousness, no matter what resonance of the cosmic rainbow of intent your evolutionary path is on.

Living Light & Your Choice

Living light is that most wondrous of things: light, with love. Light, with evolutionary intent. Light, with every nourishment that you need to grow and evolve as a human being, to become an evolved consciousness of that loving, living intent.

We all feel joy when we feel alive. Life is inherently an amazing spark of joy, as light becomes a living physical or angelic consciousness, the streams of evolutionary intent we are exploring. Joy is felt in all expressions of living light, whether planets and stars, animals and nature. Something to ponder in your own journey.

Why living light is such an important concept, in fact reality, is because it holds all that intent of evolution and of love. And this is what is often missed in human interpretation of light from a spiritual (including religious) sense in this inherent evolutionary urge.

Often times, the intent that has birthed a spiritual tradition has been broken down into emotional or mind-focussed stages, controls, or destinations. This is often necessary to aid the young consciousness, but then what? Too often, that has been as far as it goes. The path has solidified around these smaller steps, and shut the door on what lies beyond because it was threatening; because the light that stimulates spiritual, conscious awakening, whatever path is yours to explore, is living light, and constantly evolving in its expression. Therefore, institutions and concretised doctrines that are fixed in a past expression may no longer be in alignment with that nourishing light.

Living light evolves in its interaction with Earth, humanity and all life in our sphere, because all life is evolving through that evolutionary stimulus. It is simple: you would not put a child through the same grade at school year after year, simply because that was what you know and felt safe with.

Evolution challenges what you know and understand, but this is its loving embrace, and is not to be feared! As humans, we fix ourselves to too many things – whether emotional certainties (which they can never be), mental rigidity of thought, and physical things – to create that sought-after goal of stability and control.

The challenge of human consciousness is ever thus: to experience control and take charge of self, but then also to relinquish control of certainties, so to be further infused with that living light that enables us to find the true joy of being alive. To discern the pull of matter's inertia – that is, its wish to remain undisturbed and unmoved, a property of everything in the physical world – from the pull of living light's touch.

If you do nothing else in your life's journey, apply yourself to this discernment, and you will find great peace, a living peace that nourishes with inner certainty and brightens that inner flame of love and joy.

You cannot find peace in personal certainty, if you are a seeker – which you must be to be reading this far. That is a possibility only for those whose life path is to be one of the many in the ocean of awareness, where individual striving and seeking is not their path, and they simply evolve (in this life) as part of a movement and unfoldment of the greater body (the ocean) of which they are a part. This is to say, that you do not always have a life of striving and consciously evolving, and do not need to, in order to remain part of the evolving consciousness of life upon Earth.

However, there are those that apply conscious intent to the proliferation and magnification of the material pull, that draw of inertia in matter; who celebrate and revere this as the greatest achievement of human effort and the pinnacle of being human. It is not the many who become swept up in this allure, through their own young consciousness being unable to discern material pull from living light's pull, but those who lead, who promulgate, who expound and magnify this inherent property of matter – here talking about the matter of human consciousness, earthly, emotional and of mind. These are the people causing the greatest harm to Earth and her living family of beings on every level.

Choice: ever it comes back to choice. If you have passed through a certain grade at school, and have learned those lessons, use them wisely. If only it were that simple! But it is not, although there is more and more pressure now from the increased presence of living light within Earth's body – the substance of which our bodies and consciousness are made – so that more and more personal effort is required to sustain a concrete thought, feeling or action pattern that is not at least in some degree of harmony with that greater whole. Eventually, either the effort needed, or the pressure of the ocean of Earth's living light in which we dwell, become too great, and the concretised world of personal power is forced to change.

This we see organisationally and personally all around the world, and in some places, nationally. The inevitability of change is absolute. The living light is here and awakening hearts on every level, in every expression of livingness. The change will be smoother, or more fractious, according to choice: personal choice, group choice, national choice, humanity's choice. Everything starts from your personal choice.

Do not take the future of world peace upon your shoulders, but also do not underestimate the power of your choice. When you choose to open, consciously, to the evolving, nourishing grace of your living light, that presence in your heart that infuses your body with the will, love and hope for life, your own life-stream flows within and through you to all you do. And like any flow, even if faced with constriction or rigid walls of concrete, there is always a way through!

No barrier upon Earth can remain unyielding in the presence of living light, because everything on Earth is made of the substance that is Earth, and she has awakened her heart and thus become more consciously infused with the living light streaming into her being.

Everything must unfold and evolve, because that is life. Even the most rigidly guarded, humanly motivated conclave of concrete thoughts, feelings and actions cannot remain unmoved.

How long will it take? That is up to everyone of conscience and consciousness: how much living light do you accept and harmonise within your being will determine the sum of conscious living light present throughout humanity; and as the living flow increases, then so will the cracks appear in whatever resists.

Do yours, not more, and life shall unfold in loving embrace, despite challenging change.

Hope lives eternal in living light, and that will nourish your heart the minute you open that door and seek it, just as it nourishes all life, and infuses each step with joy upon the journey.

Love's Touch in Your Heart

When love streams down into your being, it can be joyful, sad, wondrous, shattering in the realisations it evokes; embracing and nurturing, motivating and encouraging, or feel overwhelming, yet never so.

This is higher love, from soul or the loving family you have in the inner worlds. It evokes, creates, magnifies the full range of human experience, because love is light, the light of cosmic intent. The light comes with all of the plan, full of vision and insight. It carries all of the past, upon which the future is built, and out of which come the realisations of your karmic journey. It carries the fullness of truth: the truth of what is and is not infused with, alive with, that intent we call love; to help you discern on your path. And it carries the fullness of will, so that you can never be crushed or dissuaded from taking your next steps on your journey.

Do not be sad if the light triggers so many different emotions and reactions within you. This is normal. This is love, like an enveloping embrace, illuminating deep corners, exposing challenges to your thoughts and perceptions, awakening you to more.

Love always evokes more, because it is evolutionary intent: evolution of beingness, of consciousness, of humanity, of earthly illumination. How can this not stir you, and thus challenge those parts of you that do not wish to move and awaken, that do not know more than the structured or staid existence they have held, perhaps for millennia?

Our journey upon Earth involves much building. Humans are beings of form, of structure in matter, which is how you get to be a human being of light, love and intent, yet also of physical body, mind and emotions. Naturally, you build many experiences into the structure of who you are. We all do, no matter what evolutionary steps we are taking.

But understand this: to hold the light of the morrow, every temple is built of the stones carved of the substance of yesterday. It takes effort to build form; but that is the pull and enticement given to Mother Earth in her journey of awakening, else no one would come and stay!

It is the inner pull of gravity, which is love. For, as love is evolutionary intent, and as Earth evolved and took upon herself that pathway of intertwining streams of life that enables nature, animals, humans and angels to incarnate and evolve, then you may understand that it is her choice, and her love, that pulls you to her – once you have chosen this wondrous experience here on Earth. This is the inner gravity, the love that pulls you to Earth, to stay and evolve upon this pathway.

You build the forms of beingness that enable you to be here. Then the loving touch of higher light comes to you, and what you have built no longer seems right, no longer holds the light you thought it had, no longer has enough room to hold your greater awareness.

Note the parallels in much of the affluent world – and yearned for in many others – for a bigger and bigger house, car or wardrobe; but for what? Perhaps it is an inner trigger to note that you need to make changes in your conscious self, and expand the space in which you dwell as a conscious being, not just as a physical being.

The journey of conscious evolution that we are all on – for that is the journey Earth is upon – requires this growth of consciousness intertwined with the physical world. Here you meet all the pulls of nature, and all the experiences that come from that. Then, when you open to that great loving presence that is your life's embrace of soul, of higher angels, brothers and sisters in your inner family, suddenly (or perhaps not so suddenly), you see a different world. Then what?

This is the conundrum of living an evolving life upon Earth. Love gives love, but also shatters whatever no longer enables you to hold and be that love.

As Buddha taught, attachment causes suffering. Yet love invites us to connect, and attach. Jesus taught that giving frees the soul, yet the pull of matter tangles us with our material world, so we find it hard to give. The truths about the evolution of our consciousness into loving, present beings can be found in the teachings of all great teachers who embody love in its many nuances, and thus give it to the world in every colour, shade and intensity.

Just know that even those words of teachers past, those steps and structures created for their gifts to reach and aid you – they are also built of the substance of the times in which they were given. They are forms, and like all forms, they must become the substance upon and with which the new temple is built.

Do not be attached to any one way or teaching, unless it nurtures and excites your soul. How do you know if this is happening? Perhaps the nurturing and stimulus comes from the holding embrace of a familiar form, familiar words, practices, ethos, principles – any or all of these. Perhaps it comes from the gentle, or perhaps a driving presence of light from your own heart, or teachings that you embrace.

How you know if this is the lighted way for you is in your heart. In your heart is all that you have learned upon your travels life after life, and the wisdom of your soul.

Make space in your life for that gentle bell of your inner voice to be heard. Not the cacophony of emotional tangles, the rigidity of certainty of thought. Go past these and listen. Listen for the certainty that is not a thought but a whole body reaction. Listen for the loving emotional touch that has no demand or pressure in it, but just is. Then, you have found love, the love that nourishes who you are as a gracious, evolving human being.

Then you have found your answers, even if they create mixed emotions, evoke sadness, illuminate with unspeakable joy, uplift with indefatigable hope, awaken realisations that hurt. No matter the complexity, recognise these are simply the structures and stones you have built with up to now. They served you well in the past.

Now, listen to the voice of true love within you, and allow yourself to rebuild your inner temple to hold the light you are to become, and you will become that. Then you evolve, and can bring greater love and thus light to those you love around you.

This is the expression and journey of evolution's light within you, and if you feel its nudge and pull within your heart, then you cannot walk away – for this is love. Pure love, of evolutionary intent. Pure love, of which your heart is made. Pure love, of which Earth is made. Pure love, of which your path is formed, so that it shines before you like a mini sun glistening upon the waters of life.

Doubt & Certainty

In the loving embrace of the universe, there is certainty, for in that embrace there is all there is to know and do, to unfold and evolve through the plan. Every incarnational breath is born with certainty, for that is inherent in the force of creativity.

All artists know this. When the sweep, the flow of creativity is upon them, there is no doubt about it: no doubt about the need to express that flow; no doubt about the force and its inspiration, at its deepest level. There are myriad ways that creative force may be expressed, but still, there is no doubt within that urge to express, whether through the stroke of the brush, the chisel on stone, the expression of colour or words, the unfoldment of shape, the sound of musical notes.

Doubt is a particularly human experience, and it comes from the evolutionary path of developing mind. This is not the day-to-day mind that processes thoughts and feelings into words, that instigates actions and reactions in daily life circumstances. Doubt comes through the development of the analytical mind, the part of our conscious self that dissects and discerns, that divides problems until there are as few options as possible, so that choice becomes easier – for the mind at least.

This is where the difference between choice of mind and choice of heart is most obvious, for in the exploration of doubt and uncertainty, this can only arise in the mind. It is so important to understand this, because doubt is one of the greatest cripplers of action and strength upon the path of unfolding consciousness, on the path to enlightenment. Doubt of choice, doubt of self, doubt of life and your circumstances, doubt of spirit/soul/enlightened teacher/God – however you relate to that higher guiding presence.

Yet doubt is also one of the greatest teachers for the human consciousness, for we only experience doubt when we seek, hope for, yearn for something to the point that our choices really matter. If you have discerned options in your life, but your mental analysis of those options yields no clarity, this pushes your consciousness to seek more depth, more information, more factors that will inform that discernment, so that the choice becomes obvious.

Here we are talking about choices of significance, not choices of small everyday things, where routine discernment will usually suffice. None-the-less, if you doubt, look into it! Treat it as a pointer, indicating a greater issue is at hand than perhaps you first perceived. How many times has a small incident triggered a cascade of realisations that create a major change in life direction? Like the saying, 'the straw that broke the camel's back,' sometimes those straws do lead us deeper into life's unfolding journey.

Doubt is the key, and not to be shunned. Uncomfortable, yes, but that is the point, for we never evolve in comfort. Yet deep within our consciousness is that place of comfort, of certainty, of clarity, of deep knowing, because we are born of the breath in which the wholeness of life before us is held; the fullness of loving expression that is ours to become.

In deep life choices, whether triggered by smaller or greater experiences, inner or outer, we experience the pressure of doubt because we know there is certainty deep inside. But how do we create certainty in our day, in our life's effort, in our personal existence?

Our mental faculties in large part evolved through dealing with and relating to our life as a physical being, with all the physical, emotional and mental stimuli and choices that involves. We learn to discern in this world, to dissect and analyse problems, options and challenges, and make decisions. However, because our decisions affect not only our human self but also the fullness of our evolving consciousness within which we dwell within our hearts, there will always come a point when the certainty of the analytical mind is suddenly not so certain.

This is the undeniable push and urge of soul, the embodying life force within you, and which is born out of, and dwells within the vibration of that Ocean of Love within our planetary being. This ocean is a microcosm of the cosmic intent, the blueprint created by the breath of life, that holds the certainty of all flows of life into manifestation. This certainty is the blueprint for our own lives, in their evolving expression.

We are not just here once, then gone. Any analysis can see how meaningless this would be: to bestow such diverse experiences, sufferings, opportunities upon the billions of people alive upon Earth, with no pathway upon which to learn and discern, such that all may eventually live in peace and wellbeing.

Soul is the fulcrum of all these life experiences. Soul is where the certainty of life's blueprint exists, and is the deepest expression of this certainty into the world of matter. The pressure of doubt is urged upon us by soul, or by karma in the early stages, where soul contact of any sort is not easily attained by the newly evolving human self. Karma is the working out of that conundrum of certainty and doubt in human life, weighed up in physical, emotional and mental experiences and choices, and gifted to us upon those levels of discernment.

However, as analytical mind develops more discernment, you cannot but reach that point where analysis simply yields no clear option, where even the most mentally acute and decisive people cannot discern the best decision. This is the doorway to deeper knowing, the deeper knowing of soul, where analysis based on the human world of physical, emotional and mental experiences and circumstances does not enable choice.

Choice infused by soul contains within it the certainty of evolution's loving intention. That which is your life stream's joy to express. That which is your vibration, love, colour, wisdom – and most importantly –

that step that takes you forward upon your journey of realisation and greater oneness with that living light of your soul, of the Ocean of Love.

You cannot analyse your way to enlightenment or soul illumination and love. You cannot evolve through mind choices alone. Mind is not made of that substance of soul, in which resonates the fine sound of cosmic intent brought down through evolutionary beings such as the Greater Hearts and Earth herself; so that you can reach that loving intent that is pure certainty.

When you cannot find answers and discernment of options, when you are filled with doubt, you can use your mind to realise that this is your soul knocking on the door of your human consciousness, reminding you there is a deeper level to go to for this choice, a deeper level of consciousness needed to experience certainty. This is the blessing of doubt!

Welcome it as that touch of love, seeking to awaken you to yet more wonders and depth of life in all its joyful unfolding. Then the Ocean of Love's certainty will fill you, and life will renew onto the next step of joyful discovery.

Our Evolutionary Choice

The thing with evolution is that it does not happen uniformly. This is seen in the physical evolution of species and behaviours within species: some evolve quickly, some evolve in vastly divergent ways, while some stay largely unchanged. Science for the most part attributes this to chance, whether a chance mutation at DNA level, or chance discovery of behaviour that is valuable, then selected by the pressure of survival of the fittest, biggest, smallest, fastest, smartest, etc. These factors contribute, but nothing happens in the evolutionary sense that is not part of an unfolding whole of conscious intention, filtered down from cosmic intent through planetary and Greater Heart intentions, angelic empowerment and embodiment. Then always there is choice.

Every evolutionary step, no matter the family of beings involved – animal, plant, human, mineral – requires choice. In those families of beings where consciousness is not developed sufficiently in an individuated way to discern a choice, it is made by the guardians of those beings. For example, animals of young development, as far as soul goes, have a group of guardian angels who hold intention and guide evolutionary unfoldment. So do plants, although do not judge plant intelligence by the attributes of human form and function, for many of the great plants, mostly ancient trees, have great intelligence and ability to choose. Scientific research has already proven a small plant's ability to learn and choose to modify its behaviour when subjected to challenges, even remembering the learned behaviour months after the first stimulus was provided.

Entities (or perhaps more like energetic convergences) within the mineral family are closely aligned with the angelic family, as are plants and animals to some degree, as already described.

The intention for the unfoldment of conscious relationship between spirit, light, love and the physicality of matter here upon Earth is present in every life stream, whether through angels, or for more individuated beings like humans and some animals, through their own souls.

There is not really any such thing as the randomness attributed to evolution and the pathway of natural selection. There is intention in the very substance of which all life is made; that is what creates life! That is what differentiates livingness from inertness. Livingness, from an evolutionary point of view, is within any matter that seeks. Even minerals seek that which is similar in vibration, so as to aggregate in electrical relationship as crystals, gems, metals, etc. Nothing random about it! This is living intention in expression.

You need to evaluate the world through different eyes and thoughts, to be part of the consciousness revolution occurring. We, humanity, cannot continue to evolve as if we are the only beings of sentience, of livingness, of priority, of importance. We are evolving as part of a whole, Earth's whole, the livingness and intention of which unfolds all around us, and to which we must learn, or re-learn, to relate and respect.

The gifts of the Earth, whether plants for food and shelter, or minerals for the creation of so many things we utilise in our world – these are gifts for all of humanity. Human greed has turned them into commodities to trade for power, oppression, wealth and manipulation, which has no balance in it at all. They are gifts for all, from Earth who gives us life, so that we may live. This is something so important to resolve, for humanity to awaken and evolve more deeply upon the needed path of consciousness.

Regarding animals – Earth has not given them to sustain human life, because they are upon their own journey of evolutionary self-determination, and thus it is, and should be, their choice whether to give of themselves to humankind. Some people work in a sacred relationship with animals and Earth to take an animal's life for food. This is at least acknowledging the need to honour, respect and give gratitude to the animal and the Earth for that life.

Mass slaughter of animals in a terrifying way that is utterly disrespectful of that life is devastating to the animal and its relationship with humanity and Earth. It is not good karmically, meaning that it is not in balance with the evolutionary imperative for loving and kind relationships to be sustained for the wellbeing of all life. This imbalance requires rectification. If not done consciously by humanity, then other challenges arise that impact human life en masse, for this is a global problem, a global attitude of humanity as a whole, and thus a global harm for all.

If you choose consciousness as your pathway of growth and enlightenment, then either do not eat animals, or give them every blessing and gratitude you can to help in the re-balancing of this imbalance of life given and taken.

We are all in this together; this is what is so easy to forget on the pathway of individuation. Humans, to develop the faculties of choice and so to become significant beings of conscious cooperation on their journey, are deeply upon this pathway. Yet the ultimate goal of realising individual selfhood, power, consciousness, is to use this understanding to consciously engage with and relate to the world in which we live, to create goodness, wholeness, light, love and realisation of evolutionary intent.

This realisation is the threshold upon which much of humanity stands, in conscious evolutionary terms. This is why we speak of the Great Change, the great choice, the shift – whatever you perceive or relate to

– this is the great revolution in consciousness, before which step we stand.

We, the conscious ones – and those of conscious development who still immerse in the ignorance of pretence that the old ways can be sustained – we are the ones who must strive and choose, empowering the forces of good to proliferate. As you make every choice that enables goodness to flow, no matter how small, you create a pathway through which that great cosmic stream of loving, nourishing intention can express and manoeuvre into this world of human and global affairs. This is the true expression of evolution. Little by little, and greater by greater, choices enable an increase in loving flow, and those of less conscious intent are nourished and able to flow with the intent.

Water will break down even the hardest substance that can be created, if it can flow. You create smaller or greater flows in your life choices, in your everyday interactions, in your daily intentions. Thus you participate in creating these pathways through which loving intention will break down the rigidity of over-emphasised individuality and self-empowerment that much of humanity is clothed in, through personal choice (where they should know better), or by simply being blanketed by these forces that others choose and manipulate on their behalf. Materialism – the yearning for things because advertising manipulates desires – is a good example of how the model of individuation expressed through greed can blanket masses of people.

If you think and notice, do something. Become that tiny pin-prick of conscious choice in the wall of feigned ignorance blanketing many. Feigned, because it is created and fed by those who have enough consciousness to know better, but choose otherwise, and let the voice of their conscience be shuttered, even crushed, by their greed for power, wealth and control.

It is always a choice. Is it an easy one? That depends upon the karma that is your personal path of learning and responsibility. It might be a hard choice, because you have amassed a great deal of personal substance formed through lives of power, need, greed, or suffering. Then you have more substance of your being to manoeuvre and shape into that which aligns with the flow and intention of loving light. This may be more difficult, but then it also gives you greater depth of wisdom and consciousness when you do so align. Harder choice gives a greater benefit.

Recognise, though, that you will never have a harder choice than what you have the capacity to rise to and achieve. It may feel like it is, but that is the nature of any conscious growth, or indeed of learning on any level. If you are not stretched beyond what you currently know and can do, then nothing is learned, is it?

Make your choices: small, great, life-changing or simply a daily smile, and be part of the Great Change in your conscious intent.

There is hope for all, when all who notice and can make the choices that really matter, so that loving light, the life-blood of Earth and all her life-streams, can flow and not stagnate into darkness.

Do your bit, open to the flow, and share it in your way to enable blessings to spread around the world for all to be nourished.

This is possible by (and is needed to enable the fulfilment of) evolution, that intentful force behind all unfoldment of consciousness and life: the loving grace that guides all; the presence that gives and needs your choice.

Choose, and be a co-creator, not a stagnant destroyer, and all life shall shine in radiant brilliance.

The Three Forces Creating Heart

There are three forces at work that are energising and giving impetus and strength to the awakening of heart consciousness. A force is directional, and is the embodiment of intent. In the context of evolution, that intent is always of a higher vibration, for that is what holds the wisdom, the oneness and the possibilities of the union of higher intent with the substance in which it seeks to resonate. It is what draws out and magnifies the already existing resonance that lies in the heart of every life-form on Earth. We are all born of the intent of spirit clothed in soul that lies resting in our hearts until the awakening call is sounded.

The three forces at work are:

1. The force created by Earth's conscious decision to open her heart, thus increasing her heart flow and its force;
2. The force of Cosmic Heart, seeking to bring greater heart flow and resonance into our earthly sphere; and
3. The force of angelic intent to engage with the building of heart in our world.

Why humanity is not mentioned here is because, collectively, the higher human consciousness of soul is not separate from the consciousness of Earth. Our souls reside in her Ocean of Love, her astral self. As Earth awakens and consciously chooses to align with and embody more heart flow, the force created by this choice embodies in her being and thus infuses our souls. Her choice ultimately guides our souls, for we are here as part of her journey – for as long as our spiritual path aligns with her choice to become a planet of heart.

Recognise that this is a long journey, which is why it can be hard to understand how all human beings are aligned with this evolution of heart when human behaviour can be so spiritually and physically destructive. In this long journey, however, there are points of great choice – meaning choice beyond that of one life's expression and action. These points of great choice are periods when the choice is not just personal, but is in the evolutionary context of humanity and Earth, in their partnership and evolutionary commitment.

We are in one such time of great choice now. Through Earth's awakening and opening to greater heart and heart flow, humanity must respond. The souls of humanity are infused with this evolutionary intent, this force of Earth's choice. It is both our personal and collective choice as to how that infusion of force at soul level manifests and reaches into our personal lives, choices and actions.

Some, who are young of soul, may not have the ability to resonate with and imbue this force individually into their human expression, but this is where it can happen collectively. Thus, the importance of strong leaders, able to compassionately and clearly resonate truth and meaning into the human world, so the younger members of humanity – those who have not walked the path of evolution for as long – can be nourished and guided to open to the resonance of heart.

As much as this seems a one-way flow from Earth's choice to embody this evolutionary force, it is also a choice she could not make without the heartfelt cooperation of the human family. This is a partnership of conscious evolution, and enough human choice has been made, and alignment achieved, for Earth to open her heart further and create that increase in opportunity for heart flow through her, and through us.

Consciousness is always created in the resonance that occurs in partnerships, whether that is between higher and lower, inner and outer, physical and non-physical, or personal and collective spheres. For Earth, her partnership is not only with us, but with the higher, nourishing, guiding love and light that embraces and infuses her being, which is Cosmic Heart. As our souls are infused with Earth's spark of love and her intent for evolution, so is her inner being infused with Cosmic Love and intent from Cosmic Heart.

Earth's choice to awaken more heart has been stimulated by that loving presence seeking greater heart consciousness, for that is the intent, the force, of cosmic evolution. Again, it is a partnership, for while Cosmic Heart sends out the resonance that stimulates and stirs the inbuilt heart light in all embodied planets and stars in this Cosmos, there is also a conscious choice needed in that planet or star to allow that Cosmic Heart resonance to awaken deep within.

Earth has made that choice, and thus the force of Cosmic Heart becomes a force in Earth's sphere, and thus a force provoking and enabling another great step in the evolutionary journey.

The third force, the force of angelic intent, is another type of partnership within the sphere of earthly and cosmic conscious expression and evolution. Angels are beings of flow. They bring the life-giving force of intent into every level of our universe where conscious intent can engage; in other words, where the resonant call of Cosmic Heart vibrates sufficiently for conscious life to begin.

Flow always has direction, and thus it is different from the stimulus of resonance, and yet they are linked. For example, through your force of intent you might throw a stone into a pond, expressing the flow of your intent in your action. When that stone, carried by the flow of force you gave it, hits the water, it sends out ripples. Those ripples are like the resonance: the reaction of the substance in which the force is applied. In this way, angels can be great agents of evolutionary stimulus.

On Earth, angels bring their intent and loving embrace to nature and Earth's physical body in many ways, stimulating points of resonance so that consciousness can awaken, and evolution unfold. This we see and feel in the uplifting beauty of our natural world, and the resonance that touches us and reminds us to care about this living planet in whose embrace we live. However, in conjunction with the two other forces of Earth's heart and Cosmic Heart, a new expression of angelic intent is now coming into being: the creation of heart. Hitherto, broadly speaking, angels have brought stimulating and guiding flow to nourish the evolution of light, the path we have all been upon in this earthly sphere. Through light, consciousness has been awakened in the substance of our world and nature; and in us, so that we have been able to become beings able to express our own will and force in this world, and thus be sufficiently anchored here to hold the increasing evolution of heart.

Angels have brought this stimulating flow, like the stone creating ripples in the pond of our world. Cosmic Heart and Earth heart have created light through the co-resonance of substance created with their evolutionary intent, reaching into our world through our souls and hearts.

Enough consciousness of light exists in our world for Earth and Cosmic Heart to align in creative intent, and seek to awaken heart consciousness in the deeper physical substance of Earth's being. In this evolutionary moment, the force of angelic intent is aligning with that choice. It enables that flow within hearts in our world, not just as ripples in the substance of our world.

A heart is a built structure that has form, yet exists only to create flow. Angels are masters of flow, yet not of form. For heart awakening to occur in fullness, not only is there need of that co-resonance of Cosmic Heart and Earth heart through our souls and hearts so that we awaken heart consciousness, but there is need for flow, so that the life-giving gift of heart flows into our world. While there may be some heart consciousness without flow, it is only the stillness of *knowing* heart, rather than of *being* heart. Angelic intent is aligning such that those who choose can awaken not only that resonance of knowing heart, but can open the door to the full consciousness of becoming a flowing heart.

To help this, many angels are seeking human embodiment, so as to better understand the form-building nature of the human self, and thus better understand how to bring these forces of heart flow and heart form together in their conscious intent.

In reality, these three forces are working as one evolutionary intention, yet they are manifest and expressed in different ways, hence the value in pausing to reflect upon these as individual inputs to our own conscious journey of heart.

In grasping the resonance of Earth's heart choice, Cosmic Heart choice, and angelic flow, we awaken greater breadth and depth in our consciousness. Awakening to flow helps us move from the more familiar resonance of knowing in a contained, form-focussed experience. Awakening to the force of heart choice resonating from Cosmic Heart through Earth heart, stimulates the reality of the evolutionary call within, and the urgency of the hour.

We are the most physical vehicle through which heart consciousness can express, because through our hearts we can resonate with Earth's heart intent as we are born with that in the substance of our being; and, with openness to angelic intent, we can learn to become beings of heart's flow, and share this love in our physical world.

We are where these three forces meet, and this is the evolutionary moment where your choice to awaken heart consciousness, in resonance and flow, matters. Find your way to make that choice in your day, your life, in balance and peace, and be a conscious part of the wondrous opportunity of this great moment in evolution's loving expression of life itself.

Consciousness

True Consciousness

When you let the sweep of love flow through your being, you awaken heart. If it is emotional love, personality to personality, it awakens astral flows, which can also be harmonious with the vibration of higher loving intent that is from soul. Emotional love can stimulate in you a resonance of that ripple of soul presence, and that is what truly awakens heart.

Why emotions alone cannot awaken heart is because of this difference in vibrational resonance. Heart is the place in your being where this most magical, mystical and divine interaction occurs: soul and matter meet and vibrate together.

At first, in the early lives of an evolving human, the vibration of soul is so fine compared to the physically-focussed human expression, that there is no medium through which soul resonance can sound. The young human journeys through many lives, and begins to differentiate the substance of consciousness in their being.

Consciousness is that mix of matter, which is the vehicle through which the vibration and light of higher intention (for example, from soul) can resonate, *along with* the perception of the intention behind that vibration.

How many times have you had that tiny ripple through your being to warn, or invite certain choices? It is so faint it is too easy to dismiss in the split second in which it arises. Only it never leaves you, and either you dismissed it and realised after making your choice that you needed to listen; or you listened and changed your choice accordingly, then to realise how nourishing that was.

This is how consciousness arises! Not only do you begin to perceive that almost imperceptible vibration in your human self, but you begin to understand the intention behind it, because you witness, and can learn from, the consequences.

This is true consciousness, which is the awakening of matter and soul in a co-vibrating whole that can express the love and light of higher intention. This is the consciousness of heart: for that is where this vibration and intention of soul lives within your physical self.

It takes many lives of learning and refinement of self for that soul resonance to begin to nudge your human consciousness, and awaken that true consciousness of heart.

There are many words duplicated in the description and exploration of evolution, and 'consciousness' is one. Many attribute consciousness, fairly, to one who is self-aware, and mentally and emotionally harmonious to a sufficient degree that there is obvious synchronicity in vibration between emotional engagement, mental directive, and physical action. This is legitimately a kind of consciousness, because within the contained system of the human self, within the personality of mind, emotions and body, there is higher intent from mind. Or it could be from highly refined, devotional emotions – devotion to any cause, not just a religion – followed by alignment of mind, emotions and the body to enable action that expresses that conscious direction.

This is an example of what we may consider consciousness; however, the human consciousness cannot develop and stay so contained in isolation from the stimulus and intention of soul. This highlights the challenge of understanding true consciousness – for it requires a break in those alliances formed vibrationally within the human self alone.

If you regularly hear the voice of your mind, nudging you with past-learned patterns and experiences, you can see this as conscience – but as it arises from within the human consciousness alone it is only able to give you the perspective of mind, and what has been learned by mind. For example, let us say, you learned that it is wise to stay silent because of uncertainty in your intellectual ability in certain company, and you do not speak out when unethical or damaging decisions are being made by others. This is a legitimate instruction from your mind because that is the breadth and depth of what you know.

However, your soul may nudge you with that little voice that requires you to speak out, to raise a voice of conscience. To listen to that, you have to break that built-up dependency on the directive from your mind.

You can repeat this example on every level, for it is the same with highly-motivated emotional inspirations. Just like with mind, unless the soul intention is stimulating that inspiration, you are only able to work from the learned patterns of the being you are now.

All of this is perfectly fine when dealing with many routine events, experiences and choices in daily, human life. But there comes a time when that is not enough, and for many humans that deep inner choice comes now, in this life.

We are in times of significant change in the milieu in which we live and evolve. Earth is evolving: her being holds more light, so we, humanity, must choose to either incorporate that light into our beings, or, simply, go elsewhere and take a slower path of evolution. Do not panic in the misapprehension that this is a once-off choice now. It may be for some, but if you have some inkling of conscience which awakens consciousness to the greater whole and your responsibilities within that, then you have already said 'yes' to some degree. Your choices going forward will be about refining that choice in your being, so that you can become an even greater vehicle of the consciousness of your soul, which comes through your heart.

Do not try to find soul through mind. That is a confusing route, for mind is the vehicle of dissecting and analysing, and soul is a unity, yet infinite multiplicity, with which the analytical mind cannot be one. Yet, it can acquiesce to it, when that voice of soul, as conscience, as the voice of intuition, gives the inner rationale with which mind can then align.

Similarly, do not seek the representation of soul consciousness in emotions. Although they can truly be of a fine and higher vibration of beauty and love that can sweep you away, emotional substance is still only able to vibrate, move and flow according to what has been learned from lessons and experiences past, and unavoidably contains conditions and limitations. Unless your emotional self is clear enough to be able to harmonise with the loving light that resonates from soul, be careful of what sweeps you to action or decisions of consequence.

Listen. Listen for the note behind these known vibrations of your human self. Listen for the little voice, the bell of your intuition – and evaluate that in your heart.

In your heart is where you can learn to discern past learned actions and reactions from the actions and guidance of soul; because in your heart is the part of your physical self that has always known soul. This is the place within your being where your life is created, and sustained, until your soul calls you. This is the place in your being that is the source of life force that sustains you. This is the only place in your human self that is constantly imbued with soul, even if only in the tiniest of vibrations, just enough to sustain life, which is what happens in early incarnations.

As your evolution unfolds life after life, you begin to hear more of that note sounding through your human consciousness. The more you allow this to stimulate and awaken you to the possibility of different mental and emotional choices, reactions and responses, the more you awaken in you the true consciousness – that of soul, with all the wisdom it has learned able to resonate within you. This enables you to take steps in life that express that higher wisdom and intent, and thus express the greatest love there is: that of soul, full of wisdom and knowing, full of understanding and light.

This is how you become a true being of consciousness, so greatly needed upon Earth, to enable the Great Change to be enacted through the voice of conscience unhindered by the limitations of mind or emotions.

Heart in Your Daily Journey

In the striving to walk a path of heart, of awakening consciousness, of striving for goodness in every step, it can at times seem unattainable, impractical, in the swirl of daily challenges and personal disruptions. It is so easy for judgements to arise – of self, of others, of the world at large. What gives balance in this striving is to know the journey, not to fixate on the destination.

Truthfully, we do not, and cannot, know the destination. As we walk the path, as our awareness and consciousness increase, we see with different eyes, and perceive with different faculties. Yet we will not undertake a journey without some sense of where we are going, or else our steps on the path may just take us wandering every which way. A challenge with this is that we may then hold up some gloriously attributed being of loving light and compassion as the being we want to be. Instead, we need to focus on finding and bringing more of our heart's wisdom into our day, because when we do that, we can both live in the present in all its challenges, yet also know the direction and goal of our striving. This allows evolutionary flexibility, without the constraints of an overly constructed goal.

Heart holds this wisdom because it is the junction of soul and human, and gives life. Life is always of this moment, never past, nor future. We are alive in this moment, and what we choose to do ripples out from this moment. Make this moment one where you seek heart, when you can. The more you do this, the more you infuse your personal consciousness with that living light that is of your heart – and inevitably you will change to become a being of more heart.

It is not much different to taking a path of intellectual learning, or of physical training: you never start at the point where you should know all of that learning, or have the physical capacity already developed.

Awakening heart is the same. All spiritual journeys are the same. What they have in common, whether intellectual, spiritual or physical, is:

1. you are aware of what is offered and the attainment that can be achieved;
2. the starting point is within your reach physically, conceptually, intellectually (or as often in our world, financially); and
3. you want to do it.

In the physical world, these are easy to quantify, assess and make decisions about. On the spiritual path, how easy is it to think we do not have what it takes, or to feel we are unworthy, or find reasons to distance ourselves from the starting point or to dilute our desire to take the journey?

These challenges are more easily created when the sense of the path, and of the attainment at the end of the journey, are held only in our mind and/or emotions. Mind is very practiced at creating things that are not us, in its processing and dissecting of life's problems; that is its forte, to objectify and create distance. Our emotional self loves to engage with a goal that creates good feelings, but is not much good at taking a nuanced journey. Emotions are instant, in that they are rarely sustained. Even if you have emotional reactions that are familiar to you, that is not because the actual emotion is still in flow around your being, but because you have formed a pattern in your emotional self that is easily reactivated, to generate the same emotional response. This works for both positive and negative emotional reactions. We remember old angers and dislike, just as much as we remember our love and care in certain situations and for certain people.

The un-patterning of these emotional patterns and mental constructs is part of the journey. However, at the same time, it is challenging to take a spiritual path when these personal forces have a strong guiding hand in our motivation and daily choices. They are rigid, or transitory, requiring us to either be constantly thinking about our path and deciding if we stay on it or not, and/or to constantly engage emotionally with it to enable us to stay on the journey. Neither of these is humanly possible in the flux and flow of everyday life.

Rigidity is the worst challenge to the path of heart at this time. As can so easily be witnessed in our world, consciousness, awareness and reality are evolving very quickly now. In past millennia, having a mentally-focussed and emotionally-formed spiritual goal that you structured into your being could work for a whole lifetime. A goal, for example, to learn and serve in a church, temple or monastery, where what you could become, and the steps on the path to get there, remained largely unchanged over time.

In its simplest expression, this is not untrue today, if you look only at the goal and the hope of its attainment. However, problems arise because of the layers of human intervention that have built increased complexity and rigidity into the pathway, and have narrowed what can be reached at the end of that pathway.

The human mind and emotions love to build and strengthen the familiar. Then you have to deal with all the human personality challenges of power, corruption, bias (for example, to women, race, gender), which build other constraints, rules and requirements. Over the millennia or centuries that most religions and spiritual practices have been present in human consciousness, this has turned the simple spiritual gift and pathway into many different offerings. Some still hold the original intent, and some people can still find that original love, simplicity and truth on their journey. On other pathways, the rigidity is too unaligned with our world today.

This is ever the challenge of a spiritual impulse, for it inevitably becomes enmeshed in the less malleable world of human thought and emotion in order to be tangible and reachable for humanity. Yet that in itself builds forms that are no longer able to adjust to the changing spiritual imperative.

Here is where the gift of heart arises: it is that place of melding of soul and human self, it is the source of living stimulus, and as such, it is expressing the living stimulus that is needed for now, this moment. When you choose a path of heart, you can be assured that the loving light you can tap into will help you in this moment, this experience, this choice.

The challenge is letting go of your need to know what the next moment, experience or choice will bring. This is not simply a detachment, because you cannot walk this path in detachment because it is a path that needs all of you. The path of heart is the path of walking in living light, the living pulse of your soul's light expressing through your living being. You cannot detach into a mind-space where emotional attachment is distanced, dismissed, or repressed. You need your emotional self to flow with this life force. Similarly, you need your mind-self involved, because life needs decisions and choices to be informed, and your mind is your go-to for this.

The challenges on every spiritual path are to be able to engage with the goal, to find the starting point, and to want to take the journey. When seeking a path of heart, the best way to meet these is to realise that:

1. The goal of heart is to be a living light that will infuse you with the fullness of love, purpose and hope, in every moment. It is a living experience, not a destination of knowledge, stillness, certainty or oneness, but a living expression that is also what is unfolding within Earth herself.
2. The starting point is not outside you, in other people's hands, in others' doctrines or teachings, although their stimulus can help and must not be shunned. Ultimately, you can start at any time, because the awakening is in your heart and reachable by all who seek.
3. The desire to take this path is, of course, your own choice. However, recognise that this is the path of conscious unfolding upon which Earth is evolving, and so all beings in her embrace must sooner or later open to this journey of heart. As the infusion of living light increases through her evolution, it becomes easier and easier for all to choose and engage with this path of discovery, illumination and love.

It is not a distant attainment, but a living experience in your day that brings you step by step further into the living light of the heart. It is not a remote shining light, but the one radiating in your own heart, that is the destination of your journey, and that is something you can turn to at any moment, in any moment of stillness and desire to be there. Open to your heart, you may be surprised how nourishing that can be.

The Difference You Make

What difference do you make?

Every soul can make a difference to the evolutionary imperative for greater loving flow to be present on Earth. How much, and how, that loving flow manifests in our physical world is a choice we have as individuals.

Consciousness

There is pressure from the inner worlds, because Cosmic Heart has sent a pulse of loving, living light, and Earth has responded. She has opened her consciousness to this flow, at least some of it, and that means the ocean of living, loving presence in her being, the loving ocean of her soul, is filled with that cosmic impulse. This is the pressure of the Great Change we are in, and have been in for over a century.

Earth's soul body is expanded, vibrant, and full of cosmic intent, blended & harmonised with the vibration of her intent: to become a vehicle through which the resonance of Cosmic Love can vibrate. This needs cooperation and alignment of her lower bodies of consciousness; which exist and express as nature, with her families of plants and animals; as the mineral family deep in her own substance of matter; as the angelic family whose role and presence we have already touched upon; and then, as the human family.

The expression through nature, and the mineral family, are closely tied to the engagement and loving flow of angels, for angels bring that flow of consciousness to guide and nourish these families and expressions. There have been crisis points where many angels have wondered if they can continue to bring that loving, evolving flow into Earth through these life forms. That has not been because of what these life forms are, or because of something in their relationship with Earth, but because of human action which, en masse, shows such disrespect for Earth and her life either through ignorance, or through greed.

Here then, comes the extremely important understanding needed: human choice not only affects how much of that flow from Earth's Ocean of Love can move through and nourish our own beingness; but we also impact how freely it can flow through the angelic guides and guardians of all other life and presences upon Earth.

This choice has already been made at soul level, but because of the particular evolutionary path human beings are on, the personal self must also choose in order for that loving light of soul to get through.

Earth has awakened her consciousness to Cosmic Love, and welcomed that nourishing, stimulating pulse of Cosmic Heart bringing loving intent into her soul. Human souls dwell in the lower (mostly) vibratory levels of Earth's Ocean of Love that holds us all in love, and guides with evolutionary intent. Greater Hearts of the human and angelic families dwell in the higher levels of Earth's Ocean of Love, holding the human and angelic aspects of this loving intent within their consciousness.

For the Earth's Ocean of Love, pregnant with that infusion of cosmic loving intent, to infuse through the depths of that ocean into her physical self, there need to be places where that flow can move through into her body.

Our physical understanding of flow gives insight into how this works. As the volume and intensity of the flow increases, then the pressure builds everywhere that flow meets resistance. From the point of view of consciousness, which is what we are exploring, the point of resistance is where evolutionary change occurs.

Hence, we have this great Ocean of Love seeking expression into our physical world, and human consciousness is the major vehicle through which that is enabled. Some flows through angelic guides, but human choice can also inhibit this. Some can flow through temples and sanctuaries dedicated to love's unfoldment, mostly held by Greater Hearts in quiet incarnation for this purpose.

However, humanity is the major expression of evolutionary consciousness that has the choice, collectively, and as individuals, to open consciously to this Ocean of Love because we hold the largest embodiment of consciousness within Earth's matter. At least, the promise of consciousness.

As individuals, we can make a great difference. The pressure is felt by all, and shows as personal, group and national challenges arise, and fractures develop as the pressure seeks release. But remember, this is pressure from the Ocean of Love, and the pressure is released by flow, and flow, once enabled, can create a cascade of force to sweep all before it.

This can be a positive and empowering experience, or a shattering one. Are you ready for more love, for more consciousness, for more responsibility as a soul expression upon Earth? Then loving flow shall empower you. You will never be given more than you have capacity for.

If you are not ready, the question is 'why not?' Many are young souls, and the pressure of choice does not weigh upon their human consciousness. Instead, they feel the pressure of the global, national and organisational (group) structures that are failing to express this needed change of intent so that loving flow can move through them, which creates societal pressures along the usual lines: international and political insecurity, financial systems, food and water supply, energy, etc.

It is not their choice as conscious beings where the weight of pressure lies. It is with those of us who can perceive, even via the tiniest voice of conscience and consciousness, that we need to change.

When that tiny voice, or the voice of changing circumstances, or global awareness, or societal pressures, tinkles in our personal awareness, it is the sound of a choice of importance to be made. That is the point at which we need to choose an uplifting, albeit transformative, shift in our expression and beingness upon Earth; or we allow the pressure to build, whereupon, eventually, the force will burst through unintended, unguided, and may shatter and crush whatever blocks its flow.

This sounds dramatic, but is fundamentally true; whether it be a significant release of pressure, or a smaller one. We have all had life experiences that have shattered, and we grow from them. We have all made choices that have led to significant changes in how and where we express our beingness. Mental breakdowns and related mental health challenges, on a significant rise throughout humanity, are an expression of this pressure; and they often lead to an awakening of consciousness. Personal and societal choices are needed to aid this.

Choosing a different job, or a different home, city or nation in which to live, can also be expressions of alignment with that unfolding pressure of conscious change. Every one of us is a unit of consciousness, no matter how developed, and as such we form a significant number of points through which Earth's Ocean of Love seeks to bring that flow into our shared physical world.

This is how the Great Change unfolds: the pulse of Cosmic Love has touched and been absorbed by Earth. Her Ocean of Love is filled and energised, and seeks to flow into her physical being. Some flow can move through angels and nature, but humanity is the major vehicle of conscious choice for that loving flow to express in this beautiful world.

Your choice, smaller or greater, enables alignment in your being to that flow. As more of your consciousness flows, others can see and perceive that, and change unfolds. Nothing we do, or choose in consciousness, is isolated from that unfoldment in our earthly and human worlds.

These choices can be inner and personal, in attitude, expression or relationship. They can be outer, in personal things such as work, and organisational effort. They can be in support of organisational and societal change, or through resistance to greed and overbearing oppressiveness, as examples.

There are many, many ways you can express your choice to align with and embrace the flow of loving intent through your being.

Simply be aware, and choose, for then you become one more point of loving flow's expression, and as we all do this, we create a wave of loving intent that shall enrich Earth life for all.

Choose well, with discernment from your heart, for there you know.

The Search for Meaning

In the search for meaning, you cannot help but turn to the inner side of life. Circumstances and physical things, in and of themselves, have no meaning; they cannot have any meaning. Meaning is a product of evolutionary intent: it is that part of you that seeks and yearns for that which holds the light, the grace, or at the very least, the familiarity that matches what is nudging you from within.

That is why, at times, just from one day to the next, or one week to the next, your satisfaction with a job, or a place you live, or even a relationship can dissolve. The job, the home, the relationship have not changed – you have. Of course, sometimes these outer influences do change and stimulate your response, but here we are exploring how it is that you experience this need to change, when those outer circumstances have not.

Within the evolution of consciousness, the expression of the greater living light, the pulse from Cosmic Heart filled with intentful love, infuses all where that pulse can be perceived. Earth perceives this pulse for she is well on her way to becoming a planetary being of greater consciousness. The highly evolved beings in her inner levels have also perceived and absorbed this loving intent, and, with Earth's embrace, help it resonate into the substance of which our souls and human selves are made.

The impulse that stimulates your need for change can be from this filtered-down evolutionary stimulus. Very, very rarely is it from the mind, even if it seems to be formed as an idea by the time it reaches your consciousness – which it often has to, for you to be able to understand, choose and respond to any stimuli. Emotions can be another driver of change, because they, unlike mind, are (or at least can be) more fluid in their movement within you and in interaction with your life's circumstances. Emotions may also be responding to the stimulus of your soul and global conscious shifts of Earth's intention, or they may be swelling and swirling within your own personal sphere due to your own human patterning, or they may respond to both.

Your task in the circumstance, where the need for change arises within you, is to discern what to do, as a step on your personal journey. Even what seems the smallest change may elicit a cascade of unfoldment in your consciousness. Or it may be part of the journey to clear some of your patterning that restricts your soul and heart's flow within you, so that the next impulse that moves through you may awaken more, both within you, and in the circumstances around you.

In talking about the basic evolutionary driver, we talk about love as that inherent quality present within all forms of life within our universe. Love drives, and enables the seeking characteristic where substance seeks connection with other substance of like vibration. Ultimately, we seek harmony, and yet it is a living harmony, able to sound a beautiful note or chord in the soundscape of life itself. It is not a static hum that never changes.

This is the fascinating edge of consciousness: ever seeking to be in harmony, and yet ever seeking to evolve. That is because, even if we find harmony in our outer world, or to some degree in our inner world, there is always part of us that is other, and thus that brings in another note, that changes the sound of our being, that nudges us to seek yet further. That is simply because we are not living beings in a vacuum: we are within a great embodiment of consciousness within Earth herself; Earth is within the embracing conscious intent of Solar presence, and all is within the living, flowing and intentful love of Cosmos.

As you experience the nudge to change your situation, you are responding to these stimuli. Even if it is a push from within your own emotions – or from what seem to be outer circumstances that are not of your doing or in your control – the inner drive is always to try to find that new level of harmony that feels right. It all comes back to your path. Each person responds differently to life's situations; your journey of heart and consciousness is to understand what is driving your response.

Go back to the source: if it is an emotional reaction, what is that from? Is it because external change is needed, or is it internal change? Is it a reflection of a deeper nudge from your soul, or is it a step on the path of karmic re-balancing to clear patterns in your being that hinder your harmony? While you could see these as being ultimately from the same source, they are not exactly.

Your soul stimulus comes directly into your heart, or to your consciousness via trusted inner teachers and guides, or both, depending upon where you are at, and how well you can consciously journey into your heart's embrace. Karmic stimulus involves more. It does arise in concert with your soul, because your soul must agree to the stimulus, but karma occurs in relationship with others, whether with humans, nature, or Earth herself.

Karma can be perceived as good or bad, but in truth it is neither. It is instead a re-balancing, a re-harmonising of your presence in the greater world of which you are a part. The determination of karma involves interaction between all parties involved, mediated by Greater Hearts who can represent the bigger picture, the greater harmony, to be attained. It is much more complex, yet follows the same principle as all evolutionary impetus: to stimulate awakening within matter, so it can resonate with the soundscape of love's evolutionary expression.

Whatever the stimulus, seek the cause. Not with endless mental analyses, for you cannot analyse your way to soul and heart knowing. Just enough analysis to determine if this has a deeper stimulus. If you keep going around in mental circles, or cannot discern what to do, that is the most basic pointer to you that this is a challenge that needs another input. Similarly, if your emotional response and movement around the situation keeps looping through the same old pattern, go deeper to review.

Ultimately, you can only find certainty on your path of evolution by seeking that steadiness within your heart; because it sounds the note that is in harmony with who you are, what you are to become, and how you harmonise with those around you and the world you live in.

None of this is instant, for just as you do not expect a five-year-old child to have the capacity to solve university-level problems, neither can you solve deep and complex life-path issues until you go through the various levels of love's schooling in this life, and in life-after-life. It takes time! But the more you know, resonate with the truth of what lies ahead, and realise the goal of conscious becoming within you, the more you are able to align and harmonise yourself within life's circumstances and relationships, and seek your heart's loving resonance to guide you.

The challenge of evolution is that we have this drive to find harmony and resonance with that which is around us, and yet, although this is always the goal, ultimately what is around us is also evolving, and so we must adjust. Spiritual maturity comes as you realise that the drive for that inner peace, that you find when you have inner and outer harmony, is only a stage in the journey. As you attain and realise one harmony, you become a being of greater resonance, and thus become aware of more vibrations around and within you – and so the path to seek a new level of harmony lies before you.

This is why great teachers who are truly upon the spiritual path (not just people who are good at emotional manipulation and marketing), have an influence far beyond the reach of the normal human energy field. They hold in their consciousness the finer vibrational notes of harmony that reach further and further into the world, and thus can be felt from afar by the sensitive student.

It is important to understand that the yearning for peace, that place of inner and outer harmony, is one step on a pathway of stepping stones. Your task on the evolutionary journey is to discern what is driving your yearning, and allowing that to guide you from heart – while also accepting that this is not a destination, and to embrace this journey with love.

Do not stress over it. All is peaceful in the loving intent of your soul within your heart. There you can find the reasons, and can gather and guide yourself with understanding and compassion on the next steps of your journey.

This is the meaning that answers all your inner questions, and that ultimately gives you hope on your journey; for here, it all makes sense, and love flows away all the challenges that stick and hinder – when you are ready, and when you say 'yes' to the journey.

Find your way to this loving place in your heart, and life can become more meaningful in the harmony of who you truly are, and the note you sound in this complex world of choice and challenge in which we live.

Awakening Consciousness of Your Path

When you open your heart to love, you open to flow, whether from soul, or from higher emotions. Desire may be motivated by a higher intent to connect, with love; or it may be created by emotional patterns only. If you seek mental connection through engagement in ideas, while not a flow in and of itself, it may be energised by a higher motivation that aligns you with a higher intent; or it may be driven by mental patterns built up over this and past lives, or by emotional need expressed through a dominant mind.

The key to evolving your consciousness is to awaken in you the discernment of the source of these desires, thoughts, actions, needs, wants. You cannot rely on what feels right, or what you consider you know as right, because feelings and thoughts are primarily created and motivated by the reality of living, creating and connecting in our physical world, for that is where we live in our human consciousness. This may be fine, and where it is not, karma will teach the boundaries and rectify any misuse of energy and force that may have occurred. This evolves personal integrity as a human being, eventually, but as the world we live in is going through such rapid change at this time, it is not enough for those who want to stay and evolve upon Earth.

To participate in this period of rapid change, to enable your capacity to contribute to positive change, to refine your actions and connections such that soul intent can guide, you first have to learn to discern between the familiar drivers of mind and feelings, and the guidance of soul.

How to do this?

Firstly, decide this is what you want. The power of decision-making in opening your consciousness is profound, because, as human beings are on a path of conscious development and not simply flowing along in the great unfoldment, there has to be choice.

Soul guidance is never forced upon the human self, unless agreed to in conscious choice before incarnation, to create certain effects. Soul is always present, and evolves by gaining the elements of higher vibration life after life, achieved through personal learning and experience from the human journey.

The paradox is that the more lives a human being has, there are both more lessons and light created that develop into wisdom in the soul, but also more patterns within the human self that build into certainty at a human level, reducing the openness to soul. This is normal evolutionary development. You could liken it to the development of a child: as they become more developed as teenagers there is the sense (commonly) that much more is known and understood than the adults around them perceive. To mature from teenager to adult, the thinking and reactions have to change. To mature from being more unconscious of soul, to opening more to soul, also requires different thinking and reactions. You can find the reflections of our evolutionary journey of consciousness mirrored throughout our single human lives, if you look.

You, as a human being, have to make a choice, and then change. This does not require great change, although it may, for example, if you choose a path of deep religious or spiritual immersion in a life of singular dedication. For most, this is not the path, so then, what does it require?

First, the choice. The choice to seek and enact the guidance of higher vision, wisdom and love. To do this you need to acknowledge there is more to life than your human motivations and experience, and for many that is not a hard choice. The rapidity of change of Earth's body of light in which we dwell stimulates both our inner reflections and questions, and the outer world where karma guides a faster pathway through the needed lessons. These bring the human consciousness into greater alignment with the loving intent of evolution expressing through soul, and through Earth's embrace and need.

Second, the adaptation of thought, feeling and action in the light and impulse of the inner wisdom that you can access. Here is where, for most, the greatest personal effort is needed. Here is where you need to remind yourself of your choice, to continually bring in that note of your higher guiding light into your daily life; because the only way you can update the patterns in your thoughts, feelings and actions is to realise there is another way; and that can only arise if you continue to impress upon your human consciousness the stimulus that gives light to that other way.

This is why a spiritual practice is always recommended, to give both indication of your human choice to your soul, and to create pathways whereby your soul and/or your inner teachers may stimulate your awakening and change.

At every step, discernment is your ally. Discernment of your practice: is it nourishing your awakening, or comforting with the familiar? Check in with yourself: is the familiar truly giving you the clarity of, and nourishment for your next step, or is it part of your human patterning from past practices? Reflect, and do not be afraid to seek something new.

Ultimately, if evolving your consciousness is your choice at this time, then you will have some place or sense in your being where you can discern what guides you, from what stagnates in you.

Whether the tinkling whisper of an intuitive thought, or the ever-so-gentle nudge of an intuitive feeling; or perhaps it will come through outer circumstances that force a re-think and re-evaluation of your path. Just do not ignore these stimuli. Embrace them and realise they are your guides, to stimulate greater awareness of your soul, your purpose, and the expression of that purpose in your life.

Find the practice that stimulates your awakening to your inner wisdom and guidance of soul, and then see how to enable that inner wisdom and guidance to be infused into your thoughts, feelings and actions. Find how to repair and adjust the patterns of your human self, so they can update to the new consciousness you seek, and not cement over you with the certainty of how you have always done things.

There is a myriad of ways to do this, but one thing is certain, you cannot change your human consciousness by being absent from it; by immersing into a new found spiritual light and dwelling there; by bypassing human life in the hope your spiritual self will solve it all.

Your journey of consciousness as a human being is not to dwell in the consciousness of your soul, but to merge your human self with your soul. Then all the valuable and detailed learning you have in your human self can be present, so you can engage with and make a difference in this world. You can be guided by the wisdom of your soul that has developed and refined life after life, and is also infused with the loving embrace of the evolutionary intent of Earth's soul, infused similarly with cosmic intent through which all evolution unfolds.

Keep at it. Whatever your path and your choice, you have the tools in your consciousness and/or are stimulated by your circumstances to find what you need to take your next steps. That is all you need to take a path of soul realisation, to experience more grace in your personal journey, to know that deep love of soul that shines in you, and bring more of that loving light into our needy world.

Heart Intuition & Discernment

If you want to walk a spiritual path in this evolving era of the awakening heart, you must develop your faculties of intuition. Think of it like the language of the heart, for it is that. It is not a wafty, fleeting impression from somewhere outside of you, but is your higher consciousness, expressing through your heart. This is true intuition, the language of the heart.

This is different from the other single, indeterminate nudges or messages that you may become aware of from time to time. These are typically from inner helpers, guides or family members, seeking to draw your attention to something. It may or may not be helpful, because, as always, it depends upon their intention and connectivity to higher consciousness; and it also depends upon your past relationship, which may create filters in your own consciousness that modify the message given. Other inputs that we often attribute to intuition arise from our emotional body, in its interaction with the environment.

If you think about our human intelligence and consciousness, we can attribute our learning and growth in awareness to the five senses we have in the physical world: touch, hearing, sight, taste and smell. These are all inputs to how we assess our situation and circumstance, and upon which we make decisions and learn.

As a spiritual being, you have many more senses, through which (if you train them) you can detect other inputs. As they are always vibrational inputs – because that is what the inner world consists of – to perceive them, you need to do two things:

1. create enough moments of stillness in your day so they can resonate into your consciousness; and
2. train yourself in their language so you can discern.

Where your emotional body is picking up energies around you and is seeking to communicate them to your physical consciousness, you most definitely need to discern. Your emotional body is of a finer vibration than your physical body and senses, but it is also conditioned by your journey as a human being. You may have particular fears, and react more strongly in certain situations than is warranted. The same can be said of prejudices, memories of past injustices, difficult relationships. You name it, and you probably have it as some kind of residual vibration, or blockage in your emotional self. We all do. First you must discern what you are picking up in this feeling world, and see if it has been over, or perhaps under-emphasised by your emotional self.

This is where you come to the heart. It is all but impossible to discern whether what is going on in our emotional perceptions are our reactions or a legitimate stimulus on an emotional level to aid us in our day – without having a still point in our being that enables comparison and evaluation.

You cannot truly evaluate intuition with your mind, because your mind is similarly structured with what you know, or do not know, with blockages and undeveloped areas. That is why we still walk the path of learning upon Earth.

Many people use their mind to evaluate what they pick up intuitively, which most usually results in the intuitive perception being dismissed. On the other hand, too many people consider that anything coming from a place other than the physical senses is true and infallible, which leaves them open to all sorts of inner rubbish.

Our inner worlds are as full of young and evolving beings as our physical world and, in just the same way, there are those of undeveloped consciousness who get up to mischief, or who may even have malevolence they have not yet cleared from their consciousness.

If you perceive on the inner levels and just believe everything you see, hear, or come to understand without applying any conscious filters, you take the risk that you will attract the attention of those who want to disrupt and create mischief. They have their own personal agendas and desires, and rarely have your journey of light in their intention – even if they may be good at pretending that they do. This may also be the case with those guides and relations on the inner levels with whom you have a relationship: do not take everything they suggest as absolute truth!

You are your own person, on your own path, and, while you can certainly be gracious to those who offer advice or assistance, you do need to discern in your own consciousness.

As the Age of the Heart unfolds, and more evolutionary impetus is given to awakening heart, this is where you go for truth. If you truly go to your heart, then you are seeking that input from your soul or can evaluate other impressions and insights you have had, in the light of your soul. Even just the tiniest of glimmers of soul light in your heart will illuminate what you are wanting to understand and evaluate: either it will resonate with that light, or it will not.

That is the wonder and brilliance of heart intuition: just like the physical heart, it either has flow, or not. Or, if working with the vibration of light, it either resonates with your soul's vibration in your heart, or it does not.

For big issues, you may need to unpack all the nuances, until you feel you have the right choice to take to your heart. You may have several, but what you obtain from aligning with the intelligence of your heart, is a singular answer: either a yes, or a no; or if it is neither, it is not the right question, or the right time to ask it, or you have blockages to clear to be able to hear the answer. The more you go to your heart, the more you can train your consciousness to learn this language and discern.

On the path of conscious awakening, this is essential, or else you can find yourself in the swirls of confusion created by your own reactions and/or the unclear inputs of inner beings not evolved enough as yet to be fully illumined. The main reasons it is essential are that your five earthly senses are built for traversing life in the physical world, and cannot guide you on a path of conscious awakening. When you seek that inner awareness, you need to learn the senses that help you traverse that inner world. You need to learn the language of your heart.

Your heart is the centre of your being where your soul touches you, where your spark of life exists, and around which your physical embodiment has been built. The intention for your life's journey is held here, for this is your soul's knowledge, manifested in you for this life's unfoldment.

When you have trained yourself to go into your heart, you bypass emotions and mind, and reach that place where truth shines, and discernment is nourished. As with any learning, repetition and gentleness are your best guides. It is more and more easily found, as heart consciousness is awakening around and within our world; but remember discernment. As more consciousness awakens, so too is there more disruption created by the gentle yet undeniable evolutionary pressure. Obvious in the physical world, it is there in the inner world too, on the lower levels of vibration. Use your discernment. You have enough to take you to your next step, and then you will learn more. Do not take any inner journey without it. Your discernment from the heart (not of mind or emotions) will enable you to learn the language of your heart, and hear the guidance of your soul, and thus awaken the fullness of loving light in your being to illumine and nourish your way.

Discerning Emotions

If you want to understand intuition, look to your experiences and the input of your every day.

Variations in vibrational tone and level are the language of your inner perceptions. The learning to be undertaken is how you perceive and receive their presence into your conscious self, or perhaps how your conscious self reaches out into the worlds of finer vibration. Either way, this is how you learn the language of your inner self.

The study and awareness of emotions is well developed for many – at least for predominant emotions – but the usual focus is on labelling them and using the mind to change them if that is wanted or needed. For example, anger is one we learn about from a very early age, as the temper of a two-year-old manifests when challenged with limitations. Then we learn from the swings and roundabouts of wants and desires, love and loss, hope and disappointment, grief and joy, and many more.

To learn the language of vibration and thus intuition, you need to go beyond the words that describe these emotions. You need to bring another level of discernment into your awareness, and that is the vibrational note of the emotion.

Emotions are fluid, mostly: being relatively quick to flow and recede when stimulated. Your emotional self is a vibrational body around you and interwoven through your physical self, and responds to the vibrations in the environment, and to causes arising in your personal consciousness.

From the environment, you pick up vibrations with which your emotional self can resonate. This varies, depending upon your experiences and learning from your many lifetimes, upon the learning journey you have incarnated with in this lifetime (where karma gives opportunities and restrictions to empower your experiences), and upon the emotional substance of the family and society into which you were born. All of these give you familiarity with certain emotional vibrations because you have grown up with them, and had opportunities to expand or refine your emotional awareness through the lessons learned.

Familiarity leads to two possible pathways as far as consciousness goes: either it leads to awareness of the familiar emotions when they arise, or they simply become part of the lived experience and do not become part of your consciousness. For example, if you grow up in a family filled with stress, you may not recognise stress as an experience, unless it is more extreme. If you were immersed in love and care, you may not have noticed it was there until something changes. If you regularly experienced fear or trauma, you may shut them down in order to reduce the challenge of those feelings (until they may re-emerge, for example, through Post Traumatic Stress Disorder). There are many examples.

Emotions that arise within you are built out of the same substance as those we have just described: the emotional milieu of your upbringing, and life in general. This is the substance available to you to work with. However, they can become qualified by your intention – whether that is to direct their flow, for example to a person or situation; or to magnify their flow; or to merge different emotions into one reaction.

We also have many experiences locked up in our emotional self that may hinder flow, stopping its expression until the flow is dammed so much that it may burst out, with unintended consequences. Or we may have built channels and confined our flows to certain well-worn expressions. These are usual in the human emotional body, and affect our ability to engage with, and work from, a higher intention of love and light that needs the freedom to express the fullness of emotional vibration, unhindered by these limitations.

What you pick up in the emotional environment could be likened to living in water. You might only notice it when there is difference, for example, it becomes cold or hot, or if you bring your focussed attention to it; or you may not notice it at all if your focus is elsewhere.

This outlines the general development and experience of emotions, although life's journey gives much more depth and nuance to your emotional development.

Now let us come to working with emotions as a language of vibration. Here, the descriptive label you may have given them does not necessarily help. What matters is what the level of vibration is: is it higher, finer in note and sound, or lower? Is it a mix, where a higher note may create a resonance with a lower note so that the two sound together?

For example, let us look at devotion. It can be a very finely vibrating quality that uplifts the devotee and touches those around them with that upliftment. Or it may be a controlling kind of devotion, where a person has been forced into that expression by their life's circumstance or by their need to repress other emotions, or both. This is not an uplifting energy, and those around them may feel constrained, criticised and maybe even condemned, if they do not apply a similarly heavy-handed discipline.

Which is best? That entirely depends upon your personal journey and karma, and both expressions have their challenges and can lead to much personal growth of consciousness. The journey of consciousness is to learn to differentiate based on their vibrational note, not on the descriptive words used.

The same can be said for many emotions. They can be finely vibrating, they may be singular and pure (pretty rare), or mixed in their levels of vibrational expression. We have plenty of emotional experiences in our lives to explore these subtleties, and this is a valuable place to begin the journey of discerning the vibrational truth, and develop the foundations of intuition.

You have no doubt already had intuitional experiences, and can also use those to review and explore how that input reached you, and what it taught you.

Emotions are the easiest inner level of our beingness to explore, because we have so much awareness in our physical consciousness of them, and how to use them. However, there is plenty more to discover, as the emotional body of humanity as a whole has just about every expression you can have in this vibrational milieu, and much of it needs a good cleanse.

Because emotions are of a fluid vibrational expression, one of the experiences we have most often is simply that: the movement of emotional substance. In and of itself, this can become something that is sought, for in its own way that can be a stimulus. The challenge comes when the stimulus is on a lower level of vibration, unlabelled, unknown, but somehow appealing. Because emotions are fluid, and because they interact with the emotional energy environment in which we dwell, they can become a current, a river, an ocean of flow, swirling around in the ebb and flow of all the people who seek, or do not resist, this experience.

When it is a lower vibration, it can lead to mass coherence of human reaction that can become a negative expression. Always, such a mass coherence of lower energy is shaped and given direction by those of more purposeful intent, who know, at least in part, what they are doing, for example, a political or religious leader stirring up a crowd.

Before participating in any mass movement, reflect on what the driving intention is – for there will be one. Dig deeper and reflect on every layer of your own response, and on what is promised, given, taught, expected by the body of energy and those who guide it.

The challenge with such amassed emotions is that they get to a level where the mass movement creates its own currents and waves of flow, and the originating intent can be hard to perceive. This is challenging for humanity at this time, when there are so many means to communicate and thus create and stimulate this emotional coherence.

The positive is that this emotional coherence is what can also create great positive change on Earth and within society; but only when enough of humanity clear their heavier emotional vibrations, through personal intentional change, or karmic experiences.

The exploration of emotional vibration not only changes you and awakens in you more understanding of the language of intuition, but also you change the milieu of human emotions globally. If we all make a little effort, then the tide of change would have more gentle and positive currents through which to reach humanity and the world in which we live.

This is a good place to start on a journey of consciousness. Heart light needs to flow, and emotions are the vehicle through which our heart's expression can reach deeper into this world, and bring that loving light.

Find ways to use awareness of heart to help you discern, for when you truly go to your heart, you can perceive those emotional energies that are not of a finer vibration, and learn how to activate your discernment.

In terms of changing vibrations of a lower level, everything from spiritual practices and healing to psychological therapy can help. You have to seek that which resonates for you at this point in your journey. Use your increased emotional awareness to discern!

When you seek with heart's intent, you will find pathways and practices that aid you – just remember to never 'set and forget' – for as you change, so too may the pathways and practices you need.

Certainty, Change & Choosing Light

You will be wrong. On your journey of spiritual unfoldment, your mental faculties and emotional maturity cannot keep up with the internal changes occurring within you. These changes create not only those inner reflections that differ from what you know, understand and feel certain about, but also have a ripple effect on the energy around you. Hence you experience the grace of karma in action, with the stimulus that brings, (most often a challenge), to help speed up the change.

If you did not find yourself in these challenging situations, how on Earth would you grow and evolve? You cannot become a spiritual being by staying in the consciousness you have already developed. You cannot become more infused with soul certainty and living light, if you maintain the constraints of your current personal knowledge and emotional capacity. Even if you do not perceive that your personal self is constraining, it most certainly is; for without constraints you cannot learn either.

Consciousness develops at the edge between what is perceived, and all that lies beyond. If you incarnated as a fully present soul in a human self:

1. your soul would not have learned from your many lives of experience how to work in this milieu, for this milieu functions very differently from the ocean of loving light in which your soul dwells; and
2. as a human, you would have no conscious awareness of how to express soul in this world, and would not be able to contribute any wisdom to that expression.

At best, you could be a little beacon of light, like a statue, but your ability to engage with the world, and express and create with light and love in it, would be pretty much non-existent. In other words, it would be a waste of an incarnation. This incredible privilege of incarnating is given to those who want to develop that human consciousness, so that they can contribute to the evolving unfoldment of conscious presence in our world; not to be uneducated, unaware, perhaps even uncooperative, regarding this global evolutionary imperative. This is a soul choice, and a dispensation given at that level, hence why so many at the human level seem so unaware of the great opportunity and responsibility they have.

This is also why you will be wrong at times in choices, insights and actions: whatever stage of evolution you are at as a soul, as a human, you have another step to take, and then another. You will be confronted with the edges of your current conscious capacity, so you can perceive the need to go beyond that in order to progress through your current challenge. Since you do not as yet have the consciousness to know, understand and enable the best choices to move forward, mistakes are an inevitable, and also valuable, experience.

As humans, we all have this curious characteristic of seeking certainty, whether mentally in rigid thought, emotionally in set patterns of perceiving and enacting feelings, or physically in the environment we set up around us; or in all three.

This is a characteristic of matter itself, and the pull it creates that binds us into this physical world, so that we can have lives in this curious milieu of human and earthly expression. Curious, because it has little resemblance to the world of souls; but none-the-less, is deeply attractive because it has reflections, vibrationally, of soul, and so we are drawn and held here as we seek.

This of course reflects Earth's choice, made many millennia ago, that resonates and hums within her: to seek that melding of soul and physical consciousness, so that the loving light of Cosmos can fully harmonise into the physical world, and shine into the universe from there.

Every soul that sends out the impulse to incarnate here within Earth, has made a choice to be part of this greater journey of consciousness that Earth has chosen. It may not look like this on a human level, with the significant number of people who demonstrate and act out of greed, the need for power and control, and what seems like utter ignorance of the needs of Earth or of their fellow humans and other living creatures on this journey. But this is also the edge where consciousness is so rapidly unfolding at this time, affecting Earth's population en masse: the understanding of our relationship with Earth. This is our personal and collective responsibility, and karma guides many opportunities for choice and response.

It is in itself a paradox, that the pull of Earth that gives us the wish and opportunity to be incarnated here, is also the pull that binds matter-to-matter, the force of love in action where like seeks like. This creates the inherent capacity of the human embodiment, to build within this pull, that which is familiar. Thus, we build forms of thought, feeling and our physical world that resonate with what we know, feel and find physical comfort within.

Then, as Earth's evolution progresses, and the resonance of her being changes, what we have built comes to be in discord with her. Similarly, as we progress from life to life, and what we have learned in each life begins to cohere in our souls as wisdom, the inner stimulus for each incarnation holds new light. We incarnate with familiar patterns built out of what has worked in our previous human lives, but now our soul stimulus resonates differently, and the Earth substance from which we gather our being as we incarnate, and within which we seek to express, is also different.

This is explained in broad terms, and simplistically, for there are multitudes of nuances in how life and consciousness unfold. However, it is important to understand the gist of it, for sooner or later you will experience the result of these changes – or perhaps you already have, which is why you are seeking.

Your task as a human is to learn and understand that what was, or what you still hold to be, a certainty, must go if you are to expand your consciousness. Not in a great sweep of dissolution, although some may take something like this path after passing away, and go through what you could call an ascension process where much of the human-built forms within the personality are dissolved. To awaken consciousness here and now, you need to make choices and consciously participate in the disassembly of old thoughts, feelings and structures you have built around yourself; and then construct new ways of thinking, feeling and being, out of lessons learned and held in the old substance.

Even just the tiniest hint or nudge of consciousness will enable this to be a conscious and positive change, because somewhere in you, you have that certainty that empowers you to face the inevitable challenges that arise from change.

This is the certainty born out of the harmonic resonance of that part of you that resonates with your soul, and that resonates with the evolving light of Earth, and thus has that deep conviction that this resonance gives. The challenge is to discern that certainty, born out of the soul-human-earthly harmonic within you, from the mind-feeling-body certainty you have from what you have learned and become as a human in this life.

This is the joy of the path, for you shall never be bored! Even if part of you wishes for this, recognise this is just old patterning and desire for the kind of certainty you had before. It is stagnant from an evolutionary sense, and unsustainable in our evolving world and with your evolving soul in this world.

Embrace the changes, seek the certainty that is in resonance with that deep inner knowing within your being, and be prepared to be wrong. This is not a judgement, simply a fact, for your mind-body-feeling self cannot possibly know who you will be in a year, in a decade, maybe even tomorrow – yet you make choices that influence your future based upon your current self.

If you cannot admit mistakes and welcome them as tools of learning, but get caught up seeing them as judgements of character, you solidify even further the structures in your knowing-feeling-physical self that resist change. Then, as change is inevitable – for evolution of consciousness is real – then the pressure to create change becomes greater, in order to break through the more strongly solidified, or even cemented, personal milieu.

Thus, Earth today: much has been solidified by those of wealth and power to sustain their old ways, and added to by those who have become englamoured by this false goal of more-more-more, in a world of finite capacity. These are the significant glamours and illusions that entrap the human self, unwilling to see the true light of Earth and soul. Thus, we see increasingly cemented forms of personal gain and societal functioning, as resistance builds to the needed evolutionary change.

We all hope and pray that enough human choice can be made to bring a loving and intentful breakdown of those barriers, and avoid the path of shattering and crushing.

Your choice matters: if you are faced with personal choice to stay with the familiar, even when it does not seem quite right, or to awaken to the possibility of a new way, a new path, a new thought, a new emotional response – choose wisely, and let loving light guide you. Become one less molecule of human concrete, cemented into the false security of past certainty. Become one who can grow beyond the challenges of past choices that no longer fit, and embrace the new that holds truth and light.

Use whatever spiritual practice enables you to give pause and space in your day so you can hear the tiniest nudge of your conscience and consciousness: and learn to recognise what holds resonance with that light within you, so you can forgive and forego the choices of the past and step forward in the certainty of the light, not that of the old and worn familiar.

Emotions & the Heart Path

In your search for inner meaning, for spiritual truth, for greater love within and around you, do not get caught in the human glamour that seeks instant solutions. It is a curious quality of the human emotional body that it can be so quick to sweep consciousness into a one-pointed need, desire, yearning, hope. However it manifests, if it arises emotionally and seeks an instant response, beware!

Instead, train your emotional self to engage in a one-pointed way with your goal as a path with many steps, and to understand that at every step, you will become wiser, have more insight and experience, and have more capacity to work with. Then you may grow to perceive your goal differently, with greater nuance, and with more clarity and depth.

When your emotional self is demanding, needy, perhaps even desperate, engage it with this reality of taking a journey that will lead to the hoped-for destination, and yet with the knowing that your path as a human soul does not have a singular destination. Your task is to take the journey of consciousness, not to be instantly conscious, loving, wise or whatever it is you seek.

Spiritual glamours flow around the world just as do political ones. Always the promise is of something that is in fact quite unreal. Yet, everyone needs to be inspired and given hope somehow, to motivate engagement. This is the tricky challenge of conscious development at this time.

Enough of the collective consciousness of humanity has been developed so that higher ideals and pathways can be impressed vibrationally upon the emotional mass of human consciousness; which is why we see similar threads of hope, intention and action all around the world, in many fields of human endeavour, and in individuals alike.

But then, what to do with it? How to respond? Recognise that your emotional self needs something with which to bond; that is its fundamental urge. It is stronger in some than in others, but inherently this is its primary mode of operation.

Emotional energy is mobile, can be labile, and can be purified enough to resonate with soul intent. If not purified enough, if full of too many predetermined patterns and rigid structures of response built of past challenges, failures, fears, angers or guilt, then soul resonance cannot sound easily, if at all. Then the sweep of astral energy stimulated by the overall impress on humanity by evolution's call and opportunity, instead of inspiring positive evolutionary action, can get funnelled into these existing channels, magnifying the old.

We all have astral patterns, so we all have this experience to work with. However, if you take the emotional impression you receive into your consciousness as something to explore, not rush into, you give yourself space to perceive the nuances, and reflect on your own personal reactions – also known as 'constraints'.

This is all about the bigger issues of life, and not the smaller emotional ripples that occur within and through us in daily life –although this can be applied there if you choose. It takes effort though, so from an evolutionary point of view, from a spiritual consciousness point of view, apply your resources and effort to how you handle the bigger issues.

Emotional drive is needed to create personal change, and spiritual evolutionary growth, because it is this medium in our personal sphere that we can fairly easily recognise, but that can also resonate with soul. In addition, it is the closest energy milieu to our physical selves. It pervades our physical selves, and as such is the greater vehicle through which we may effect change within our physical selves.

Much is made of using the mind to discipline and control emotional urges – and this is true and good, to a certain degree. But if you choose a path of heart, you cannot work with your body by mental discipline alone, because it simply is not close enough in vibrational level to be able to harmonise with your physical self. It can condition and shape your emotional self, and impress upon your brain certain thoughts and perspectives that you can enact through your body. The energy field of your mental body – which is not your mind, but may impress upon your mind – does not nourish your physical self, and you need to nourish your physical self to be able to walk a spiritual path.

Your body is your temple, built out of eons of experiences and lessons learned, and it is the only means you have through which to be here and effect positive change upon our world and your own future. Even if we perceive ourselves as thinking beings, and live much in the mind, we cannot do any of this without being anchored in the physical world through our physical self.

You cannot fully incarnate spiritual intent without emotional matter: it is part of your human embodiment, and it is the loving embrace that keeps your physical temple sustained and engaged in the journey of discovery that is life.

This is where the melding of the two major pathways of spiritual development needs to occur. The devotional path, relying much on emotional engagement to draw the aspirant along the path; and the more mentally-focussed path of detachment from the emotional to create the stillness and illumination for the journey.

Both are (and have been) excellent pathways, but neither of them is the pathway of the heart. You cannot walk the path of heart utilising strength of mind alone; neither can you engage with this journey using emotions as your primary driver.

Heart is the in-between energetically, and physically, when you consider we mostly feel emotions impress upon our solar plexus and lower chakras (gut feelings), and perceive thoughts in our head.

Heart is a different vibration to both mind and emotions, yet it infuses, and needs, both. And your body needs all aspects of your consciousness to be sustained in walking a path of heart.

When emotional drivers touch you from within or from around you, and you want to walk a path of heart, then you need to engage your heart's discernment to give the fullness and intention to your way of responding. Do not rush off in the first flow you perceive – yet do not stop the flow, for your physical self needs it; that is its life force, and lets your temple shine. Then you can become like a radiant cell, present in Earth's body of consciousness, and illumine the possibilities for others around you.

Take your emotional journey with heart, embrace your mind, and you can find your way through the sweeps and flows of emotional movement within and around you, as the Great Change unfolds upon Earth.

Mind & Wisdom

Your mental body can be a clear illuminating light in which pathways of logic can be developed, because it consists of a particular energy that enables this. The astral emotional body has its characteristic capacity to align and move like a fluid with a stimulus, human or spiritual.

The part of the mental body most commonly accessed by the human self is a lighter substance than astral liquid, and is more like air. Unlike the emotional body, you do not get responses that continually move like waves or currents, washing over you then back again. This is peculiar to the emotional body, where a stimulus may set off a movement of that watery element, and then the momentum in that water of feeling may continue to move and perpetuate the feeling, or the backwash of the feeling. This is something to be worked upon to create clarity and to avoid unnecessary exacerbation and magnification of feelings upon the spiritual journey – while still recognising and allowing their very valuable presence in your consciousness and actions in the world.

In the air element of the mental body, you have two possibilities of response: a storm, or a crystalline structure that aligns the molecules of intuition and thought.

A storm of activity in your mental body could be a spiritual infusion of a mentally illuminating stimulus, giving breakthroughs to solve challenges in any field of human endeavour; or it could be a stimulus from human reactions, emotions, needs, that stirs the creative power of the mind. Note that motive here is essential, because a negatively motivated but mentally developed person can be creative in a negative sense. The mental body in and of itself does not discern. It is a builder of crystalline structures and a vehicle through which stimulus may move mental substance.

This is the great challenge of the current societal dominance of the mind, and here also, the difference between mind and mental body is important. The mind is that aggregate of feelings and reactions turned into words and thoughts, of learned knowledge, and of patterns based on emotional experiences.

Do not conflate mind with the mental body of your energy self.

You can never separate mind from your emotional self. Even if you have a purified and developed mental body, it reaches (for the most part) your physical consciousness in your brain through your emotional body. Your emotional body is fluid and permeates the whole of your being. Your mental body is like air, and is less able to permeate the astral and physical substance of your being. It can, just like in our physical world, stir and move the waters it is near, and then rely upon those moving waters to convey the information. Or, as you build knowledge, you may refine your ability to still the waters of your emotional self such that you may see or perceive the knowledge structured in your mental body. Your knowing always comes through the emotional milieu of your being.

Hence the validity of the term 'hidden bias'. People may think they have no prejudice or judgement, but as psychological studies have shown for decades, this is never true. It just demonstrates that there is so much more within our brain, mind, emotional self and mental self than that of which we are directly conscious.

In stillness and one-pointed focus, you can build much in your mental body of learned knowledge, and can then use that knowledge to build further and extend and expand those structures of what is known.

Humanity as a whole has developed a great collective body of mental capacity, having had such a significant focus on the reductive model of knowledge for so long, in seeking answers to the journey of life and consciousness and all its challenges.

The challenge that arises is that the knowledge is built like a crystalline structure on the mental levels. In an evolved being these structures can be stored as energetic fields, imprints if you like; however, in the earlier stages of the evolving mind, the knowledge remains as this built and more rigid crystalline structure. The paradox – and ever they exist in human conscious development – is that in order to create an energetic imprint of knowledge in the finer vibrating ethers of the mental body, the crystalline structure needs to be built and rebuilt, strengthened and energised by repeated use, which can then appear as rigidity of thought. Eventually, however, the imprint will be created in the ethers of the mental level, and the rigid crystalline structure can be dissolved, as it is no longer needed to ensure the knowledge is sustained and accessible.

On the journey of developing the mental body, you build a lot of concrete knowledge, where the crystalline structure is strong – and fixed. The problem with having fixed knowledge, is that the world we live in is evolving, we are evolving, and so what we know and can access to respond with wisdom, needs to be able to evolve.

To change a strengthened, rigid crystalline form requires it be dismantled, consciously, or to be broken. Neither has appeal to the human personality, which inherently (for most people) seeks clarity and certainty.

When your certainty comes from what you think you know, yet that knowing no longer solves your problems, or enables you to contribute in the world, it is a shattering realisation. Humanity en masse is also going through this. Our societies, our search for answers, cures, and certainty have built a vast body of collective knowledge, but most of it is far too fixed in the crystalline structure that has been built out of what worked and could be understood in the past. This has to change.

The model built by those focussed on the power of the mind, and that now entraps most of humanity, is one that enables power, poverty (not just financial), and narrow-mindedness to envelop in rigid constraints. Change requires this mental construct to let go of old rigidity, and perceive the reality that the old model of reductively deduced knowledge is no longer sufficient to sustain Earth, humanity and all life. The challenge is that it has been so used by the minds of humanity, that it is not only a rigid pattern crystallised in the lower levels of the mental body, but it has a great deal of emotional substance adhered to it.

Knowledge has been and still is seen to be the hope of humanity, solving problems and providing for all. However, the faculty of knowledge, the substance of the mind, does not discern on motive, on care, on global responsibility, on anything. It is a vehicle for refining until a clear crystalline structure can be built into what we call a 'fact'.

But then what? How do you discern whether what you have distilled into a fact is useful, or whether it must be expanded to give a fuller picture, where the single fact is given context and thus the possibility of more meaning and value for life on Earth?

The most useful way is to let soul conscience be the evaluation, not your mind. Knowing in and of itself does not amount to truth. Knowing in the whole context of meaning, evolution and conscious care of others and the Earth is the truth that enables both certainty of that knowledge, and its value in the human journey.

We have a vast amount of knowledge in the human consciousness of mind – but you need to always ask yourself, 'then what?' Knowledge without care invites disasters, and that crystalline structure, whether personal or in humanity as a whole, must change.

Here is where mind can be your helper, because your mind is not just the place of knowledge in your being – far from it. It is where knowledge and feelings merge. Even if you do not think you are influenced by emotions in your thinking, you most certainly are. Emotions can constrain, energise, expand, colour and dampen your thinking. Your opportunity on the evolutionary journey is to realise this, and work with the gifts you have.

Purify your emotional self and train it both to create stillness and to nourish you with the ripples of love and care that come from your soul. This creates a milieu of conscience and harmony within you, so that when you think and access your knowledge, or humanity's collective knowledge, you can discern in your mind what has light and love in it, and thus what is positive in its value for you, Earth, humanity, and all life.

If you do not apply your purified emotional intelligence to knowledge, it can never become wisdom. Wisdom is the living truth: that which knowledge becomes when each discerned fact becomes part of a living whole, within the bigger picture of influence and impact that enables positive change.

Let emotions be part of your thinking journey, and help you discern what is wisdom out of what can be known. Then you are better equipped to evolve and contribute to the Great Change unfolding within and around us.

Without the transformation of knowledge into wisdom, knowledge can be used for good or evil. A mind without conscience can justify anything; just look at history, if today's world events are not enough.

The amount of knowledge in the world today that remains unshaped into that which serves positive change is a challenge, but also an opportunity. The key is to become flexible, so that rigidity does not build up around what you think you know, cementing your thinking into the past: enable those crystalline structures of your mental body to be adapted and adjusted to incorporate the conscience needed in our world today.

This is how you become wise, and enable your soul to work more fully through you.

Earth Consciousness

The Last Kumara

In the journey of light, you evolve as a soul. In the journey on Earth, you evolve as a human soul, or as a human angel.

Humanity is gifted with the yearning to seek reasons and understand, but the world we see through human eyes makes little sense and gives little rationale for those significant events that shape life and consciousness. After millennia of traversing this landscape of physical existence, your physical, mental and emotional faculties as a human being are developed enough to know there is more to understand, because we have learned that behind physical events and experiences are causes.

The world of soul is the world of causes. That is where the intent of evolution, the force and love that guide the existence of all life, can interact with the physical vibratory levels of human and earthly life. Why do they seem so separate to us?

To bring evolutionary intent into matter – that is, the consciousness that is able to span light and dense matter – the matter has to be qualified first. That is the whole point of evolution: to bring them together. You cannot simply bring a stimulus of light, or any finer vibrating energy stream, into dense physical matter that has no points of resonance, for the light will either bounce off, or pass straight through, and all the vibratory intent within that stimulating flow of light goes nowhere within the body of matter itself.

What seems like a long journey on Earth for humanity (and for nature with all her expressions) has given us the breadth and depth of development that enables us, collectively, to be ready for the guiding light and love of evolutionary intent to reach into earthly substance in much greater ways.

There have been great teachers who have become points of light, because they have been able to refine their own consciousness and the substance of their beings so that the world of soul becomes available to them. However, from an evolutionary perspective, it is not the single points of light, but the mass attributes of living consciousness within Earth's body that matter: all that humanity has attained en masse, and that Earth has absorbed and awoken through angels and nature. This includes the family of animals, which, as many already understand, holds many evolved and soul-aligned expressions.

This illumination of matter proceeds through humanity's search for meaning, because that conditions the lower matter of substance, and brings alignment with the vibrations of higher light, where answers are held, and causes can be understood.

Earth has her own search and meaning to embody, but is on a very different path. Long ago she was conscious enough to make a choice to take this path, and so her being was already imbued with this evolutionary intent before humanity and most expressions of nature and life began their journey, or else we would not be here.

In the first instance, her choice called in the loving presence of great souls of cosmic grace – already evolved as agents able to wield and express evolutionary intent – and thus the journey began. Now those souls have largely moved on to other spheres; but of those who remain, the Last Kumara is of most importance. She holds the blueprint of evolutionary intent, that initial outpouring of Cosmic Love that was gifted in response to Earth's choice.

Many Kumaras have come, and then moved on to other spheres, for each of them has had a specific role to play in the expression of that Cosmic Love and how it may manifest within Earth's loving body. They have, for example, helped humanity develop mind, the substance of logic and analysis that enables and develops the capacity of choice – a most crucial element of awakening and taking responsibility for conscious action.

Other Kumara embodiments have held light within the emotional substance of Earth, enabling the upward yearning of emotional substance, which would otherwise have been too attached to, and too enmeshed with, the pull of physical matter to allow the budding consciousness to seek anything beyond emotional and physical life.

This pull on the consciousness by physical matter is inherent in all matter, just like the force of gravity. It is what enables light and life to evolve here, but can also be a trap for the young soul, who cannot get through to the entrapped human who finds reasons in the entrapment to stay there – like familiarity and love, great attractions for any young consciousness. Earth's love is present in her being and draws us to her, but when manifest in as yet unillumined astral emotional substance, it can become a bind, not freedom in light.

Now we have the embodiment of the last Kumara of the Venus family. The Venus family were the major family of souls who responded to Earth's call, and cosmic evolutionary intent. The last Kumara of this family is the one who, in full consciousness, embodies within the substance and matter of Earth herself, so that her consciousness and intentions align and become one in that intention and conscious expression. Thus, the Great Change evolves from stimulus of mind and stimulus of emotion, now to stimulus of heart and body, in the great unfoldment of evolutionary intent.

Heart and body go together, for without heart, the physical body cannot live; and without a body, spiritual love cannot manifest. The great awakening of consciousness proceeds as the awakening and stimulus of finer vibrations of physical existence through mind and emotions, to stir in human expression that yearning and seeking that lifts human consciousness away from the gravitational pull of matter itself.

Then it comes as the final stimulus, to awaken heart in matter, which does two things: it enables human life to align with cosmic intent and soul love in each heartbeat, and express that loving intent into the physical world; and it enables the substance of the human life in physical matter to be so infused with intentional consciousness that it is no longer entrapped by gravitational forces. Thus loving intent can live in full and free expression, humanity becomes a conscious expression of living heart light, and Earth shines like the jewel in space we know she shall be.

This is the reality to unfold, and the vision to enable your journey to have hope and strength. There is much to unfold before this may manifest, but without vision, how can you align?

The purpose of the Last Kumara is to embody this reality in loving embrace with the consciousness of Earth, so that we all may evolve in alignment with cosmic intent and Earth's loving choice. It is her choice, not ours, how she evolves, something humanity often forgets in its grandiose glamours and self-righteous expressions of personal power. But this is the journey, and we all undertake it together.

Then the great golden age shall emerge, when the first Kumara of Earth shall arise, born of the deeply loving and consciously aligned intent of Earth, nature, humanity and angelic flow, infused with Cosmic Love that is evolutionary intent. Then shall the next Great Change unfold, that of Earth's expression as a full body of light, reaching out into Cosmos, to send teachers and loving intention to others who call.

This is the vision and reality contained in the very substance of Earth herself, imbued with cosmic awakening brought by the Kumara who embodies with her. Thus, we all may see, hear and respond to this great evolutionary force of love that embraces every living soul, in every family of life in our world.

Seek, and it will become a resonance within you, and that resonance can then become part of the song of Earth, the soul of light, and the rainbow of expression of life itself in this wondrous universe.

Seek, and I shall find you, for I am here, the Last Kumara, and you can know me when you want to in your heart. Then you will not just see or hear the vision, but you shall become it, as I have, and such love shall touch you that you shall have found that promised land: heaven upon Earth, for that is what I embody, when you seek.

I am here, for the lost and the searching ones, and for the loving and kind ones, and for the angry and closed ones alike, for we are all of the substance of this world; and now I take all my children through the great healing, so that light may unfold, unhindered. Take the journey with me, and loving light shall be yours.

Choose, that is all, and know the journey is not just this life, but many lives to come, for that is the horizon of such Great Change, and the life span of soul's intention in this evolutionary impulse. But if you do not choose now, you will not catch up. Now, in this life, make peace with your heart's yearning, and seek that which you know to be true. No matter how much you may or may not manifest your choice in your outer life, there is time for that to come. I seek hearts now: the hearts that have chosen, the hearts that are willing, the hearts that do not close to love's intent that is my love. For I am evolutionary intention in this world, embodied by Earth's love such that we merge in unity, and two become one, for this time of Great Change.

Come with me.

I am the Last Kumara of the Earth's great evolutionary leap, and I speak so you may find my love, that resonates in every heart no matter what God or teacher or hope you have, for I resonate through all who shine truth and the loving vision ahead.

I shine, and so shall you. Choose, in your heart, and Earth shall sing with choirs of angels, such that nowhere in the universe shall that magnificent sound be unheard. Thus the next Great Change is awoken, and universal love comes into being through more and more planets and stars, until our universe is glowing with light, and the next great coming of cosmic intent may then unfold.

This is the vision I am given. This is the vision I embody. This is the great evolutionary intention that creates the pathway upon which we all must journey. No matter what belief or hope, this is what the very substance of our universe is made of, and thus our destiny contains this blueprint down to the expression of life in every cell; and I come to awaken what is mine to love: little Earth and her great heart, and all who live in her grace.

Thus I come. Thus I am, the Last Kumara, awakening the last great moment of change so love's light can truly be in our hearts, from Cosmos, to human, to Earth, and back; and love's intention becomes alive in all life.

(please note, this was written as a direct communique,
and 'I' does not refer to the author)

Meeting Global Crises with Heart

Thoughts and feelings are challenging enough at a personal level, let alone at national, racial, or organisational levels (such as some religions). Here you have not only the aggregate of the personal thoughts and feelings of those contributing to these group expressions, but you also have the magnifying effect that occurs when a mass of energy coheres. In astral emotional matter, that coherence enables it to be more compelling, more dampening of any other emotional inputs or expressions within it, and more manipulative of thoughts to move them to compliance. When there is enough astral matter so aggregated on a lower level of vibration, even the good people involved find it hard to stand up to the force created.

This is the model of political power that has been in use for millennia, sadly but truthfully, because humanity has not had enough collective consciousness to counter the great amassing of emotional force. There have been many periods in history when this has occurred, and there continue to be, because those seeking power continue to work with what they know, this old way of wielding power, to achieve their goals. Their motives may be justified by a vast array of reasons, from quite negative, to what could even be seen as somewhat positive, but the means remain largely unchanged: manipulation of emotional energy.

The fulcrum of how power is expressed and actioned on Earth is the last to change under evolutionary pressure. By its very nature, it is strong, resistant to any other inputs, and single-pointed in its energy makeup; whether as a personal expression – at its worst in an abusive relationship – or as a national political expression through the manipulative conduct of single individuals, or of the few that aggregate in leadership groups and feed each other the reinforcing glue of misplaced thoughts and feelings. The latter expression also applies to organisational and racial groups.

Any act of leadership that evokes human response risks being this. However, if the motives are pure and as much light as possible is brought to those being asked to join and follow, then the same lower astral energy is not evoked and created to blanket and blind those involved. Energy of a higher astral level acts the same as that of the lower: it can aggregate and become a mass of lighted and uplifting intent, to inspire people to be part of positive change.

The problem is that not only is there still so much unworked out lower astral energy in humanity, as individuals, but also there are masses of the same, aggregated and adhered to in racial, national and organisational psyches. To wait for the personal purification and illumination of astral matter throughout humanity such that these racial, national and organisational emotional coherences of lower vibration can be dissipated is a long journey. Too long.

To hope for enlightened leaders who would sweep the world with positive change and cleanse the lower astral of all these problematic aggregates, even the expected second coming of a religious leader, is unrealistic for two reasons. Firstly, there is no possibility of cleansing these heavy emotional aggregates – whether personal, organisation, racial or national – with any speed without shattering, because the lower astral is so much a part of, and intertwined with, our physical awareness of self. This is not desired. Secondly, this is an aggregate of human choices, and as such is the darkness in our corner that each of us must cleanse.

However, we cannot wait for individual personal purification to release the problematic aggregates.

What to do?

In the new age of consciousness, birthing now around and within us, leadership will express in a different way. The model of single-pointed and narrowly-expressed power will not be the way forward, where one leads and others follow.

The expression of power will come through the heart and is a magnetic pull of life-affirming vibration. Those who lead will show and emanate greater heart vibration, so that others around them may be able to perceive this note and presence of living light, and make their own choice in their own heart.

It may sound similar to the astral method, but it is vastly different. When lower astral energies are magnified and manipulated by powerful leaders, this sets up emotional currents and waves that can be impossible to resist by all but the more conscious of those in that flow. Many will think they have chosen to be part of it, but instead, they have been manipulated by the compelling, seemingly irresistible forces of the emotional energy in which they are immersed. This is not a choice; it is a reverberation of the surrounding emotional intent that filters into the mind as ideas.

An emanation of heart energy does not set up waves and currents that can get magnified by an emotional charge. Heart energy expresses as a hum, a vibration of light that just is; or as a flow. As a flow of heart it pulses, and the space between each pulse gives stillness, in which you can become self-aware and bring heart awareness to your choices and actions. Clarity and strength of heart enables others to perceive it, and as more align and choose heart, it will become more radiant and diverse in its presence on Earth.

While as yet not strongly formed in the psyche of humanity, this is the way forward for those who seek to contribute through consciousness and energy stimulation:
1. Find your own heart resonance and work from that;
2. Find those around you who similarly seek and care, and create a space where your collective heart resonance can be nourished and grow; and
3. Seek those of great heart on the inner levels, and sit within their loving embrace.

Then take action, whether through meditation where you can send heart light to heal, release, transform and create resonance in the awakening consciousness of those around the world in need; or through your own personal or organisational actions, to bring heart intent into those actions to create positive change.

If you are not in a dire situation of conflict, war or famine, where focussed physical attention may take all your effort for survival, try to make effort in your day to hold the presence of heart alive in your consciousness, and with it, energise the positive change you hope for in the world.

Because the note of heart is energised by evolutionary intent, it can create greater change than if we try to change old emotional binds simply with other emotional energy; or with the mind, which is usually bound up in either the emotional patterns of the past, or the power-wielding patterns that no longer enable the degree of positive change needed, as already explained.

This is not to say that an illumined mind is not beautiful and enlightening; but mind enlightenment is not the means by which egregious leaders will be moved from their path of action. Their mode of power and manipulation, while it may be driven by a certain brilliance of mind (if you can call it that), is astral, which is how they seek to sweep all those into compliance around them. This is also not to say that heart energy will miraculously lift their consciousness, intention and mode of operation.

However, this is the best option for those of us who work in an energetic way with the evolutionary forces that are active now.

Not only is heart the centre of evolutionary expression at this time, but it is also the vibration of life. No matter the mental or emotional binds any individual wraps themselves in, ultimately life force is what keeps them alive, and heart is the vehicle for that, so it can never be closed down as a source of light.

Work with your heart however you can. Fill your intentions with heart-felt prayers, affirmations or mantras; use heart-centred meditation as your gathering place and from where you send out that heart intent by whatever means you have access to.

At this point in time, every heart-intentioned effort is desperately needed. Please do yours.

The Blood of Humanity & Earth

In the blood of humanity runs the blood of the Earth. Of course it does: she is the living being within which our life is possible, and all life streams made of her substance are in her care.

All complex life forms circulate life-giving nourishment through their beings, whether via what we call blood, or sap in the plant family. This is a product not only of physical necessity, to enable the circulation of nourishment and the retrieval of metabolic waste, but also of spiritual necessity. To grow consciousness, you need movement of that which gives life. To awaken the heaviness of matter – which in and of itself is not radiant with soul's light – you need to circulate that which can infuse that matter with the life-giving light of soul, wherein consciousness is nourished.

There are many ways in which that soul presence first develops, and then resonates down through the octaves of matter's precipitation into human form. The same occurs for all animals and all plants with the engagement of the angelic family.

Matter does not hold or become light on the evolutionary path: it builds the forms in which that light can flow, and it becomes refined enough so that it can resonate and harmonise with that light, but it is not ever light itself. It may shine and radiate, like beautiful trees and places upon Earth, and like highly soul-infused human beings, but matter in and of itself, as a substance of the universe, is the solid-state of existence, not the moving wave form.

One can become the other when you review at the minute, sub-atomic level of physical existence, as physics has shown and continues to explore. One can become the other at greater levels of vibratory coherence too, but that takes strong intention to hold the matter in that coherence, and enough purification and refinement of the matter in all its vibrational expressions, to be able to hold resonance throughout all those components.

The simple truth is that if physical matter has become a vibration of light, it is no longer a physical form.

This describes the ascension process! This will occur for many, who will be aided by their karmic opportunity, by many other beings, and by the intensely, intentfully-held vibratory flames of transformation that enable human matter to be taken through the ascension process. We must be honest, human matter is not so coherent or purified as to achieve ascension by its own intent for most people, but karma can enable this great grace to be given.

Naturally, you are then no longer a physical being, although you may reincarnate should your path of service be thus.

The point of elucidating this process is to highlight that matter cannot become light, and a human can only become light by enabling that light to infuse, resonate within and flow through the physical form.

This is why the Age of the Heart is of such profound importance in the journey of physical evolution of light. Heart is the source from which light can be circulated through your being. Heart is the part of your being that has the capacity to resonate with soul, and thus, if you consciously or karmically walk this pathway of heart awakening, then your soul will infuse you with light, through your heart, through your blood.

This is how we feel such upliftment and hope in times of need, or of giving, or of faith, or of deep knowing of the universal truths of life. All actions and choices that bring our attention to that which is greater than us as little personalities in this vast world of life – these will awaken the matter of our being through the yearning, giving, immersing or seeking. As soon as we make that intent alive in our human selves, our physical substance is brought into coherence around that action; and, through the more coherent vibration that we setup in our beings, we attract the outpouring of soul's light, which can then infuse us, and illumine our beings with the hope, love and truth we seek.

None of this occurs in isolation, for we are built of Earth's substance; our consciousness evolves in her being, and our souls resonate in her Ocean of Love. As Earth's heart awakens and evolves into much greater presence within her physical being, her substance and matter is held with greater conscious intent; it vibrates with greater coherence; it resonates with greater clarity, and thus her soul's love can infuse through deeper and deeper layers of her physical self. Thus, the substance of which our beings are built is also enabled to awaken to this living light that is Earth's Solar and soul intent in manifestation.

The Solar intent infusing Earth is the Solar will and love that holds Earth in grace, giving life, awakening her being to the pulse of Cosmic Heart, creating the presence of higher consciousness that can guide her awakening. And thus resonate, eventually, through her soul.

This is the milieu in which we exist. This is the Ocean of Love and the physical substance in which our life is created and nourished. The intentful force behind this is the heart of Earth, which pulses this Ocean of Love through deeper and deeper layers of her physical being, enabling, and requiring, greater and greater alignment of the substance of our beings such that the great Ocean of Love can flow fully through her body.

This is why we see such great opportunity for conscious awakening, and/or ascension, for so many of humanity, for we are in and of this great transformation of Earth's body, and can be infused with her love.

This is her blood flow: the very love and light of her being, circulated by her heart and soul intention. We, humanity, form a major proportion of the substance of her physical being that is able to respond, align, and resonate with that loving harmony.

That is our journey, and soul's intent. If not, then your pathway is not to be of this Earth substance in the journey to come, and off you will go to other spheres of learning.

However, to stay here and evolve upon Earth, then the more you awaken and align your intention to the love and intention of Earth, the more you can be nourished, uplifted and infused with the joy of her awakening being. If you do not choose this with consciousness, you may still evolve in this loving pulse if you do not resist it.

Resistance through constructed thought or aggregated and solidified emotion can never hold strength in the loving light of evolution's flow, although karma is the coordinator of how that journey of awakening shall proceed – whether personally, nationally, globally, in the world of human affairs.

We are not, cannot, evolve outside Earth's intent. Therefore, seek her loving flow. Seek her loving presence. Nature bathing can infuse your physical and etheric body with that love, if you let it. Nature awareness can nourish your emotional self. And consciously intending to care for Earth, and our collective future, can open your mind to her living flows. Then your whole being can become more infused with her nourishment, and thus shine with more of the light that she is, and you do yours to be part of the conscious awakening so desperately needed in these times of Great Change.

Be of Earth, align with her heart flow, and shine into our collective physical existence, then the blood of not only Earth, but that of Cosmos, the greatest loving intent of our time, can infuse your soul, and awaken your heart in the utmost joy of life itself.

Love the Earth

When you love the Earth, you establish a relationship with her, just as you do when you love other people. When you love, you send out that vibration to whomever you love, and the one receiving that vibration will always perceive it and respond. That is because all life on this planet is born out of the loving impulse of Earth and Cosmos, that guide evolutionary intent in our world. Every life form holds the memory of this vibration, and needs no training, development or knowledge to respond, thus establishing a loving contact that nourishes both.

In human-to-human love, we know that love and relationships are complicated and not this straightforward. This is not because the ability to send, receive and respond with love is not there in every human. Rather it is because of our layers of learned behaviour, reactions, fears, hopes, and expectations; in other words, all the patterns we have built into our human selves in life after life that condition how we perceive and how we respond.

Earth, however, does not hold these patterns with us as individuals, and for the most part we do not have them with her, so, with intent applied, we can love and be loved by our beautiful Mother Earth.

Sometimes there is karma involved that may affect this relationship, for those who have taken actions in the past that have been harmful, either to Earth herself (including nature and her creatures), or to people in particular locations, where the karma is aggregated in that location, and thus affects Earth. For example, mining operations that leave toxic waste behind them, with no care for cleaning up and rehabilitating what has been destroyed. Or places like the concentration camps of WWII. Those who carry responsibility for these choices and actions will carry the burden of karma that impacts their relationship with Earth. It does not matter if they seek to hide behind a corporate structure where no one seems to be responsible, or a political machine structured to do the same.

The responsibility of every soul to care is never diminished, and so when that care is not enacted in life, the imprint returns to the soul, and karma is applied accordingly. No organisational or physical structure can shield you from the karma that is yours to learn from, and that guides you to balance past actions of harm. This applies for all actions, of course, but in this instance it relates specifically to those actions and perceptions that hinder our ability to relate to the Earth. Note that this does not affect Earth's wish or ability to love you, for you are born of her substance and walk her journey, and her love is all encompassing.

If you find it hard to love Earth, it is within you that you must seek understanding. Do not instantly attribute to yourself heinous deeds of the past, because most (well over 99.9%) of humans do not carry responsibility for these. At most you may have witnessed, or had a minor role; or simply be picking up on the collective guilt and grief that does exist within Earth's and humanity's combined milieu of conscience and consciousness.

If you feel these pressures, work on them. And the best way is to find yourself a place where you can touch Earth: a garden, a beautiful tree, a forest, waterfall, a flower, etc. It can be anything of Earth, and as soon as you view it, touch it with hope and love, you will open that conscious stream that joins your heart with hers.

Why seek this, perhaps some of you say?

For two reasons: you need the vibration of Earth's love to resonate in you so that you can evolve, and you need to clear any constrictions that hinder your relationship with her, so you can consciously contribute to the incarnation of heart consciousness within her being. This is the evolutionary task of every human, whether undertaken through personal conscious effort, or guided by the flow of mass intention to do the same. If you do not feel love for Earth, and have no wish to explore and heal that restriction in your conscious journey, then perhaps Earth is not the home for you in the next phase of your, and her, evolutionary journey.

In the not-so-distant future, this choice will become manifest for everyone, whether at soul level, or at personality and soul level, depending upon the degree of consciousness awakened in the human self. The choice must be made, because Earth has already chosen. Your whole opportunity to incarnate here is because of her choice, to become a beacon of physically-expressed heart consciousness in Cosmos.

Your incarnation as a human is made possible by having a heart that keeps you alive physically, in the substance of Earth; and spiritually, through your soul's vibration radiating into your human self. Life is only possible because there is heart on all these levels.

Therefore, you must engage, with love, in relationship with Earth so that your heart can continue to be a life-force in your being.

Earth gives us all the substance we need to incarnate, and our souls dwell in her Ocean of Love and give us all the love we need. Turning away from this is to turn away from that which gives life.

Humanity is the only family of consciousness that has this choice, for we walk the pathway of evolution that will unite us as humans with our souls. Other families of consciousness upon Earth have different roles and responsibilities. Plants, for example, are an expression of both Earth's living, loving intent to create life and beauty; and are a key expression through which the angelic family brings its love, which is essential for Earth, for us and all life. Plants and angels do not have the possibility to say no. They evolve in consciousness through immersion in the loving milieu in which they exist, and can become great and wise beings (more than many humans).

Humans evolve through contrast and thus choice. That is our role, for that also enables another level of consciousness to be developed, which in turn creates a flow of strength and determination in the application of love's expression. This is not about human evolution alone, far from it. This determination and expression of love, with will, is needed throughout Cosmos, and is the expression of loving light that Earth has committed to become.

Many animals have an evolved consciousness, but they, like the plant family, do not hold the responsibility for direct and conscious choice that incarnates love-will.

Thus, humanity, you need to learn, relearn, heal, clear, and energise your loving relationship with Earth, for that is essential in your, her, and our collective journey of evolution that nourishes every life form here in this world. This is love in action, which will speed up your own evolutionary journey. There is nothing upon this Earth like love, for cleansing relationships and releasing karma.

Love heals all: the love of souls not emotions alone; the love of commitment to and responsibility for the conscious evolving of self and the world in which we live. Then you live in the brilliance of Earth's nourishing, living light, which is the love resonant with everything living, from Cosmic Heart, to Solar heart, to Earth heart, to your heart.

In gentleness and without glamours or expectations, love. Love Earth, and let yourself feel her love, and you will never look back.

The Trap of the Absolute

On your spiritual path, never work with absolutes. That is the one absolute that is worthy of your consideration!

On every step you need something that is one pointed and decisive, but to take the next step those skills of discernment and one-pointedness may no longer have relevance. When in the past you could align with one spiritual dogma, then set and forget for the rest of that life, now spiritual unfoldment is awakening with such rapidity that this is much less possible.

The milieu of our conscious world is evolving, and is presenting us opportunities for different journeys. The dedication, one-pointedness and clarity you have that enables you to reach one spiritual stage of development, may not enable you to journey further. You need to awaken to this possibility, yet at the same time not take a smorgasbord approach of trying a little of this, a little of that. There are a million options today for what might take your consciousness another step further along your path: whether through religious or spiritual devotion, study and practice; a deep healing journey, physically, mentally or both; a nature connection through awareness and ceremony; or a life journey of reflection and pondering.

Unfortunately, what are presented as helping you to evolve, are often astral convolutions driven by emotional needs and wants, where the appeal is of emotion, for emotion. For example, a strong desire to leave life's pain behind may make a path of instant illumination or complete karma release seem realistic and very appealing, when the true causes of the pain are life lessons that require reflection, learning and personal change to achieve lasting results, including illumination and karma release. Because the mind is largely entwined with the emotions, and not as separate as many hope and think, a strong emotion can evoke a linear mental argument for certain actions, seemingly then being thought out and justified, but instead they are astral manipulations.

The challenge is that when we have strong emotions, and when we dabble in the expression of spirituality, the personal self unavoidably creates alignments internally to seek to be one with both. The human body of physical, emotional and mind substances, is a builder of form, so it is our natural impulse to build that which holds, guides and represents the life force we perceive, within the framework of what we want.

This is perfectly natural as part of the journey upon the path, but it must be filtered by conscience, and evaluated to ensure it is harmless – harmless to others, and harmless to Earth. If it is not, then you must evaluate and discern much more deeply. Sometimes your spiritual path may need you to not be harmless, in the face of others who cause destruction of lives, Earth, hope. But you must evaluate deeply, and take your action with heart-motivated conviction.

We live in a world where the forces of materialism, expressed through the culture of wealth and greed, reach deeply into the psyche of so many. The pull of matter in its most basic sense is like the pull of gravity, and is what enables us to incarnate and journey through our lives upon Earth. However, when the emotions of greed and selfishness attach to that pull of matter, the path you take is one of descent, into lower and lower vibrations. If you seek heart, spirituality, awakening of consciousness, peace in life – however your higher, inner yearning manifests – you need to disengage from the emotionally-charged pull of materialism, and stand up to those lost in its thrall in the way your inner conscience and consciousness guides.

The catch always is the emotional self. On the one hand, it is the vehicle through which we engage with and experience life in ways that motivate us to seek, strive for and take action in our inner and outer world as human beings. On the other hand, it is subject to the swells and flows of all the fluid, emotional substance of the human world in which our consciousness mostly rests. Sometimes you need to stand in steadiness and strength and let the flows and swells go by; other times you need to let go and go with that ocean of movement.

At every stage, you have to choose, and you do choose, even if sometimes you may feel you do not engage consciously. In every choice, you have an opportunity to apply discernment. This is not to suggest a mental and emotional struggle for every little thing in your day. This is for those choices where you can perceive the weight of conscience nudging you, where the bell of intuition tinkles in your inner hearing, where a still point in your heartbeat makes you pause. Our lives of experience give us many lessons, from which we discern and learn behaviours, thought patterns, emotional patterns and reactions. From those lessons we build our personal selves, full of options, some wise, some still reactionary; some open, some closed – but all are built in to the substance of who we are as humans.

In this milieu, we step into this world of rapidly evolving conscious change. The patterns of past ways do not necessarily fit so well, and abiding by them can create inner or outer conflict that we may not understand. It is hard for the developing human consciousness to understand what is outside its sphere of experience. That is the paradox of evolution: we build certainty into our beings in order to incarnate and live, yet we incarnate within this evolving planet where the certainty-of-what-was is usurped by the presence of what is.

That is why, in this rapidly evolving time, we cannot adhere to absolutism of any sort that is built of certainties learned in the past.

At this time, certainty comes from the heart, because that is the current evolutionary stimulus of our Earth, infusing us all, nature, everything. You may find this an uncertain certainty because it is unfamiliar, but you can change that with practice.

If you struggle with doubt, this is where to go – to your heart. Weigh up your options, assess if they light up or sink, if they flow or stagnate. Whatever way you can bend your consciousness, this is the practice that enables certainty. It is never absolute, though, for as you evolve, as Earth evolves, then adjustments will be needed. However, heart-aligned adjustments do not cause you to waiver on your path, for in your heart you stand in the flow of consciousness, and so your path is one of a living certainty, not the personality certainty built only of structures of past lessons and experience.

As the tide of human emotion and thought swells and ebbs in these changing times, seek the certainty of heart so that you can stand with strength in the midst of human attachment to the old that no longer serves life.

There is nothing absolute about the way of the heart, except that the living light of the heart will nourish you so that you can discern and act in alignment with your dharma, your heart's flow, your service to the world, and your next step on evolution's loving path for you.

Any other certainties you feel or think on your journey of consciousness – be careful of them. There are too many astrally-motivated constructs that have no evolutionary life force in them, but that are amassed by those of ill intent for their own self-aggrandisement, or distorted sense of evolution's need. These cults of emotional flows are distorted and will not awaken heart in you, or in the world, but instead hinder the achievement of everything humanity ultimately yearns for, of peace, equality, hope, acceptance.

This is the evil of the world today: the lure of absoluteness, built of distorted thoughts and feelings that themselves are nothing but an aggrandisement of that which was constructed in the past, even if prophesied to be the necessity of the future. If there is no adjustment to this, just more reasons given to justify, if there is no heart, just more emotional and mental manipulation, then this is not a force for good, whether manifesting nationally, or through some would-be leaders or movements. Their certainty is not that of heart, and is not one to follow.

There is always a choice, and in these complex and rapidly evolving times, make your major life and belief choices with care and in your heart.

Discerning Higher Truth

Whatever higher source you believe in for light, hope, meaning, guidance, truth, it still has to reach you, here in this physical world. Even intuition, which some perceive as being directly from a higher source, must still resonate in the conscious realms of your being in order for you to grasp it in your human self. Do not be deluded by those who claim to be in direct contact with certain spirits or higher beings of any sort, because that connection can still be made only through their consciousness, and can only enter our human world through their human beingness.

This is not to say that many people are not capable of perceiving and sharing much that is divine and truthful, and of light, hope and love. Of course there are, and have been many throughout history, or else humanity's and Earth's evolution would have progressed much more slowly.

The point being made here is that for anything that is true in the worlds of light and divinity, it can only be realised as truth in our world if it can resonate in the world of human beingness, in our physical, emotional and mental selves. This is the vehicle we have to work with and through, as souls, and no matter how wise and connected that soul is, what matters is how receptive is the human self.

Through this, the journey of consciousness begins: as we get glimpses of reason and meaning behind life's challenges, or healing for great ills, or direction for life's journey, we search for more contact with that source. Being human, we like to build certainty into uncertainty, and seek to codify how that higher perception can be attained. For example, specific practices and rituals that must be performed, or certain types of training given to chosen individuals who then become the givers of what is provided by higher perception. This gives opportunity for development to those involved or chosen. However, recognise it also solidifies the ways and means by which the higher light is accessed, which can only work for as long as the conscious milieu stays the same. Of course, it does not stay the same!

In current times, many people find they have spiritual realisations, intuitive touches, or callings from within that they feel to act upon; and do not need those solid structures created over millennia to house our access to the divine. But then where does their training and development come from to facilitate development and discernment of their intuitive perception? It rarely comes from the old structures in these rapidly evolving days, although a more developed soul may use such well-trodden pathways to re-develop their intuitive and divine-connecting capacities. For the majority of those receiving intuitive stimuli, there is much need for development of one key factor: discernment.

Everything that comes into your consciousness from a place you do not know, must be evaluated. The simplest test has been enunciated for millennia: is it true, is it kind, is it necessary, is it the right time? If you step back from what can sometimes be a rush of inspiration when intuition nudges you, and sit with your intuitive perception to see if it passes through these four gates, that is a good start.

Sometimes we connect with others who seem well connected on the inner, who bring beautiful words, or perhaps truths we are seeking. However, you must still ask the same questions!

There is no human being upon this Earth that can avoid bringing their higher inspiration and truth through their human self, and, as we know, our human selves carry so much programming and so many patterns – some of light, some of history as yet unredeemed – that inevitably we colour our words and expressions with that fabric of our being. Unavoidable! It is not to say this prevents light and truth getting through, it means that you need to discern so that you are sure.

Today there are so many who seek to express their perceptions, claiming they are from a higher source, yet they come with impure motives. Attractive motives in some cases, like those who focus on wealth creation, or racial or religious strength. Some are more controversial to many, such as those motivating people to align with conspiracy theories, to belief structures that go beyond strengthening racial or religious alignments to create radical divides from others of humanity.

The truth is that inspired actions, beliefs and organisations are usually initiated by a touch of light, whether a vision or realisation, and there remain truths in some of their expressions. But you must discern, and not just believe.

The world today also has many people developed enough to build emotional and mental structures, and then seek to align people with their ways. You do not need to look far in the current business or political worlds to see people doing this, and in extreme ways in some nations. These people are rarely inspired by light, truth or reality, but are building upon their perception of the history of their nation; or structuring their efforts based on the expectation of societal forgiveness and tolerance, and the delusions in many political and corporate endeavours. Forgiveness, because we, humanity as a whole, have attached ourselves to the vehicle of money and wealth as the great saviour of the challenges of human life: we accept the behaviours of those who profess to be aiding others while they amass excessive wealth. The same paradigm applies to political leaders, who promulgate a state or national vision to replicate the history they want to live in, and ask people to suffer for the greater good. Whose greater good?

This is the journey of consciousness, and we are in this journey together. We must all make individual choices based on discernment in our own hearts. Even if we feel powerless in the world of political or corporate affairs, we are not powerless in the human world of consciousness. Never underestimate what individuals can do.

Yet, every path of light into our personal consciousness has to come through our own human self, and all our emotional and mental substance with all its pre-programming and life-learned patterns. Where do we obtain that substance of mind and feeling? That comes from the Earth. Our physical bodies are built of her molecules and atoms; so too are our bodies of mind and feeling built out of the global milieu of these vibrational levels of substance.

Every time you apply discernment and choose from heart to the best of your abilities, you are qualifying the vibrations of mind and feelings, not only in yourself, but having a ripple effect throughout this global milieu. If you then consciously direct your love and care into these inner worlds, you have even more influence on how much light and truth resonates there. Every time you act thus, you help build that which truly holds the real light in mind and feelings, and you disaggregate those vibrational illusions and glamours that some leaders use to oppress, repress and distort the truth of our evolving world.

Choose wisely, trust your heart, and bring more light into that which nourishes us all as human beings in our efforts to create and sustain a world of equity and peace for all.

Creating Change through Heart

In every moment when the lust for power, the ignorance of selfishness, the hatred of otherness, the sheer lack of humaneness within human beings creates tragedy and grief, face it with hope. Lift your response to your heart, infuse it with the flames of courage, hope and compassion that enflame your inner being with soul's intent, and express into the world from there, whatever it is your calling, your dharma, to do.

The heart does not dictate any particular action, just that your action be infused with that will, certainty and intent of soul, that your heart can give. Then you bring into the world the very vibration that counters the forces of fear, hatred and power bent to selfish wants. You bring in the forces that enable evolution.

Human hatred and destructiveness can never be an evolutionary force, whatever the motivation. Whether attributed falsely to national need, for which it can never be – for nations are nourished and sustained in completely other ways – or promulgated as if for human need, which is also completely false, for human need is never to cause harm, destruction or devastation to others or Earth.

The capacities of human leaders to cause such grave wrongs to people and Earth, all around our world, are motivated by the remnants of the forces that brought human souls to Earth in the first wave of evolution's call: the forces of involution, the forces that attract the resonant soul to emerge from the Ocean of Love into the dense substance of earthly matter. Like the pull of gravity, these forces are motivated by love; for ultimately their call could only entice the human soul to incarnate if the song of that call resonated with the truth that soul knew.

The forces that draw the soul to Earth, are for that purpose only. The challenge for all life on the conscious path is that the first forces you become conscious of are those that have influenced you in your first awareness, so many humans remember this pull to incarnate upon Earth. This in itself is not a problem. The problem is the destruction and cruelty to Earth and all her creatures, which is caused when the human chooses this pull to incarnate as the one force they believe in, and closes off to the force that draws their consciousness upwards to refined insight and understanding, from where wisdom and compassion can arise.

Perhaps this seems too esoteric for the great challenges facing the world today. Unless you are in a position to act on the global stage in ways that can create positive change, your only option to help create peace, equity and hope in the world is to bring your heart's motivation into the milieu of human affairs, and let your heart add to the shining, resonating vibration of care that can overwhelm those who have chosen to say 'no'.

If you lack heart light in your consciousness, then the lure of power, greed and separateness can go unhindered, and your personal motivations can become cemented around these destructive, earth-bound forces. Earth-bound, because they only tie you, and all you influence, to the lower worlds of human existence, in the realms of mind, feeling and physical expression. This is not the journey of the human soul, nor the journey of the Earth and all her creatures, on the evolutionary path. This is bringing the forces of a coherent, but lower, consciousness in alignment with those forces that bind souls to Earth – but not for the positive journey of evolution's call. Instead, they serve the personal motivations of one who seeks power over light's call; material wealth over global prosperity; total control over life's influences personally, racially and nationally.

The bind to Earth comes from saying 'no' to the influence of light in the heart, and from choosing to work with those forces that are of this involutionary intention and purpose. These forces will exist upon Earth until such time as humanity has evolved sufficiently to be able to move freely between soul and physical expression as evolution's journey needs – but this is a long way off.

For now, we need the aid of these forces, this coherent pull of involution's force, to bring us into incarnation. Then we have a choice. In every life, we have a choice as to how much we align our mental and emotional selves with these involutionary forces, which make us look to matter for all our needs, wants, hopes, dreams; and how much we let our heart's resonance be felt and heard in our consciousness. This choice is not a conscious one for most, for evolution's journey and the guiding embrace of karma give each human small, but usually obvious, options, so that the evolution of conscience and consciousness can proceed.

Most humans are not, in fact, captured by the force of involution's pull to matter. It is the ones who have evolved enough consciousness to encompass positions of national, racial or corporate power that must choose. The whole structure that gives them their power is invariably, although certainly to different degrees, created by the forces that bind life to things material and of the lower worlds, where power and greed manifest in the worlds of feeling and thought. The physical body itself has no need of these excesses of greed and control, it is the emotions and thoughts that pervade it where the choices lie.

Some leaders have made the choice to work with this false power and to close to the light. They are no longer in any balance at all, and it shows. There is no longer any light to be found anywhere in their eyes, for they no longer lift their gaze to the infusing grace of evolution's, and love's, call from their soul. The complex path of human need and want has caught their awareness and they have chosen to ignore the light.

No path of personal power, wealth and control serves evolution's grace. Those of us who hope for peace, care and equity can be of service, and we make up the majority of consciousness upon Earth. We can choose to resonate from heart, and make the sound of the heart's call louder and louder until it smashes through the lower vibrational barrier, with which those of materialistic focus have shrouded themselves.

The darkened ones who say no to soul, can only build their personal world of greed and power out of the substance afforded them within the milieu of human thought and feeling. Bring your conscious intention to changing that milieu, so their edifices of oppression, hatred, greed or whatever light-less driver motivates them, have less and less substance with which to build.

Do not underestimate the power of light that you have, for as with all things upon Earth, it is the resonance of the collective human consciousness that enables change – both from within humanity, and from the worlds of higher consciousness.

Life and light evolve in vibration; that is the means and expression of all existence. As soon as enough human conscious intent is applied to awakening the awareness, need and hope of heart, then the resonance will grow, because every heart adds to the harmony of that call, and increases it in tone and volume. Then the call of the heart is more easily heard by those still learning that language, the language of life's call, the language of soul and hope. As the chorus sounds even louder, then this resonance in the milieu of the consciousness of the human family is able to resonate in harmony with Earth's vibration, which enables the loving embrace of higher beings to send more loving light into that milieu, to respond to that call in our hour of need.

Thus, the sound of the heart is magnified, and the edifices of materialistic self-empowerment will have less and less substance from which they can be built and sustained, and they will crumble.

Therefore, in these times of great global distress, work from your heart, whether in meditation, prayer, action, donation – however your heart guides. Let your heart resonance be one of the many that will change the milieu of the world, so that those who do not choose this path of evolution's grace, will be shaken out of their castles and empires of involuntary motivation, and will remember that we are all souls with a responsibility to Earth and all life.

The sound of the many can only be loud enough when every individual with love and hope so chooses. Do yours, from heart, and be empowered with the knowing that this is a moment where great change can occur within Earth's evolutionary awakening, and humanity can take a major step upon the winding path of love's evolution, and see the vistas of true hope and loving care that lie ahead for all.

We can all make and act upon this simple choice, for it lies within our heart, and we all have access to that or else we would have no conscience or wish for the world to be better.

Be empowered, knowing that the voice of every heart, no matter how expressed, resonates with evolution's call, and that creates the harmony of sound we need to awaken the lighted future we hope for, and can thus create.

Be your heart, give it everything, and make your difference now.

Soul

Expressing Soul on Earth

The greatest step taken in the development of your human consciousness is when you realise you are not alive for your own personal self-focussed gains.

Souls are fully aware of the global milieu in which they live, and within which they have responsibilities. It is not in the nature of a soul to be singularly focussed on self, even the youngest of souls. That simply cannot happen, except in truly extreme and rare circumstances resulting from repeated human choice to deny this necessary step in conscious development, which then invites an intervention of spirit and Karmic Law.

Why it cannot happen is because the vibrational milieu in which soul is created, and in which it resides, is the conscious milieu of love created by Earth and her family of greater souls and cosmic agents of evolution. It is a milieu of amazing properties, for it has the ability to resonate with spiritual stimuli (that is, from spirit, the higher fire of creation), and to just reach, ever so gently, into the depths of human life in the physical, mental and emotional levels of vibration.

The Ocean of Love in which souls dwell is a unique vibration that can hold and resonate with this great span of vibrational stimuli. When you leave this life, you do not take with you all the density of thought, feeling and physical vibration, for that cannot live on the level of soul vibration. You take the refined seeds of each level of your human experience, wherein the wisdom gained, and karma earned from lessons learned and new ones created, are held in suspension until your next evolutionary step, whatever level of vibration that is on (physical or inner).

As a human, we earn and learn all these experiences and lessons within the milieu of human earthly life, and it is in this milieu where separation exists. This is another spiritual paradox, because we are not ultimately separate beings, yet our journey needs this experience so that we can truly learn to work within the physical world with the love we have as a soul.

It is about consciousness. A soul cannot know separateness, because the vibrational milieu of which it is made and in which it exists, is one of a certain kind of permeability. There is no resistance at soul level to lessons, guidance, requirements, and the giving and receiving of love. Thus, at soul level, no matter how unevolved the soul of a human being, there is an intrinsic understanding of the need to love and care for Earth, for it is her Ocean of Love in which the soul exists.

As you enter the deeper levels of denser vibrations, wherein we are created and exist as human beings, then you enter the worlds where vibrations are not as easily interactive or permeable. For example, it could be likened to the difference between rock and air. The benefit is that you get your very own little sphere (your self) in which to play with this dense matter in which we live. You can learn and mould the substance of your being, to change it from an unqualified and single-coloured portion of Earth, into a multi-coloured radiant gem through which light can shine.

If you did not have your own sphere in which to experiment with cause and effect, care and hostility, love and separation, light and dark, hope and action, then you would not learn to hold and mould this dense matter of human life into light-giving substance. But in this sphere of matter in which you live and learn, the reality of being part of a greater whole, of having responsibilities outside your sphere, is not inherently present.

Through our hearts, where our soul is anchored, we learn to reach out and connect with others, and to care about family, friends, other life, and this gives valuable stimuli on the path of learning. Indigenous cultures often have a strong element of Earth care in their societies, for they have evolved that through wise souls teaching this for millennia.

However, cultures that have become industrialised, focussed on economies, not Earth – on civilisation as a human attainment of mind and emotion without soul, where the inherent human need for their loving soul has been contained and restrained into material need and greed – these societies cruel the evolution of life, light and soul upon Earth, and of Earth herself.

It is the balance that is needed, for a certain amount of containment is necessary in order to learn and earn the capacity to become light. This journey can never be completed until you recognise that you are a part of Earth's loving embrace, and that you have a duty of care to her and all life in her sphere of evolutionary force.

This is the great step of awakening, and as Earth suffers under the prevalent need-and-greed focus of human activity of this time, this is a choice that is desperately needed. This is a choice of evolutionary imperative. This is a choice of heart – for in your heart you do know. Unfortunately, most societies do not teach this or even encourage this – whether in its most simple form of caring and sharing with others and Earth, or in its spiritual expression through meditation, self-awareness and service.

Even many so-called spiritual journeys are little if anything more than self-contained expressions of need-and-greed, coloured with spiritual words, but of little impact upon the needs of soul or Earth, or the evolution of human consciousness.

If Earth cannot evolve into the next phase of her journey, because too many humans choose not to acknowledge and act upon the basics of human life as a gift of her being, then perhaps she has to fast and purge to detoxify herself. As above, so below.

The Great Change we are in is a time of sickness and choice: Earth suffers, humans suffer, nature and all life suffer. This is the sickness, brought on by too much self-focus and greed in the human family.

It is our responsibility, for we are the primary vehicles within which soul can resonate here upon physical Earth, and create that loving, caring balance that our souls know, where all life is celebrated and nourished. We are the vehicles where consciousness can enable choice, and choice can enable loving heart's flow, and we can become those beautiful gems of brilliance, where our own journey is manifest as colour and light, and our souls can hum through us. Such a joyful life awaits, when we choose this!

It is not a far-off path or destination, it is possible now for everyone, for everyone can say 'yes' to loving light. Even if that light is small, and still evolving, you can still shine.

A great step upon the way is to see Earth for what she is: your home, your nourishment, your shelter, your caring Mother of heart. She is not inert, not endless in what she can give, not a resource for the greedy, and not a place for selfish attainment.

Remember this and choose wisely, then no matter how long or deeply you have journeyed, you can be a gracious presence of care and love, where you own soul can shine more greatly through you. Then your life can be part of the solution, not more of the challenge threatening all life through self-centred, deliberate unawareness.

Journey of Soul on Earth

What is soul?

Soul is the fulcrum of a conscious life, the central point from where life's guidance is directed and nourished, and into which spirit's flame ignites that life force around which life itself is created.

Spirit is the fiery element of life, and the universal element of life's expression as a force of creative intent throughout the universe.

Soul, however, is an element of flow, and is only created when spirit's intent is to incarnate with consciousness into the denser matter of Cosmos. That is because the soul has a water-like characteristic that can more readily enter, and, most importantly, engage and mix with the denser elements of an expression in physical life. The expression of spirit, as a spark that ignites the flame, is not so friendly to matter: it burns and transforms immediately. It is also not a vehicle of consciousness, but a vehicle to manifest intent. Soul is the vehicle of consciousness, and is intentfully fired into action by spirit, but yet does not contain spirit.

It is all a sequence of layers of deepening vibration, where the fire of creation is infused in just the right dose to spark life, but not burn it; to give will and intent, but allow evolution to enrich that expression with conscious choice in the worlds of matter. Soul can only come into beingness when there is an intention to incarnate into a world of matter. Note that for a soul, incarnation means inspiring and nourishing the expression of life on any of the levels of matter below it in vibration. This includes the mental level of mind, the astral level of feelings, as well as the physical and etheric level of manifestation. Not all souls have a physical embodiment, some express only on the inner levels of mind and feeling, learning and becoming a refined consciousness to contribute to the illumination and qualification of these levels of life's manifestation in matter.

On Earth, souls are created in, and dwell in, the Earth's Ocean of Love – which is the equivalent of her emotional (astral) body, a finer-vibrating milieu that embraces and infuses her physical self. Her physical self is the substance in which our mental, emotional and physical self comes into being.

Planets have a conscious journey that evolves on another level of the life force of cosmic intent. Earth's astral body has become purified and energised enough over her evolutionary process, to enable the birth of consciously intentional beings through her. The fire of the spirit of these beings does not burn her, for she has purified the substance sufficiently to absorb that intention, clothe it in love, and enable the descent of life's spark into the physical body of her existence – our mental, emotional and physical worlds.

Some souls have come to Earth already developed to a lesser or greater degree from journeys on other planets, where they have gained experience from incarnating on an emotional or mental level. A physical existence, as we know it upon Earth, is not required from the soul's perspective. They have been called by the increasing intent in Earth's self, in alignment with cosmic intent, to aid her being to become an expression of loving grace into the depth of physical life.

Other souls have arisen in her body of light, by the direct will of the spirit drawn here similarly, to align with cosmic intent and take the creative journey of evolving Earth's physical being into a beacon of loving light.

Spirit dwells in the fiery element of cosmic life in physical expression, and is infused with the direction and intent of Cosmos. Cosmos and Earth have aligned in intent, though Earth's evolutionary journey and choice to become an expression of Cosmic Love through the depths of her being. Thus, she prepared by purifying and qualifying her astral self into the Ocean of Love that it is today – with the aid of many other evolutionary forces and beings, including the Kumaras.

Spirit's intent is a spark that enters this Ocean of Love and sustains its presence there, until the vibration it holds attracts substance of a resonant vibration around it. This is a new soul: a core of spirit's spark, with a surrounding vibratory sphere that resonates in harmony. Time is taken to do this, to build coherence with the note of that initial vibratory intent in the spark of spirit. Once enough coherence has been established for the newly developed soul to have capacity enough to extend itself, then the process of physical incarnation begins.

In concert with Earth's will – for it is of her body that physical life is built – the soul sends out a vibrational seed into the physical levels of vibration: into mental, emotional, and finally etheric layers (if that is the journey). Then a similar process of building occurs, as that initial seed draws to it the matter with which it can resonate. Thus, the new soul develops mental, emotional and etheric spheres of energy within which it can resonate. From there, if spirit's and Earth's wills so align, the physical incarnation can begin with the final building of the physical matter occurring around the blueprint held in the etheric seed.

This new soul, now with garments of physical existence, is still largely an unqualified energy vehicle, as are its garments. The intent that created it is the spark of spirit, and that lies within all, because that is the note that has enabled all levels of coherence to occur, aggregating like-with-like in resonance from soul, down to the dense physical. However, the qualities that enable that soul and its physical expression to form a conscious being – where that initial intent can be expressed and magnified in loving expression – that is the journey of life after life, as evolution of consciousness proceeds.

Every lesson learned, every experience that qualifies your journey as a human into more love, becomes a resonance that can cohere with the seed atoms of your etheric, astral and mental self. Eventually, when refined enough, these vibrations rise into the milieu of your soul, and bring those qualities into the foundation of your being. You evolve from being a soul of one vibration, built of the Ocean of Love of Earth's being, in resonance with your spirit's intent, to a soul of many resonant vibrations, showing as the splendid colours of conscious development.

Similarly, your emotional and mental selves become developed in intent and vibrational differentiation, showing not only in colour but also in brightness. The difference between soul colours and those of the mental and astral selves, is that the soul colours are permanent, for as long as that soul exists; whereas the mental and astral bodies are rebuilt each life, and their expression can be nuanced to contain the opportunities and lessons given by karma, and by your soul.

Ultimately, the core of beingness is always there, for that spark of creation that brought your soul into beingness, and then your physical existence, remains steadfast throughout evolution; for that is your guiding light, the silver cord that keeps you aligned with soul, no matter the human blunders you might make.

This, then, is the journey of soul, in concert with the will of spirit, and the love of Mother Earth who has birthed us all. Even those who have come as souls already, with some development and qualification in their soul and lower bodies, can only be here at Earth's call and acquiescence, for all the substance required to incarnate here is of her body.

Incoming souls will bring the resonance they have qualified on their journeys elsewhere, both in their soul vibration and in the seed atoms of any other bodies of expression they have developed, but they must still cohere their new bodies of soul and physical selves out of Earth's loving matter.

The core of your being is always aligned with Earth's call, your spirit's response, and your soul's creation or reconstitution; so, deep within, you know why you are here. It is a sacred and utterly blessed opportunity. Remind yourself of this every day, and slowly the whole resonance of your being will become aligned and illumined with the light of who you truly are, and why you are here.

Find ways to let the still sentience of your inner self shine. This does not have to be your soul, for that fine vibration takes time to perceive, or if perceived, to handle with balance in the vibration of your physical self. Know and trust that the core inspiration that brought you into beingness lies also in your etheric, astral and mental seeds, so that anything you do to still your outer vibrational busy-ness, created by dealing with outer life, will allow you to bring more and more of your awareness, and then consciousness, into alignment with who you truly are: the self that hums deep in your being, with love.

Differentiating Darkness & Evil

In our world we have evil, and we have darkness, and they are quite different. It is important to understand and differentiate between them because both can cause the evolving consciousness concern and perhaps fear, which is not always the best response.

Darkness is very different from evil, for true darkness, like the deep darkness of space, is simply unillumined, unqualified, unconscious matter. Evil, however, is a combination of the materially-focussed forces, with emotional and sometimes mental forces aligned with them, magnifying the downward pull.

We all have darkness within, until such time as we have brought the vibration, illumination and coherence of consciousness to all parts of our being in our physical world of mind, feelings and body. This is a darkness we should not fear or shy away from, for this is simply the small part of our planet and our universe that we have taken on, into which to bring the loving embrace and vibratory resonance that is consciousness. The darkness you find within needs exploration – with help if you need it – so that you can cleanse, clarify and bring your harmonic resonance into that part of you in such a way that it enters your conscious milieu.

Our inner bodies (mental and astral) are the vehicles that enable us to discern and intuit the higher vibrations of life's existence. Yes, we wobble on the way, because it takes time to refine and qualify the vibrations within our physical consciousness in order to perceive them. This is normal, and is simply the journey of exploring and learning about what is unconscious within us. While it may appear dark, it is not evil, even if we have done wrong by others or by Earth, in our lack of knowing. It is unillumined substance that may hold some memories, some qualification of energy that differentiates it a little from the deep unknowing of matter itself.

The journey of evolution, the lessons and grace of karma, the choices we make to keep striving for positive change will help awaken, purify and redeem any emerging, undesirable patterns. This is the foundation of forgiveness, for we are all on this journey, and stumble and fumble around in many lives as we learn this great lesson of evolving consciousness within matter itself.

However, we take a dark turn when we align our emotional and perhaps mental consciousness, with the downward pull of the involutionary forces. This is so very different from stumbling on the evolutionary path as we learn. This is a deliberate choice, although as portrayed in the opera 'Faust', sometimes the choice is seen as a means to an end, and the consciousness pretends not to realise the consequences.

Primarily, turning to evil can only occur when the emotional self is developed enough to register the pull of involution, and, usually through imbalance, to attach to that pull, and attribute to it benefits on which the emotional self has fixated.

Do not fret if you have strong desires for things – everyone does in one way or another. However, be careful if those emotional pulls extend beyond you, and involve people en masse. If you do wrong by others individually, that is sorted by your own karma, conscience, and life journey. We all make these steps and mis-steps, but they are not the creator of evil.

Evil is that which becomes so strong in its pull to matter, unqualified and unillumined matter, that it shrouds all in a lifeless darkness, denying the glimmer of consciousness to spark the realisation of light, and true life. Yet it is energised by a coherence, built around an emotional desire, or, in darker evil, around both emotional desire and mental vision – if you can call it that.

Sometimes, to the emerging consciousness upon the evolutionary journey, the presentation of a strongly-cohered emotional vibration together with an enunciated vision can seem very appealing. In the fog of life without heart's spark of light giving us personal guidance, with the lack of any religious guidance and/or relevance to fit our current times, we search for meaning. Meaning can seem present in a coherent and vision-driven presentation – but, how does that vision affect others? How does that vision affect nature and Earth?

It is quite remarkable how so many fall for an enunciated vision, filled with emotional sweeteners. Yet that vision is neither coherent, life-affirming (in the evolutionary sense), motivated by kindness, or even built in reality.

This is too often the start of what entraps the human expression of young souls, and those older souls who should know better, upon a downward-focussed journey that glorifies the material, not the truly spiritual.

There is never a spiritual impulse of light, love, hope, that requires divisiveness and isolationism (as in 'us and them'), or cruelty in words or actions, or incitement to anger and hatred. Never!

On rare occasions there is a spiritual impulse to destroy evil, and that can come with a decisiveness and forcefulness that can be confronting. Look at the meaning and consequence, and you will understand.

If you feel drawn to something that offers an emotional coherence with a vision that appeals, look very carefully.

One of the greatest drivers of evil in this world is greed: people with an unfettered greed for more power, more wealth, more land, more people aligned with their vision or in their control, more self-aggrandisement.

This is born of the pull of the forces that create us, the involuntary forces that draw us into incarnation. Beautiful forces for which we must be grateful, but not ones that we should re-energise with conscious intent and emotional charge when we are on the evolutionary path. This is the distortion that is anti-life, and thus what we call 'evil'.

These are complex times, and multifaceted in the opportunities presented to us to awaken our life force, and grow in consciousness. This is a product of both us and Earth (and all her life streams) reaching a point of great transition, where the great unfoldment of spirit may deepen into the world of our existence. This is a great and profound change, for it shall bring into closer reach that touch of the true light that uplifts and nourishes us all – but we have to choose it. Earth, all life, humanity – we have to choose this, for the light of spirit is never imposed, else it will burn and harm, and not enable the evolutionary process that is underway.

This is the magic of consciousness and choice: when you choose, the door opens and light floods in. It is as simple as that, at a soul level at least. It can be this simple in our personality selves, but usually our patterns from previous lives, and the presence of our unconscious substance (darkness, as we have described it; the old experiences and lessons not yet completed), restrict the inflowing light to small rivulets or trickles.

Whatever our experience, ultimately there is only one simple fork in the road ahead, needing one simple choice: to walk in the light. Then, however your path evolves, whatever your past and future require you to learn, know that you will be on your true evolutionary path.

If you pray for this, meditate upon this, or simply hold this as your mantra – to walk in the light – then you will. You will receive the help and nudges you need to avoid the entrapments of those who have not chosen light: those who spin stories that empower themselves, for their own grand vision that holds no light or love; those who weave entanglements of personal desire and greed in with religious motives, which is ridiculous and should be called out for what it is, for material yearning will never achieve spiritual salvation; and those who weave emotional confusion into conspiracies to disrupt soul and light, to create division and disillusionment.

If you seek, want, pray for, meditate on, affirm in your day that you want to walk in the light, and then review your choices in your heart, you will give yourself every chance to see and differentiate what is true and necessary (even a disruption, when caused by the light and evolutionary forces), from the entanglements of the dark forces – that is, matter unillumined, and clothed in manufactured human desire.

Thus, you help Earth and all life: for the more who choose this path of light, the less substance those who have chosen to bind themselves to greed of one sort or another shall have with which to work.

On this choice: never rely on your mind, for mind alone can justify anything if the emotional drivers are strong enough. You can see this frequently with otherwise intelligent people who become completely immersed in conspiracies, who cannot enunciate a thread of logic to cohere their theories, or the theories they believe, yet they do not notice; or they attribute the gaps in logic to some great divine intervention or plan yet there is no divine energy within it.

Sometimes we cannot understand or make sense of upheavals in life, yet somewhere there is intention behind it. However, there is never spiritual intention behind people who cause devastation, destruction, oppression or divisiveness; or who incite hatred, greed, selfishness or separatism on the world stage.

You will know in your heart! Your task is to make sure you give space – even just the shortest of quiet moments can be enough – where you still your thoughts and emotional impulses, and listen. Listen to the deep core of your being, the resonating light in your heart, the resonance of truth in the light, and follow that.

In this time of Great Change, you cannot blindly follow or rely on other human beings in roles of leadership, or organisations, or theories about the plan for the world, unless you verify their authenticity in the light of your heart. Your choice, your evolutionary step, your enlightenment for Earth and all.

This is the difference between evil and darkness: evil drags all in its grasp back into the dullness of unevolved matter, shrouded in and bound there by emotional binds and mental contortions. Darkness is unevolved and unqualified substance, and in you it is simply that substance ready for you to illuminate and love.

Our yearning as humans for coherence and resonance with others of similar thought and feeling is natural and positive, just make sure that yearning does not draw you into groups where you no longer find your own light, and discern carefully in your heart, for your sake, for the sake of the Earth.

There is much resistance to this incoming light of spirit in some who hold or yearn for power. Beware.

Justice & Sticky Guilt

Justice. What is it really? Many feel justice is achieved when someone is punished by the law, and often that is true. Of lesser validity is when justice is meted out personally, when one feels justified in mistreating another – leading to violence, racism, misguided nationalism, religious intolerance, and other acts of prejudice.

As indicated in the word 'prejudice', this arises from a *pre*-judgement, making it inevitably personal – whether individually, or collectively by the group involved. A picture is formed, and promulgated within groups, based on personal perceptions, assessments, experiences, all of which are filtered through one's own memories and knowledge, and the constraints of one's own karma and consciousness.

The inevitable failure of this to align with and empower true justice is why humanity has long sought and created laws to bring order, and has invested in the value of wise citizens to make judgements based on the agreed laws, but this is all changing now. Change is obviously needed, for even though most countries have laws and a legal system that enable justice in most situations, there are two obvious failings: the power of individuals and corporations to manipulate law to enable their continued unethical exploits of people and Earth; and the need for more pervasive and effective global law, as the global community grows in interactions in both positive and negative ways.

The difficulty with the law, is that it is one of the hardest expressions of social structure to change, when it is on issues of societal interest. Unfortunately, many laws are changed to suit certain empowered individuals and corporations, but society at large does not notice, or perceive the need to care. Ultimately, it is conscious human change that must occur, to enable the re-imagining of what a lawful society means in the unfolding Age of the Heart.

The laws present in nations at this time are largely created and interpreted mentally. Some nations still apply laws on an astral level, but very few. The challenge with both is that they are, and must be, implemented through the assessment of mind and emotion, for that is the milieu in which they exist. Emotions we know can be swayed in many ways. The mind too, as it unfortunately can justify anything if so pre-conditioned.

In society we choose those who make judgements of law in the perception and hope that they will be impartial, and many are. But they are human.

Some people turn to their god to mete out justice, trying to find a higher administration of law, but there is no god in charge of physical law courts, or that can justify humanly motivated retributions.

True justice comes from soul, because this is where there is both insight into the pattern of causes, and interaction with the Board of Karma, which holds and implements the justice of soul.

On Earth, soul is the giver and taker of life, in concert with the Law of Karma. Soul is of the Ocean of Love, the milieu of life's birth itself, upon and within Earth. When soul breathes out, life is created; when soul calls, that life is drawn back from human expression into the sanctuary of love's embrace.

Karma is the law that enables consciousness to grow, through the experience of constraints and other lessons to balance life's journey, if the law of life and love has been broken.

There is a great distance between the administration of karmic law, actioned from the world of soul, and the machinations of law on a human level, although you would understand there is much intermingling as karma manifests in our personal lives.

The challenge is as described: too many individuals and corporate entities wield power over human law at this time, and their greed, their materially-focussed idealism, is causing harm to Earth, and to many souls. On this scale, it goes beyond the implementation of karmic law on an individual scale, and great global challenges arise.

Humanity needs to wake up and care on this greater scale. Some, many in fact, are awake to this need, but not the masses needed to turn around the sluggish and entrenched systems of law, to force change and to meet the needs of both human and global evolution and their challenges.

The forces of involution that draw souls to incarnation become something completely else when overly energised by the emotional and mental drive of greed.

Greed is the one primary driver that sucks people into actions against the law, against the law of soul. When the laws of the land do not align with the justice of soul and karma – at least enough to enable re-balancing under the law of karma – then justice is not achieved.

As the world of souls evolves into greater presence in the consciousness of humanity, as the great shift to heart consciousness unfolds, then the justice of soul must be embedded more deeply into the laws of nations, and those who administer them, and into the world as a whole.

This can only come from human demand, for too many legal systems and those administering them, are enmeshed in either the rigidity of tradition and society of the past; or, of more challenging and worrying concern, have been captured and are manipulated by political greed, typically the lust for power.

To do yours to help this transition: meditate on justice, true justice, that of heart and soul. In that, you redeem and release guilt! So many of humanity fail to act, out of the oppressive weight of guilt that feeds doubt, even fear; and let darkness creep by into greater and greater amalgamations of lawlessness on a group, corporate, national or global scale.

To discern justice, you must discern guilt. Guilt is the great awakener of conscience, but unfortunately it is also sticky in that it is hard to let go of, even when the conscience, and thus consciousness, has been awakened.

Humanity as a whole is burdened by many layers of guilt, whether consciously apprehended or not (as is most usually the case). Much of this guilt arises from the wars of the 20th century, where evil and the combat of it has left many human life streams with residual trauma; or where political greed has unjustly waged war and entrapped many in the clutches of their own wrong deeds.

Therefore, when you meditate upon justice, apprehend any guilt in your being and seek to learn the lessons of conscience it has for you. If there are no lessons that you can perceive, then let it go. Guilt is our own internal prejudice; we pre-judge ourselves based on the residues of past memories we have not yet released. Now we need to for-give: to give to our future that which we can offer from our current place in time, whether in our day, or in our life. That gift is the freedom to become soul, unencumbered by the weight of burdens past.

The paradox is that the stickiness of guilt arises from our human uncertainty about justice: we rehash the past, from this life, or often unknowingly from past lives, because we either do not remember, or do not believe that justice has been meted out by soul and karma, and its lesson has been finalised. If it is not finished, then we can work to perceive our wrongs and rectify them consciously. If it is finished, we can release it.

This is the path forward, as individuals, as groups, as nations, as a global community, so that we can release the sticky binds of guilt that hinder our ability to fight for and demand the true justice we need for our times. The justice that holds both the light of soul's intention for individuals, and global heart for our world, so desperately needed at this time.

In your heart you can find the understanding of justice, for there your soul nourishes you with truth, and from there you can free yourself from guilt's fetters, and trust in your strength to empower positive change within and around you.

Incarnating as Soul

In your heart, in your physical self, is the part of you that resonates with your soul, your living, loving, nourishing source of life's vitality. It may be the only part of you resonating with soul at this point, but it is always there. You will not usually find bits of soul consciousness reverberating in your being, as you refine and develop your personal self to resonate with that consciousness. It takes a long time for more of your being to hold the resonance of soul, because that is the end point of the human journey.

The most usual path of development of soul consciousness is to build and refine the wisdom, insight and self-awareness in the mental and emotional self, and the purity of the physical-etheric self, so that when the inspiration and strength of soul is needed, your whole being can hold that resonance as a vibrating light into the physical world. If you are not developed in the fullness just described, then any expression of soul must be guided by soul, and is therefore not a conscious expression of the personality; this is the saviour model of spiritual growth, where the hope is for a sudden possession of all things illuminated, loving and wise without the conscious engagement of the personal self.

There are times on every spiritual journey where you may feel a sweep of uplifting energy fully infuse and embrace you, and help you gain insight or healing – but the truth is that this is rarely brought to you by your soul. In almost every circumstance, this great inflow and embrace is given by your inner guides, helpers or teachers.

Soul is not involved on a daily basis in your life – in your human day at least. A day in the life of soul is your life from birth to passing, the active period of engagement before the inner retreat between lives. The inner retreat may also be one of busy engagement in further learning and development, and usually is for those striving forward on the path; but still the soul is not involved in every detail.

There are several reasons as to why soul is not engaged in every moment of our personal life's learning and journey. The first is that soul vibration is on another octave, if you like, from the vibratory notes of our lives.

While in our personal self we develop mind, body and feelings within a limited range of vibrations (because that is the milieu of human life), soul develops on a completely other vibration. Connected in resonance, yes, but not in the same range of notes.

Second, you have to consider evolutionary purpose. Soul is not there to save you, the human self, but to learn in concert with you, so that when time is right, you can merge in consciousness and become that beacon of loving light and presence that is a soul-infused being.

Your soul helps map out the key lessons for any one life, and may engage in certain moments to encourage, or illumine certain options, but most likely these are given by your helpers, friends and teachers on the inner or physical levels.

Third, your soul may not yet have the wisdom and capacity to engage in human life in its physical detail. Your soul is learning too, and while at all times it is the source of the living force that enables you to be alive in this physical world, and energises your life journey, until it (and you) are very far along the path, your soul has limited know-how that it can apply directly in this human world. That is your job!

You, the human personality of mind, emotion, etheric and physical body, you are to become the expert at navigating with wisdom and love in this human world. When you do become a wise and loving person, then your soul can resonate in you, and more to the point, you will have developed the refinement and qualities with which your soul's resonance can set up a harmonic vibration. Thus, you will walk on Earth infused with your soul's presence that you can radiate into the world, and give to Earth in the denser levels of vibration.

This is the journey to mastership, where the gift is to become that presence of living light here in the physical world. There are many other journeys, though, and the primary goal is to understand what your journey is, here in any one life.

At every point your soul love is there in your heart, so you always have that loving presence into which to retreat when you need that nourishment or healing, but you need to be realistic about becoming light. For the majority, this is not the path. The path is to become a loving human, in whom light can harmonise, and soul can resonate, and you shine in the world as that beautiful and loving human.

The path of becoming an incarnated soul right down into our physical world – compared to incarnating as a human being with your soul's loving presence awakened within you – is not the path for the majority either. Nor is this needed by the Earth. We are all at different stages of human and soul development, and while in every life we can learn to become wiser and more loving as a human, and to develop in consciousness so we can be a more positive citizen here within Earth's evolutionary journey, the path of becoming soul fully incarnated in our human self is not necessary for either.

To reiterate: soul is the loving, nourishing life force that enables you to live and evolve here upon Earth. Soul is the vehicle that accumulates and re-gifts the consciousness and wisdom you have gained from life to life, and works within the Law of Karma to help you become that wise, strong and loving human you wish to be. That is the evolutionary journey.

Beyond that, it becomes a choice of your soul. In broad, the choices are to stay here on Earth and help on the inner levels, as a guide, mentor, healer, teacher, etc.; or to stay and continue to incarnate, to nourish human and earthly life with the gifts you have gained; or it may be to leave Earth, and journey elsewhere in Cosmos.

Then there are the very few who have the opportunity to evolve further in such a way that they can incarnate as souls – something only possible with Earth's direct request and consent – and undergo the specific training and development that is required for one who has chosen this path. Examples are the two great beings we know from the incarnations of Buddha and Christ Maitreya (who overshadowed Jesus). These two great souls have long walked the path to enable them to stand upon Earth as humans and as souls, and thus the reverberation of their teachings and sheer presence are remembered and revered through millennia.

Certainly there have been great, caring, illumined teachers since, but they have either been overshadowed by great souls from the inner world of the Greater Hearts, or they have expressed their own soul wisdom in periods of illumination; but in neither case have they been a fully-incarnated soul upon Earth. Many of these are great female souls who have, and will incarnate. It is all about timing and need of the particular vibrational stimulus that a great soul in incarnation brings.

It is perhaps disheartening to understand how rarely any soul fully incarnates here in this world; but only if you have been caught by the illusion or glamour of the weekend workshop that will turn you into a purified and gloriously soul-infused being; or lost in the hope of escaping this life's journey by letting soul take it all over.

The utter, glorious beauty of human life is the ability to be here, fully functioning as a human being, taking the journey of the evolution of consciousness, and learning how to resonate with soul; so that love and light can filter through all the colours of your personal expression, and help make this world one of peace and equity, love and hope, consciousness and care for all life and Earth herself.

Understand soul, for that is your life source. Seek to resonate with soul, for that is your greatest loving expression. Take the journey gifted by your soul, for that is your journey to freedom, the true freedom of living and serving in oneness with the law that defines our alignment with soul and Earth.

This is your path to becoming the most beautiful, radiant, loving, soul-infused being you are to be in this life – and that is your path to pure joy.

Start in your heart, where your soul resonates no matter at what stage of development you are. From there, become more heart conscious, and in every tiny or greater choice, you enable soul to infuse you more and more, and that is the gift and blessing of a life here upon this beautiful, nourishing Earth.

Involution to Evolution

The yearning for soul, whether you experience that as the yearning for a higher love to embrace you in times of need, or for illumination in times of uncertainty or doubt, or for healing in times of challenge, or for meaning and purpose in life's journey – this yearning is born out of the Law of Attraction.

It is the Law of Attraction that enables us to work with the involutionary forces, and to incarnate and build a body of human existence. Equally, it is what constantly pulls our hearts to that deeper, higher yearning that leads us on the fullness of the conscious journey of evolution.

On the journey of involution, the descent into matter, the forces of attraction are garnered by those nourishing and deeply focussed beings that build form in these dense levels of Cosmos that Earth embodies.

In its most basic expression, the force of attraction is what we see at work in gravity: the basic pull of matter to matter. However, in order for a human soul to be influenced by this, it must have matter that resonates with the matter of Earth, so that this force can work. Remember, like attracts like; this is the inherent nature of every molecule and subatomic particle in our universe, because that is the life expression our universe embodies. All matter is created within, and imbued with this basic blueprint.

When you bring life from one level of resonance into a denser level, you need more than the inbuilt force of gravity. For example, to bring the resonance of soul (dwelling in the Ocean of Love) into the denser vibration of emotional, mental and physical substance, another force is needed because these levels of substance are not resonant with each other.

Thus, the guiding beings are formed. In Earth's situation, they form in response to her call, and through the supporting intent of Cosmos and its response, expressed in consciousness from Cosmic Heart, they are held within the energetic sphere of Sirius.

Consciousness is the one other force of Cosmos that is able to coalesce matter and resonance, and build intent into that creation. In terms of the journey of soul into manifestation as a physical being: when the soul is young, it does not have enough, if any, consciousness to build a human form in the worlds of matter. Highly developed souls who came to Earth in response to her call, can build their own vehicles for conscious expression as human beings, or angelic beings in some situations. Young souls, however, need assistance, and so the great involutionary builders came into being, to enable Earth's choice to be an expression of loving intent in physical matter to be fulfilled.

To create and build in matter when the inherent forces of attraction are not activated, i.e., when there is not enough resonance between the level where the creative force arises, and the intended level of creation – for example, a soul creating a human life – this is an act of will. Will takes effort, rather than the natural process of coalescence that happens when resonance and the forces of attraction are able to build. Some of the greater souls who came in response to Earth's call used this method in earlier days. They used their own will to incarnate, in alignment with cosmic intent (which is a type of will). Because this takes effort, there is a limitation on how often and how long that effort may be applied. As humanity is slowly learning (too slowly, in those who do not treat Earth with respect or value sustainability), Earth is a being of contained, and thus limited, resources. It is the same on the inner levels: there is only so much will that can be embodied within her ring-pass-not.

The great involutionary builders are created and sustained by Earth's will and the intent (will) of Cosmos. Their creation was energised for a period throughout which enough souls could incarnate, evolve, and become sufficiently developed that there was enough resonance developed between soul and earthly levels that the involutionary builders would no longer be needed. A soul could then choose to incarnate (in alignment with the Law of Karma that balances all expressions of consciousness), without needing the great conscious intent of these builders to constantly be involved. This has largely been achieved, and is the point at which we find ourselves at this time.

This is the evolutionary journey we are on: to become a conscious flow from soul to human and back, such that Earth becomes that living pulse of love that the circulation of her Ocean of Love through her physical substance will achieve.

We begin with involution, and here is where the great choice of our era arises. Humanity and other physical life forms as a whole, have achieved enough resonance with the higher worlds to enable incarnation to continue, without the massive effort needed by the great builders created to fulfil involution's intent. However, the memory of that force that brought us into being is strong in some, especially for those lured by the human emotions of greed – for greed can only express in the manifestation of things in the physical world, such as property, money, power. None of these have value to the soul.

If greed captures a person's emotional motives, and it becomes strong enough to subvert the decisive mind, and hide the yearning heart, then that person may create such a strong intentional vibration in their being that the forces of involution resonate with them. With enough conscious development, yet with heart closed off by the intensity of emotional greed, this person becomes one who wields some of the forces of involution, motivated by their greed. We call this person a dark magician. The forces that should naturally draw us into balance between involution, the force for life's creation, and evolution, the force impelling us to seek higher and more loving consciousness, are subverted by the distortions and cementations of an overly greedy and inhumane emotional self.

Rarely does this occur, for the Law of Karma is there to create opportunities for, and at times to force, a person to re-take lessons and evolve the consciousness to choose more wisely, and heal and purify the greed they have strengthened in their human self.

However, you cannot evolve consciousness without choice, so there is always an element of risk on this path of evolutionary growth – risk of making dark choices.

Two great periods have arisen upon Earth where that choice has been magnified beyond an individual, when whole populations and civilisations have made consecutive and increasingly dominant choices, succumbing to the lure of greed over communal equity and shared evolutionary care. One was on Atlantis, where, as human myth and reality in the Akashic records states, the continent and civilisation were broken apart. This was the first great intervention, and was an act of Cosmic Will, brought into manifestation by the hearts of those of greater consciousness, who are the guardians of Earth's evolutionary path. These are the Kumaras, and in particular, Sanat Kumara, who has held Earth's evolutionary intent within his consciousness since he came from Venus many millions of years ago to fulfil this role.

The forces of involution are established through an effort of Cosmic Will. If these forces are bent to human greed in manifestation, only an act of Cosmic Will can correct this, and it must be brought into focused action by an embodied heart within Earth's sphere of consciousness.

The second great period of the challenge of greed, and the need for careful choice, is now. This last (approximately) 150 years has manifested much harm to humanity, Earth and all her life streams, as a result of an increasingly coherent force of greed, that is pulling into action the forces of involution.

You may wonder, where are the great builders who wield these forces for humans and soul, and Earth's journey of consciousness? Can they not control these forces, so that they are not misused? These great builders were created by the will, to bring souls into incarnation. Outside of this, they have no role; for that is not their evolutionary journey. Humanity has to make the choice, individually and collectively, and then that combined intent can become the force that uncouples the massed coherence of greed from the will and intent of involution upon our planet.

We all experience wants beyond our needs. That is an aspect of our emotional nature that seeks attachment with the world around us. However, this creates the fertile ground upon which choice becomes conscious, and evolution occurs.

The great choice and the Great Change of our times requires this personal choice to be magnified through alignment with the force of attraction that is within our hearts, drawing us to the light and love of soul. It is not enough to simply make a human choice at this critical time, for that does not create enough wilful intention of evolutionary force to break through the layers of greed that enshroud Earth and life at this time.

We need the intervention of greater forces. If enough human beings, the vehicle of the majority of conscious choice in our earthly world, yearn for this positive change for the sake of all life and Earth herself, then the Greater Hearts can respond. This is the first stage, where the call and response are enabled by the Law of Attraction: enough human heartfelt yearning can attract the forces of love from these Greater Hearts. That may be enough. Those who remember, or resonate with the memory of Atlantis, hope so.

If it is not enough, then divine will shall intervene, this time through the great female Kumara who is preparing to embody for Earth's next great evolutionary step: to embody heart. If humanity's call is not great enough to enable the forces of attraction to undo the manifesting evil in our current era, then the Greater Hearts will themselves unite and call for this cosmic intervention, and the emerging Kumara will have to take upon herself the wielding of this great force of will, to shatter evil.

Let us not get to this point, not only for the sake of Earth and humanity, and all life which would be strongly affected, but because it dilutes the importance of this moment of evolutionary choice, and thus the opportunity of the great step forward that can be made upon the conscious journey for every soul upon Earth, and for Earth herself.

Follow the yearning in your heart, temper any sense of greed in your being, and pray, meditate, attune in whatever way you can to magnify your heart's call for peace, and for dissipation of the excesses of greed manifesting in obscene wealth, nationalistic oppression, unfettered political power, and the brutal destruction of people, nature, nations and Earth.

The time is now. The call from a million conscious hearts could be enough, if personal will is applied, and clear choices made.

Do yours. It is urgent.

Living a Soul Life

To live a life of soul is to live infused with loving purpose, to flow with energised service, to relate with insight and wisdom, to understand and act with perspective and compassion.

Who doesn't want this? This is what lies as the promise of life to be, in your heart; for your heart resonates with soul, and is your guide on your evolutionary journey of conscious awakening. Your heart is also built of physical matter, and creates and sustains your physical life, and so it also resonates with those forces that build life out of matter. It is the place where we balance those forces that pull us into matter, and those that draw us to soul and the refined light of evolutionary intention.

Heart is what awakens now, in this evolutionary journey upon Earth. In the past, spiritual and soul stimuli were filtered down through mental and emotional structures, built by evolved and inspired beings with insight and at least some resonance with soul and evolutionary intention. Religions and spiritual traditions are the most obvious of these structures, built as they have been through millennia of human yearning, searching, insight and hope, and often inspired by the radiating presence of an incarnated soul of light in the past. These structures have given pathways, guidance, and opportunities for a human young in soul to grow and develop upon their path, when they do not as yet have enough personal conscious development to find soul and light, and to follow that guidance directly.

Other structures, not so obviously of soul intent, are many and varied, because soul and spirit are not just interested in the spiritual awakening of humanity. For human life to continue to exist and be of service upon Earth, there needs to be carefully-considered and caring expressions of life's development and management in every sphere: for example, in politics, law, science, education, art, music, medicine, psychology – the spectrum of health, wellbeing and social structures in all their expressions.

To seek to live life immersed in soul and ignoring all other aspects of human life and responsibilities to Earth, nature and all life, is as unbalanced as living a life of greed and unillumined materialism – unless it should be your specific dharma to seek that isolated soul life, but that is rare.

Soul infuses our heart and sustains our life upon Earth because we have the honour and privilege to have a physical incarnation, which in this universe is rare; and we have work to do here.

If you wish to dissolve into the world of soul, then you may have that opportunity – but it will cost you, as a human and as a soul.

Everything in life is balanced, life after life, by the ebb and flow of soul, and human intent and actions, encompassed and guided by the Law of Karma.

To incarnate here upon Earth is a great gift, and requires cooperation of your soul with the loving embrace of Mother Earth, and with the laws of life and those who hold and implement them. For example, the laws that guide the forces of involution so that you can physically incarnate; the laws that guide your development and evolution such as the Law of Karma; and the laws that enable and guide interaction and learning through relationships to others and Earth, such as the Law of Attraction. These laws are impregnated into the substance of the universe itself, for that is the great living being in whose presence and body we live.

Our life here within the physical realms is not about just finding God and going to heaven, or finding illumination and breaking the wheel of dharma, or sacrificing self and returning to the light – or any of the other pathways elucidated, and unfortunately in many expressions, cemented, in the teachings and practices we see as spiritual.

Yes, seek soul. That is essential to illumine our minds and awaken our hearts and consciousness so we can evolve. But it is not enough!

Some spiritual practices and religions embrace the need for engagement with and service in the world. However, the traditionally non-spiritual aspects of life, society and Earth-care are not in and of themselves seen as part of our spiritual journey, but just as places we can bring our own personal spirituality. This is what must change!

Until we see every expression of society and physical life's structures as part of the illuminating evolutionary expression of spirit's unfolding, we are spiritually by-passing the needs of the hour. These structures are seen as something necessary for physical existence, but irrelevant to the spiritual journey. This is not so!

Furthermore, this does not give leave to those of any narrow-minded dogma to seek to dominate social structures so they can impose their way upon others. We see this too often when those who pretend religious or spiritual allegiance, create division and separatism in groups and nations. This is not an expression of soul, of light, or of loving evolutionary intent. This is religion convoluted by greed into the power politics of darkness. No good shall come of this, in any sphere.

We are a diversity of human beings upon Earth, to enrich the path of evolution and learning. We would learn nothing of evolutionary importance if all were the same, for we would have no choices of consequence to make. There are masses of people who do not actively seek an evolving path in life, and for whom sameness holds the appeal of false certainty, but it is not them upon whom the urgent need of the hour rests. It is on those who lead, in all endeavours of human expression, and on those of conscious intent who have choice.

All human structures of life and society need to become vehicles aligned with the inflowing evolutionary intent, and reflect the reality of soul. A long way off, perhaps, but until the seed of this reality rests in the human consciousness, even to just the smallest degree, it shall not even begin to be realised.

The paradox of living a spiritual life is to enable that infusion of soul and loving intent to give you vision, and then to put your feet back upon the ground and strive to help that vision manifest.

Humans are exceptional creators and builders, with excellent problem-solving capacities. The key to the path forward is to avoid greed. Greed is the manifestation of the pull of the material forces of involution, when not balanced by the pull from the heart to the light. From greed, all other anti-light characteristics can develop, for you can only fulfil greed when you create separation from others, so that you have more than them. From this arises almost every human challenge: for example, war, famine, racism, nationalism, oppression, poverty, pollution and destruction of Earth herself.

As heart awakens through this period of the Great Change, greed is confronted in all its expressions. The only hope is more heart, which means more choice every day, for every human. Then we do not disappear into a life of soul, but we express the loving, balanced life of soul in our human world in this hour of need.

Soul's Loving Embrace

Soul is love, but what does that mean in your day-to-day life?

Does it mean soul is present when you love your children, parents, siblings, partner? Does it mean soul is present when you love a cause, or perhaps a religious figure through your faith? The answer is maybe, but usually not.

Let us explore what soul love means in the human world. Soul is of the vibration of the Ocean of Love, Earth's milieu of loving intention that coheres her conscious existence with the incoming and present souls, drawn to participate in and contribute to her journey as a loving, living expression of heart consciousness. That is her evolutionary goal, as it is of the universe in conscious intent, and that is the expression of her beingness that draws other life streams to her through the Law of Attraction.

Soul is the medium, the level of vibration that can respond both to spirit's call, and to the resonance of physical matter. In this way, it is a unique medium for conscious life: it both gifts life into matter, energising the spark of intent that gathers substance into human or other physical forms; and it resonates with the guiding intention of higher life, be that spirit, or Earth's intent expressed through her body via her astral self, the Ocean of Love.

It is a creative force. It creates life, and/or it creates intention to stimulate growth of consciousness. In this way it is a loving expression of life itself. When you think about love as a vehicle of human connection, it is about relationship, comfort, caring, nurturing, and support. There are many words that can describe the fullness of a loving relationship, but very few relate to the primary purpose and vibration of soul love, which is to create under the guidance and impulse of spirit's and Earth's intent. Even the human creative process to bring new souls into incarnation is not often directly linked to earthly or spirit-aligned intent.

The primary reason for this is because the fineness of vibration of soul is neither easily perceived in the dense vibrational nature of human life, nor, if it were, would it be easy for the human self to accommodate.

You may wonder how that can be, if soul is the creative force that brings all life into incarnation. It is simply the fact of the vibrational resonance: a fine vibration will, in most cases, either simply bounce off, or pass straight through, a denser vibration. This is a physical fact. That is why spiritual healing only works for some – and for some it challenges – because unless the vibrational input is exactly harmonised with the resonance of what needs transforming, the vibration will have no effect, or may be disruptive. Thus, the skill and training of the healer is of paramount importance, as it is for the inner healing guides who work with and through them. This is not to say spiritual healing always invokes soul vibration, it rarely does, for the very reasons we are exploring.

If a higher vibration of light and love, or whatever focussed quality is held in that vibration, is brought into presence around a human being, through a healer, a life circumstance, or direct soul intervention, there are two possible outcomes:

1. no effect at all, because the vibration has found no resonance within the vibrational structure of the human being, so it passes through, or bounces off; or
2. there is resonance within some part of the human self, such that the incoming vibration can set up a harmonic vibration, and change the note, if you like, in the human consciousness and/or physical milieu of the body (including the emotions and mind).

In any circumstance, too much of a different vibrational note resonating in your being can be harmful. You are a vehicle of complex and interconnected emotions, thoughts, and physical substance, and your journey is one of evolving consciousness.

If, for example, soul simply infused and took over your human self, your soul would be in charge of your human life, which it can only be capable of if you have had millennia of lives of learning such that your soul has enough knowledge to do this; and you would no longer be on a human journey of developing consciousness.

That is why this almost never happens. Only when the soul and personality are capable of co-resonance to the degree that enables complete soul infusion, and when global and personal karma enable, can this occur

– such as in the incarnation of the soul of a great spiritual teacher for a particular global impact. Note that this is totally different from the work of many illumined and/or inspired people of spiritual intent, who influence a smaller or greater number of followers. Very few souls incarnate as a direct presence here on Earth, because it does not have an impact just on the human beings attracted to that light, but upon the whole Earth herself. Thus, it is only able to occur in concert with the choice and evolutionary path of Earth herself. That is very rare, but spectacular when it occurs, when seen as the expression of light that it is.

Furthermore, this light has various effects. In the complex milieu of the human personality of mind, feelings and physical-etheric self, an infusion of a finely vibrating light unavoidably stimulates change, for that is inevitable in the mix of vibrational notes that ensues. If you have the capacity to perceive and welcome this change as something with which to resonate further, then you can take that journey and evolve your consciousness and your physical being to be more resonant with this vibration. For example, in those followers of Jesus, or of Buddha, two great conscious beings who incarnated the vibration of soul into the world. However, this always requires change, which is what evolution is about. Change such that you can resonate more fully with their loving soul intent, and change such that you dissolve, transform or dissipate those parts of yourself that do not resonate.

This is where you choose. All spiritual stimuli, whether directly from soul, or circumstantially through karma, show you what to change so that you evolve. The very structure of a human being is built in the worlds of physical, emotional and mental matter, held together by the forces of attraction that enable incarnation. The very substance of your conscious and personal self is cohered by this structure and containment, which is what makes you who you are, as a human personality.

How should you choose to resonate with something that will forever change the structure and inner containment of your being? The first reaction of physical matter to the force of change is to resist, and the force of inertia is strong. This is the basic interaction of soul with dense physical matter. That is why it takes life after life of incarnation, learning lessons, and achieving enough consciousness so that the opportunity of choice is not overruled by the very inertia of physical existence, but instead can be informed by the consciousness that can drive acceptance of and cooperation with the light of soul or circumstance. As we know from history, very few have been capable of this choice, and most have adhered to the familiarity of inertia's force.

However, times are different now, for two reasons: Earth has evolved more consciousness; thus, the milieu in which we incarnate is more infused with that which can resonate with soul's call; and humanity has also evolved, both en masse as a collective consciousness (still a long way to go though), and in the number of individuals with a more highly-developed consciousness who hold incarnational intent into this physical world.

Thus, the period we call the Great Change is here. Change can only occur through conscious choice; although note that for human evolution and the impact that has upon Earth as a living, loving being, this can occur both individually and collectively. Meaning that not all humans need to consciously choose the path of individual change, but if there is enough combined intentional alignment of the masses, with the desire and hope for positive change (however that takes form in the mind or emotions), then that is also a choice for change in the milieu of earthly and human existence.

This is the field of influence and expression of soul: the loving infusion that is the instigator of, and creator of, evolution of consciousness. Soul is the force of love that coheres spirit and matter, because it can resonate with both. Soul is the force of love that enables creation, and evolution, and thus makes change in the world of substance and matter. Soul infused the love Jesus and Gautama had and still have for their followers and chelas – the soul love that invited and still invites conscious change.

If you have evolved enough to have some resonance with your soul, then it will shine through your heart and infuse subtly, or more greatly, the loving expressions you share in all your relationships. If you, like most of humanity, are still learning to resonate with soul to this degree, then rest assured you can still be a most loving being, for human love is most fully expressed through emotional, mental and physical alignment of your being with the forces of attraction that build our relationships in the first place. Then, in time – perhaps not such a long time in this era of great change and infusion of evolutionary opportunity – you can bring soul resonance into your relationships. Then, not only you, but those you love, can hold and resonate with that evolutionary force and creative intent that is soul love, and grow in that loving embrace, not resist in inertia's ignorance.

If you want more loving soul in your life, start in your heart, for there you can refine your consciousness to apprehend the vibration of soul, for that undeniably exists in your heart. That is the very loving, creative force that keeps your physical heart beating and infusing your existence with not only physical life, but the loving life force that is in resonance with Earth and soul, aligned with the conscious intent of evolution in manifestation through the Law of Karma.

This is soul love, and how much you experience and bring it into your day is your choice. Not how much your hopes, dreams or wishes seek – but your conscious choice, for that is how the revelation and resonance of soul is enabled in your human conscious self.

If you want soul love, choose it, in whatever smaller or greater way your heart guides.

Do not force it, for that can harm. Align with it, through your heart, your intuitive perceptions, your loving instincts, but most of all, through a wholesome personal choice. Then it shall shine in you, through you, and not only into your relationships, but into the milieu of humanity's collective consciousness, and make the understanding of, and choice for, soul's loving resonance easier for everyone else.

Thus, the Great Change can occur, and Earth's loving path can embrace all, instead of human hatred, destructiveness, and war on whatever level it might otherwise manifest. Do yours, and great positive change can and will occur in soul's loving embrace.

Our Soul's Flow to Nature & Earth

Where is the soul in nature?

There are many times, and places, where you feel the nourishing presence of nature uplift you. This is a two-way thing, because the flow of loving, uplifting intent that you feel then radiates out from you through your re-energised inner self, and that light nourishes nature.

Everything we feel, see, do, is moving energy. We absorb it, we create it, we emanate it, we expend it; but we rarely see anything other than physical exertion as being this energy movement. We certainly do not look at our presence in the world as being one of energy interaction, but we need to! For two reasons at least: we create impacts all around us, and not all are positive, and we need to become conscious of them and take responsibility for changing them; and, we need the nourishment of nature and Earth; but we do not recognise and therefore attend to this need if we do not see what we receive from nature and Earth and how it assists us.

It is all about exchange, and this is one major lesson that nature teaches us: in nature, whether through basic ecology, soil science, the cycles of life, death and decay, the balance of what grows and what is eaten; or in exploring whole ecosystems. No matter at what level we see and learn about nature, we can see that nothing exists on its own. Every component has interrelationships and interdependencies with others, and the energy exchange is obvious at a physical level.

It is also significant on the inner levels. For example, the sharing of physical-etheric vitality from trees that absorb and share that vitality from the Sun with all living entities around them (including you, if you stand near one strong in this activity, such as a eucalyptus or pine tree). Then there is exchange emotionally, because this occurs in the cycles of expression of all life. A flower is not just a vehicle for the plant's reproduction, it is an expression of joy, and it creates an exchange of joy and nourishment for those who see and feel with this awareness. A bird does not sing a complex song just to attract a partner, or to communicate about food or safety, it expresses joy and love in relationship with Earth and nature.

These are some of the obvious outflows in nature's expression of light and energy, but how much do we pay attention to our role in this cycle and exchange that sustains life, rather than just take what is given?

Humans evolve as containers of physical, emotional and mental substance, and our journey is one of learning how to infuse that container with wisdom, love and light. For much of our evolution, we are learning about who we are, with little relationship to nature. Of course, many do have a relationship with nature to find and produce food – but that is usually very one-way. Nature is seen as our resource, not our partner, and we give back little other than minerals and fertiliser so we can get more out.

In some indigenous cultures there remain meaningful relationships with nature, but not for humanity as a whole. Generally, we rely on cities and supermarkets for shelter and food, and while this in itself is not the problem, it facilitates the problem, that is, that we simply do not relate enough to nature.

In part, it is because of the domination of mind, for mind does not relate. Even if you have a wonderful exchange of ideas with another like-minded person, it is the emotional connection that nourishes the relationship. Mind can become very radiant as it evolves, and that can be a form of exchange when it is understood, and especially when consciously energised.

The development of mind has been a major focus of evolution's intent, for it is the vehicle that holds and contains the personal self. It is the component of our consciousness that can guide and direct our actions upon the physical level, eventually with conscious alignment with the soul's intent. However, it is not a vehicle of flow. It can radiate, but it is structurally, vibrationally, not built of a substance that flows. As humanity develops with a certain focus on mind, then the containment of consciousness creates separation from the reality of life upon Earth, which requires a relationship with nature.

Our emotional self, which is of a substance that flows more easily, is the part of our consciousness that can perceive and relate to nature. We relate to others for that exchange of energy and feeling; that is what our need and love in relationships is all about. Through our feelings we can perceive the gifts from nature, where we feel nourished, replenished, revitalised, uplifted, soothed – but what do we give back?

All life in our physical world arises from soul stimulus, for that is what sparks and sustains existence for all in Earth's evolutionary embrace; everything from her minerals to trees, ocean life to humans.

Some life streams, like us, are more directly on the path to consciously engage with soul, and our evolution guides us through experience and learning to activate this. Many life streams evolve in groups, and are collectively nourished by soul that way, rather than individuation being a focus. Other life streams evolve with angels as intermediaries, such as most of the plant family. Their purpose is not to become sentient radiating beings of soul consciousness, their purpose is to receive and exchange the loving flow of soul's grace with the loving flow of Earth's physical life force, and as such they work greatly with angels to manifest and magnify that flow, for the sake of Earth.

Trees are of massive importance to the health of Earth's physical body, because of the work that they do. They enable the energising of the physical substance of Earth's body, with the inflow of soul's love, such that Earth's etheric body, and thus her health, are sustained. It is not only vital to keep trees and forests for the sake of sustaining animals and the diversity of life, and because of their positive impact on the global oxygen/carbon dioxide balance in the climate, but also because they are essential to nourish Earth's body itself. All of nature performs this role to some degree, but trees especially.

Humans, however, do not give enough back to Earth, hence the turmoil and imbalance in life's journey for nations, races and cultures alike. We need to learn to exchange and flow with loving intent, if not conscious purpose, both in our relationships with each other, and in relationship with Earth.

The era of mental dominance that has arisen very recently in humanity's evolution, and which drives such disengagement from Earth and nature, is not the path forward for continued evolution. We have developed enough mental capacity, collectively; now we need to bring that mental capacity back to the reality of our life upon Earth: we are here in relationship with her, and we must give back and not just take.

All soul creation evolves through relationships. We incarnate through our soul's relationship with Earth, and evolve through that relationship life after life. Now, as we stand at the threshold of the evolutionary step to greater heart consciousness, this is the step into the full consciousness of that relationship with Earth, and with nature.

Heart creates flow, and heart consciousness can only exist in flow. Flow can only occur when there is a source, and a destination. Our source of life's intent is soul, and it flows through us to Earth; that is its destination. Not to us, but to Earth. If soul existed just to pour life force into us as human beings, where would the relationship be? To some extent, there can be flow between soul and human self, but the majority of that relationship is soul in flow to Earth.

Nature shows us how life force manifests, loves, shares joy, expresses in every diverse form there is, and flows that life force into and receives it from Earth herself. This is the soul of nature in expression.

Now we need to be part of that, and relate consciously to Earth, and nature, and take upon ourselves the responsibility of becoming radiant and flowing soul presences here in Earth's body. If that were not our purpose, and why Earth accepted us in the first place, then we would simply not have this journey of physical expression.

Soul is about relationship: make your relationship with Earth meaningful and two-way. Love her; that is a start. Give to her in healing and meditation. Love nature and all her creatures, and protect them, for that is the great living body of Earth, and the nourisher of our home on physical, etheric and emotional levels. Our role, and humanity's, is to nourish her in conscious intent, with purposeful mind, and emotional care. That way we open our hearts to that magnificent flow of life, heart to heart, that is the ultimate expression of soul.

Nature's soul expresses without fear or favour, through all her life forms, fulfilling their earthly dharma. Now we need to do the same, and be part of the living, loving planet that is Earth, not just be visitors here to take for ourselves alone.

The more you relate to Earth, the more you will open to that loving flow in nature, and in turn be more nourished. Like attracts like. Love resonates with love. Flow joins with flow.

Take your shoes off and stand upon Earth. Feel not what is touching the soles of your feet, but what is beyond. Feel your connection. Hug a tree, and feel not only its presence, but its loving, flowing life force, and love it back to share your flow in return. See the beauty of flowers not just as colour, shape, fragrance, but as the living joy of plants, and love them back with your joy.

Refine your senses and see how nature shows you how to deepen your relationship, and strengthen your own loving flow, with Earth, for that is the evolution of heart that awaits all. Earth and her living world of nature desperately need us to make this conscious and deliberate step now.

Nature's Song & Your Purpose

When the soul of nature sings, the whole Earth sings, for nature is her voice. Nature is her expression in this physical world. Not us, human beings. We are not of Earth's song, with rare exceptions, because we come to Earth as a physical incarnation of soul, and though that soul was born in Earth's Ocean of Love, it is created from the spark of spirit and bears cosmic intent. All human souls are created this way, as are those of other beings that circulate through Cosmos.

However, nature is of Earth's intent alone. Nature is her expression of life and consciousness. Earth's consciousness has been enabled and stimulated by the spark of spirit that has taken her on her journey of evolution, but because nature is not on the path of individualised consciousness, as humans are, then Earth remains as nature's soul, and her spark of life is what creates life in all of nature.

There are some creatures who have what we call a 'group soul', where there are many incarnations at the same time, and the collective experience is gathered into one soul and shared with all future incarnations. This is a soul created by Earth's intent, through differentiation in expression of the evolutionary stimulus she has in her being from her divine spark. These group souls are creations of her spirit, not cosmic spirit.

In the past, humans could evolve this way, through group soul experience, refining further and further until individuation was possible. That is when a spark of spirit of cosmic intent descended and energised the creation of an individual soul from the group soul, thus taking that soul out of the group soul of Earth's creation, into an individual soul on the path of incarnating cosmic intent through its own spark of spirit.

One thing we forget forever as human beings: we are here, incarnated upon Earth, to participate in the global and cosmic evolutionary plan. We are here to learn how to manifest that in our physical world, which is why Earth invites us to incarnate, and why our souls are born in her Ocean of Love.

We are not here to amass wealth, power or land, etc. We are not here to live a life of self-focus and greed. We are here to learn and understand, so that our true reason for being here – that which is held in our souls – can resonate through us, in concert with the harmony of Earth's song, her song that sounds through nature.

It is a tricky medium in which to hold the resonance of soul, here on Earth as a human being, for two reasons: soul is a vehicle of consciousness, so we have to become conscious enough in our human self to resonate with soul; and we have to understand the call of the Earth to understand her journey, and thus our purpose for being here.

The journey of becoming conscious takes place under the Law of Karma and the guidance of soul. This proceeds reasonably well, as far as the masses of humanity are concerned. Recognise that for human soul-consciousness to resonate through its human vehicle, the human self does not have to become an illumined, wise being; but simply to have learned the lessons on its path, and become purified enough in its manifestation for the soul note to resonate. What that soul note is, and whether you need lives over tens of thousands of millennia to learn to sound a complex harmony in your human self, or a shorter journey to learn a single note, is to do with your relationship with Earth.

This is the bit most do not understand: you are not here to become glorious in the resonance of your own soul, you are here to be part of the great and glorious symphony of sound of Mother Earth herself, as an incarnated vibration of Cosmic Heart, which is her path and choice.

Your search for purpose is good, your search for soul is good, but it must relate to Earth for you to continue here! Here is where the sound of nature is revelatory. Nature sounds Earth's call, her note, her need, her love. If you learn to listen to nature with attunement to the loving light and embrace that is her gift to us, you shall hear Earth. When you hear Earth, you have a whole new vibratory resonance to hold in your being, and thus refine and align your own note to resonate with her. Then you can truly become the glorious light of your soul, and live in the resonant sound of your note in harmony with Earth. That is true purpose.

So often we only look up, and so many religions teach us this: the heavenly worlds of the illumined and the divine are our goal, and they are far above us. True, sort of, if you only consider your path to be one of becoming soul or higher light – whatever way you conceive this – but not true when it comes to realising your true purpose here upon Earth. As stated, that is not to become soul, it is to become your soul in resonant harmony with Earth.

Is it not just taken care of by your soul? Is it not one and the same, because surely your soul is in harmony with Earth, so if you become soul, you are automatically in that harmony? The reality here, is that as a human being you are never just soul. Only on rare occasions will a direct soul incarnation happen in the physical world.

We evolve as human beings so that we can resonate with our souls. However, we are still human, with all the nuances and refinements that our human consciousness brings. That is what we need to bring into our purposeful life on Earth: all the gifts we have learned, the wisdom we have gained, the light we can shine, the love we can share, in all its complexity in our human self. That is what makes our life resonate with such beauty in Earth's sphere. If it were just Earth's purpose to hold light and love at our soul level, that would have been achieved long ago. But she has chosen to become a beacon of heart and light through her physical self, and therefore, so must we, if we are to achieve the highest expression of love that we seek.

Listen to nature. She sounds Earth's loving chorus, shows us her many variations in harmony, even if through our human eyes we see creatures and systems we do not like. Look and listen with the eyes and ears of your conscious self, and understand the whole picture. Then look to what the note is that you need to add to that harmony; then you are upon your purposeful path.

A path of soul purpose will give you some direction, but it is not enough in this era of unfolding consciousness of heart, for in your heart you resonate with Earth and soul, with your human self upon Earth, and with the loving intention of your soul infused by spirit. A remarkable and truly beautiful thing!

In your heart you can hear the note of soul and Earth, when you train and learn to refine and still your personal self. Still, but not dissolved.

Be who you are and celebrate the note of your being, and become part of the symphony of Earth, singing through soul and nature, reverberating love and the path of heart throughout our universe.

Why Loving the Earth Matters

Love is that expression of divine care from one to another, when the Law of Attraction builds the bridge for that flow. That bridge always exists between a soul and its human self, and between Earth and every soul here upon this planet – for no soul can be here without being drawn here by the Law of Attraction, and sustained here by Earth's love. That is the gravity of spirit, that draws spiritual fire closer to earthly substance, such that incarnation can occur under the cosmic intent of life's expression into all realms.

Then we have love in our personal world, enabled by concordant resonance created culturally, racially, spiritually (between teachers and students), nationally, organisationally, idealistically, and in families. We build bridges of coherence so that we can share love and the grace of relationship with others, on whatever level that relationship is expressed.

As human evolution has occurred, we have experienced the bonds of love, and then also the breakdown of love and resulting separation, as the complexity of human relationships weaves through and around us. Through this we learn more about ourselves, and seek deeper within to understand and grieve, and thus we find the deeper, more permanent presence of love within – which in turn expresses more deeply in our relationships externally. It is a continuous and renewing experience, from a soul's point of view, for so much is learnt from these experiences! Even if we all wish we did not need to experience loss and separation, unfortunately without it, and from an evolutionary point of view, we would take too long to notice our inner world, and look to build the conscious bridges to and of soul.

We understand a little of these complex interactions and relationships in our human world, and how we evolve from them. But what about our relationship with Earth or with nature? These are just as important, if not more so, than our interpersonal relationships, but in our human-focussed world and the urbanised existence of most, we immerse ourselves in our human needs and foibles, and the needs of Earth and nature are pushed away and forgotten too easily.

The curious thing is that in doing so, we leave a great gap in the flow of love in our existence – for the needs of Earth and nature for our loving connection are utterly reciprocated by our need for the same. Without that, the Law of Attraction would not build the bridge of resonance that allows love to flow.

Many are awakening to this lack. It is not as easy to realise, for it is more subtle than the intensity of human-to-human relationships in our daily awareness. Much of this is because, in general, our whole society is built on human endeavour and human-to-human relationships. We not only have our own personal drivers and karmic journeys to experience in our connections with others, but society expects and conditions us to do much more. Yet this is all to do with the bubble of human life itself, not human life on Earth.

We know we are missing something, when confronted with the fragility of human relationships. We are missing the love that sustains us day-to-day, as souls upon Earth – the love that many religions and spiritual practices put in the hands of their deities to bestow upon the good and the faithful, and withhold from the disconnected and disengaged. The love of higher beings is a wonderful thing that guides and inspires us to learn and seek further on our spiritual path, and that is very sustaining. But we are here upon Earth, not in the elevated worlds of light, so all spiritual nourishment can only go so far, especially in these days of evolving and awakening heart consciousness.

You cannot awaken heart just through spiritual and devotional practices alone. This is not only spiritually, but physically impossible – 'physically' meaning the physical world of spiritual evolution, that of body, emotional and mental substance.

Here we are talking about heart as the spiritual centre of every living being, that receives and sends out nourishment, and that lives within the physical heart of every incarnated being. This is not the heart chakra, which is another matter altogether. The chakras are points of resonance between levels of personality substance, for example, between mind and your mental body, between emotional energy and your physical response. In time they can become purified enough to also resonate with different vibrational inputs from higher realms, and be a wonderful vehicle of evolutionary stimulus and awakening. However, impurified and undeveloped they can become unfiltered doorways to lower worlds and mischievous spirits. A lot of utter rubbish is promulgated by people who fail to filter their inner perceptions, thinking anything that stimulates the chakras and inner perceptions must be of a higher consciousness. Unfortunately, it rarely is, and the true spiritual journey is clouded and muddied by the untruths spouted in this englamoured certainty of false light.

Do not confuse the heart chakra with the heart that we speak of, it does not have the function of the heart centre. The heart centre is your wellspring of spiritual life – but only because that life force flows through your heart. Heart only exists in flow. In its most physical expression, this is the life force and spiritual vitality that keeps you alive, for you are not a living being by virtue of a heart and blood alone. Your whole existence is an expression of your soul's intent aligned with Earth's intent, and your inner heart flows that intent into you to attract and sustain the physical, emotional and mental substance that creates your human self. Thus, you come into existence. But this is a physically-focussed existence, and the flow is limited to your body and inner vitality.

That is not enough now. Earth is evolving, humanity en masse is evolving (even if it looks otherwise from the behaviour of some on the world stage). We are at an open door of human and planetary evolution, and that doorway is the heart.

Why it matters so much is because we can no longer safely evolve human mind, bolstered by emotional alignment, without the conscience of heart. Emotional conscience is too easily overridden by strong minds, and great harm comes to Earth, our home, through what is now too many unconscionable choices humanity is making, allowing and following.

Heart is the fulcrum upon which soul, and planet, balance; upon which human and nature balance, because it is the point through which all life is created, energised, loved and sustained. Realisation of this in conscious choice saves our planet, and saves our spiritual existence.

We can no longer continue as incarnated souls upon Earth, if we treat her like an unlimited resource for our greed that is not of need. We cannot stay if we refuse to seek heart conscience in our own decisions and actions, and of those we allow or support in our world.

Your choice really matters, for at the end of this life, and over the next short phase evolutionarily speaking, this choice will be an evaluation used to determine who has future lives here. Many do not believe in or care about future lives, but that does not change the fact that the impacts of our choices will occur.

Earth's evolution to become a planet of heart is proceeding, and we, humanity, are part of that. Our role in this unfolding development is to bring consciousness into the deep worlds of matter, the physical, emotional and mental matter of our human existence, and of Earth's physical body.

Now Earth needs more spiritual vitality in her physical body, just like you do when you evolve to a finer vibration; so that your whole being resonates with that greater love, and not just with your mind or emotions, for that leads to disconnection and illness.

We, humanity, have a significant responsibility to enable, support, and magnetise the loving flow of spiritual vitality into the Earth. Nature does this – but we are destroying nature. So not only do we need to become more aligned and cooperative with this spiritual flow, because that is our spiritual dharma here upon Earth, but we must magnify it to make up for the amount of loving vitality needed by Earth that we destroy in our abuse and destruction of nature.

This is the call of nature, the call of Earth, the call of our hearts. If we align with this loving flow to Earth and nature, we too are nourished, and step through that doorway of conscious evolution to become beings of greater grace and light.

Heart consciousness and love happen through flow. We need to realise and consciously engage in the greater loving flow of humanity to Earth, our home, and magnify that with our intent.

Then the great circulation of spiritual heart on our planet will build in flow, and sweep the darkness of stagnant cells, whether humans within Earth's body, or cancerous cells within our own human bodies, into that flow – there to be energised, revitalised and re-infused with the love that is life.

Love nature, love Earth, and open to this great cosmic flow that is life in its fullest loving expression, flowing all the way from the intent in Cosmic Heart, through the life force of Solar heart, to Earth; there to reach all the way to her physical heart through nature and humanity in conscious cooperation, bringing that flow and vitality into the deepest depths of manifest incarnation. From there, it flows back, and the circulation that sustains and awakens all life becomes complete.

This may be a great cosmic picture easily dismissed – but you are here, here upon Earth, and you are part of this great unfoldment through the simplest of balanced and personal actions: to simply love Earth, love nature, and make your earthly choices accordingly.

This is not hard, and it will create great positive change.

No sweeping brilliance of an illumined soul teacher can achieve this, because it requires the choice of humanity. Do not abdicate your personal choices, assuming your god, prophet or teacher will return and make it all right. This infusion of heart needed by Earth and all her life (humans included), can only be achieved by heart cooperation of the many, because every small and intentful flow enables cooperative change and global infusion, and every positive choice magnifies the outcome.

It is your small every-day choices that matter, in this Age of the Heart, as to whether you stand in love upon Earth, or remain separated from the one loving flow that sustains us all, the flow of love to Earth herself.

Conscience through Heart Consciousness

What is consciousness, compared to knowledge, wisdom and intuition? All of these are rightfully spoken of as attributes of value on the human and spiritual path. But to awaken spiritually for this new age that is upon us, to help it to come about, we need to develop heart consciousness.

Consciousness in general has and is part of the teachings and goal of some spiritual pathways; but most reference or require knowledge to progress on the path, and develop the conscience founded upon that knowledge.

Conscience is basically an assessment of right and wrong, and thus needs a framework in which to operate, whether that is through knowledge, or emotional development and refinement. This framework is limited to what is known or emotionally conditioned; hence why some consider themselves to be upstanding citizens of conscience because of their adherence to religious frameworks, or societal frameworks, yet fail to demonstrate any conscience regarding the welfare of the environment, climate, or Earth herself; or in consideration of groups of people other than their own.

This is why conscience alone is not enough for us to continue to develop in loving harmony with each other and Earth; and love, as we know it, is still mostly conditioned by an accepted framework. This is unworkable when there is need, as humanity has, for peaceful respect to be created between people of diverse religions, races and nations.

Knowledge is part of building a framework for conscience, but it can also be developed in such a way that all conscience is disbanded, in the illusion that knowledge will solve all and save all, without discernment or choice. Knowledge for knowledge's sake can result in this. Scientific exploration is full of people with this approach, where just because something can be explored, dissected, tested, experimented on, it is. This is not in itself a problem, for surely this has led to many benefits for the world at large. However, too often that pursuit of knowledge is driven by money or power, and any possibility of conscience tempering what is done, to ensure it does not create more harm to people, other life or Earth, is abandoned by the lure, or narrowing constraints, of this expression of greed.

All of this expresses the complex relationships and entanglements between mind, knowledge and emotional values, and they play out every day in our personal choices, and in the choices of governments and leaders, corporations and groups all around the world, for the betterment or harm of Earth and all her life.

When it is defensible to kill others for political gain, when it is defensible to destroy Earth for corporate gain, you know we have reached a point where change is urgently needed. Humanity has behaved thus for millennia, but the impacts have for the most part been localised. Now, these last 100 years or so in particular, the impacts not only affect humanity globally, but seriously and very detrimentally affect Earth herself.

The conscience developed and held by many societies through their religious or spiritual practices has been dispersed, diluted, or denounced in the name of development. What replaces it?

The mind is an analytical tool, which can only analyse what it perceives: it can easily dismiss perceptions if they do not fit the value model that it has accepted. This is why so many continue to utterly devastate the Earth, in the name of the financial gain accepted as the model essential for life. Without Earth thriving with a balanced ecosystem and climate, we will not have life, yet that is not accepted by too many of those wielding power.

To see the pinnacle of decision-making as through the mind and knowledge alone is completely nonsensical. Not only does this assume that what is available to the mind to analyse represents all the factors involved, but it also assumes that it has not been conditioned by emotional reactions, conscious or unconscious. Just because something exists as words in your head, just because you can develop an apparently logical argument based on the knowledge you have to justify the point of those words, provides no measure of whether it is valuable or complete knowledge. This is the failing of many with significant intellectual power, who have allowed themselves to be captured by an emotional driver that filters and conditions, and thus limit what the mind can analyse and decide.

Then we come to intuition. Many say they have been jolted out of certain thoughts or emotional frameworks by a sudden flash that reveals another perspective and understanding – or it may come in dreams, meditations or prayers. Intuition can increase the depth and breadth of our perception around issues or problems, or it may simply be an instantaneous warning not to do something. We bundle them all together, as something that arises from outside our consciousness.

Our ability to perceive intuitive nudges, whatever they are for, depends upon our psychological and energetic openness to them. Many people dismiss intuitive insights because they are captured by their concrete mind, or emotional prejudice, and do not accept anything else. At the other extreme, some people are so desperate for spiritual contact that they accept anything that seems to arise from outside their consciousness, and believe it without discernment. You can develop a balanced and valuable capacity to use your intuitive abilities by using your heart to discern, and by using physical and spiritual practices to refine and purify your physical and inner self to better perceive what is offered.

Intuition is a valuable tool for awakening consciousness, for it can stretch your perceptions, just as knowledge can – yet it is not consciousness itself.

Wisdom is another sought after attribute for seekers. Differentiating wisdom from knowledge comes down to experience. If you have learned something through the teaching of another, or through the agility of your mind to accumulate and organise information to create a meaningful framework for your life, you have developed knowledge. But knowledge in and of itself is only that, until it is tested and validated in the world of experience. Wisdom arises when we have tempered our knowledge with enough experience to discern and adjust its application to the world we live in. It can be spiritually infused, creating spiritual wisdom; or it may be humanly focussed, creating human wisdom. Often these overlap.

Mind has a tendency to seek more knowledge, when what it knows proves to be insufficient to solve the problems of life's journey. However, at some point, the accumulation of knowledge simply does not offer enough depth with which to understand and solve life's challenges. Depending upon your journey and the frameworks within which you function, sooner or later you will come to the need for more depth and wisdom in your life, either easily or through challenge, but it will come.

Experience tempers run-away knowledge and enables adjustments; intuition and conscience open pathways for reflection and choice, and allow for life expression with more depth and wisdom.

What, then, is consciousness? Consciousness is what coheres all of these elements into a meaningful whole. Consciousness enables intuition to be perceived and discerned with meaning; for knowledge to be used as a tool not a goal; for wisdom to reach into the fullness of who you are.

We consider the time we are conscious in our daily life as when we are awake: when we can consciously utilise the five senses that enable our interaction with the physical world. Consciousness on the spiritual path means awakening your awareness to the senses you have in the inner worlds. Both require a certain ability to focus. As you most probably have experienced, it is possible to be physically awake without being conscious with all your senses. It is also possible to be awake but focussed on the inner worlds such that you are no longer conscious of physical experiences, something some seek through meditation.

Consciousness requires choice, whatever level it is on.

Consciousness is a synthesis of all the knowledge, wisdom, intuition and perceptions we have, such that we can make sense of all these factors, or at least have the opportunity to do so. That is the path.

Why heart consciousness is of such importance is because it is so vastly different from the path of consciousness evolved on the human journey so far, where for most the focus has been upon developing consciousness on the level of mind and emotions. Now, however, that is not enough. It is difficult for those with wisdom and insight to dissuade people in power, whether corporate or government, from pathways of destruction and harm. Unconscionable actions proceed because the mind is distorted by knowledge based on past frameworks, or limited by emotional desires not in harmony with life on Earth today – and they are untempered by the conscience required to meet our current earthly and human needs. For the most part, humanity is not living in sustainable harmony with Earth, let alone fulfilling our purpose here, and this requires a shift.

The consciousness humanity primarily lives within is a bubble of mind, emotion and physical existence. When mind and knowledge are seen as the pinnacle of human development, and there is no perspective higher than this, we cannot develop the global conscience we need now. The religious and spiritual traditions in our world mostly foster individual thought and emotion within their frameworks of belief, and while some awaken and develop a societal conscience, many do not seek to lift people into a higher perspective that would stop hatred and destruction of others and of Earth.

However, through heart consciousness, so much will change, because heart is the point in your being where your soul resonates. As you awaken heart consciousness, you cannot but awaken perceptions of higher meaning, beyond the usually well-intentioned but nevertheless constructed frameworks of meaning built in the human world of existing religions, spiritual pathways and thinking.

Through the awakening heart, we learn to wake up in the world touched by soul, where true meaning and purpose of life arises. We learn to expand the senses we work with to those infused with soul, not just what we know or intuit in our physical world of thought, emotion and body. Through awakening our perceptions to these finer vibrations of soul, we will awaken our loving relationship with Earth. Some have this already, but not enough. The machinery of the false economy built around money alone, and of power built of control over land, possessions and people, is not yet disrupted enough for those who should know better to choose more wisely.

Soul presence is inevitable, it is just a matter of how long, and how destructive, is the path humanity takes to get there. It is not that everyone will suddenly become soul conscious – that is not the next step. Rather, it is to awaken to whatever degree of soul infusion is yours to receive, and live in resonance with that in your life.

Soul is of the Ocean of Love of Earth's being, and it knows the plan of Earth and your part in it. Heart is the vehicle of resonance in your being where you can perceive that vibration of soul. This is where conscience will develop that includes Earth in the evaluation; where knowledge will be stimulated to expand beyond that which is constructed in thought alone; where wisdom and experience will align more and more of your being with what is right, just and loving for Earth and all life. And where intuition will bring the gifts of the heart, where the focus is not on self-development of love and light, but on global development of love and light.

Utopian? No, because Earth's choice has been made, and humanity's path has been formed; the choice and variation come down to how much every one of us chooses and strives for contact with that infusion of heart that will awaken our consciousness to all there is in the world of love to be. Then we become part of that Ocean of Love here upon Earth, and make the transition of consciousness easier for everyone else.

Love, Care & Peace

One of the greatest stimuli of conscious development is when you do not get what you feel is yours, or you lose something you want or need. It does not matter if it is of material origin, or personal opportunity; and it is not to say that what is lost, or not given, is wrongly grieved.

We cannot become conscious of anything if we have no interest in what lies outside the sphere in which we exist. Unless we are driven to seek outside our sphere, we remain unconscious. That drive, in the first instance, comes from physical need for food, shelter, warmth, shade, etc. From a physical point of view, this builds a connection of awareness between us and Earth.

To develop beyond this needs soul stimulus, and that comes from the inbuilt presence of emotional need for connection and the response from relationship. Why it needs soul stimulus is because anything beyond physical need is not drawn into expression through the involuntary process that enables us to incarnate. That process draws our soul spark down into matter, and clothes it in body, emotions and mind, but it is only the body's needs that are triggered, for that is for survival, where all the other elements of our earthly presence are in the realm of evolution.

Our body is our anchor here on Earth. All our inner elements are what stimulate our yearning and seeking for the home of souls, in Earth's Ocean of Love. Thus, they are not activated until the soul stimulus resonates through heart, to awaken those initial seed atoms around which our emotional and mental bodies are built, and begin that process of evolution where we seek that which we remember – or at least that which we know exists outside our current conscious sphere of physical existence. We seek it because it is born of love, soul's love, which is ever there to sustain us on our evolutionary journey.

This is simplistic but essential to know, because unless we understand more about the mechanisms of evolution – meaning the full expression of evolution, which is our journey to become conscious vehicles of our souls, not the Darwinian evolution of physical forms – then we take so much longer to become conscious participants in our evolutionary journey. On Earth, now, we do not have time to dilly-dally, because she has made her choice and our conscious cooperation is needed. Hence the speeding up of those stimuli that magnify the pull of evolution – and conflict, confusion, oppression and inequity on every level from food to intellectual opportunity are stressed.

Why is evolution not a product of love and care? Of light and peace? Because, unfortunately, if we already lived in a world where our needs were met, we would not seek, and our journey and responsibility is to seek and become conscious, such that our individual and collective life upon Earth is an expression of light, love, care and peace, not just an immersion in it.

Our journey requires consciousness, because we are to be contributors to the creation and sustenance of the world of soul in the physical realms of mind, body and emotions on Earth – something many do not yet apprehend in a spiritual sense. We seek it, and hope for it, and often fight for it in our physical world, yet still there are so many injustices in the realm of physical equity. Not only equity where all humans have equitable access to what meets their physical needs, but also that we consider and weigh our needs in relation to Earth. Most of the human activity on Earth today has little consideration for her need for balanced give and take. Although many have lifted their consciousness to understand this, and action to balance this does proceed rapidly, it is still not rapidly enough.

Contrary to what many think, it is through our emotional development that we can evolve most rapidly in this current and emerging era. Hence why it is also the medium through which the most distress arises, on a global scale. This is not to downgrade the very real distress of physical needs unmet, but the way to change this is through our emotional purification and response.

Emotions are our vehicle for caring, and without care, it does not matter how much we know intellectually. Care can arise in response to many situations, for it is a basic human capacity. It is an expression of love, resonating with the seed of soul love in our emotional selves. This soul stimulus awakens our need to seek outside ourselves for emotional connection. It may first be expressed as wants, where we want to draw to us the nourishment that connection brings, but it is quickly (evolutionarily speaking) followed by care – which is the outflow of love, and this is where we realise the fullness of love, and feel the grace of soul resonate within us.

All love is a flow from one heart to another, whether Cosmic Heart to our Earth's heart, our Earth's heart to our hearts, or our hearts to each other. However, it can never be an expression of love until it circulates, because until then it is not a flow, and the living grace of love cannot be bestowed. It is like expecting a person to live without blood flow: the body can survive a short while on the residual nourishment in the cells, but that is quickly depleted. It is the same with love. Love is a living sustenance for life, and it must flow.

We must learn to consciously choose to be part of that flow, and we do that through our emotional responses to needs and grievances, hopes and oppressive experiences, opportunities and defeats. There are many emotions that we experience, but the key is to differentiate them into inflows and outflows; into positive loving expressions, and negative reactive ones. We circulate all of these to a greater or lesser degree in our day.

It is not to suggest we immerse in our emotional journeys without focus on mind, but mind is a vehicle of learning to facilitate conscious awakening, it is not a vehicle of flow or of love. An illuminated mind can infuse a loving emotional embrace with radiance, but without the emotional element it cannot be a vehicle of love in our human world.

Our path is to become a vehicle of loving flow. When enough of us choose this path, and apply our conscious effort to evolving rapidly on this journey, we can change this world.

People and the races, nations and religions that are the aggregates of people's needs and wants, are seeking in response to soul stimulus, because that is the evolutionary moment we are in. Humanity, as a whole, has structured much of its response to these needs through a financial medium; but although money can facilitate care and the supply to meet needs, and must be supported, on a global scale we need more love to foster a change of consciousness such that care and equity can be empowered, and bring evolutionary change.

Many people and organisations work with great love and care, but globally it needs to be more – to sustain those on the front line, and to infuse those still fighting for what they want through war, aggression, oppression and greed. This is the great imbalance in physical expression, for to take without giving on a national, racial or other aggregate scale is not positive.

There are too many minds in charge of these aggregations of human expressions and needs, who do not care about Earth and humanity as a whole, and most frequently do not care for their people either, other than as supports for their own self-aggrandisement or deluded nationalistic isolationism.

Justice must and will prevail, but only when enough people enact their own choices in daily life, to be part of a solution to world challenges based on care for humanity and Earth, and not just care for self and nation.

The tide of change will arise from the emotional response of humanity, when that response is sufficiently infused with love and care. But, as with any ocean, it is the wave that offers the power for change, and it does not need the whole ocean to change.

Have hope, and join the wave of change through your own concerted effort to care, whether in five minutes of daily prayer or meditation dedicated to world peace, or in the fullness of your life given in service to this cause, or any expression in between. This is how you magnify the loving flow through, and thus resonance of, your own emotional self; and become a vibration that magnifies the wave of change so desperately needed in our world today.

A wave is created by every small water molecule receiving, and vibrating with the infusion of energy around it, and giving that energy on to the next. Do the same with the loving grace that is here in our world, and let us not let the darkness of stagnant and un-flowing emotions expand their non-living presence further in our world. Instead, we can be part of the conscious wave that gives nourishment and equity, through love, not greed.

Unfortunately, it is not an instant switch, but it can be a rapid change; that is our choice to enact.

The Full Moon's Grace

On the special days of the year when the moon is full, not only is the physical ocean of Earth moved, but her Ocean of Love is also drawn into greater movement, her inner ocean of flowing matter in which our souls dwell. Especially at the moments of the great full moons: those that have been energised in Earth's aura by the great teachers embodying her

Ocean of Love here in the physical world; in particular Jesus Maitreya, bringing the Christ light of love, and Gautama Buddha, bringing the Buddha light of illumination.

It is not that we have not had other great teachers and way-showers upon this Earth, but their role has been of a human spiritual focus, whereas Jesus and Gautama incarnated for both humanity's *and* Earth's spiritual journey. They not only brought insight, wisdom and healing to the human consciousness, but they incarnated an element of Christly or Buddhic love and light into Earth's physical body. They gave Earth a profound healing that was not just a rectification of imbalances and a soothing of ills, but an inflow of spiritual life force to stimulate the next global phase of evolutionary growth.

All true healing is a spiritual awakening, even if you are not conscious of it at the time. It is the same for Earth. On her journey of evolution, she has ills and travails, and healing is needed. In time, humanity can become a balanced force for love and light that will enable Earth to be in good health, and that is the harmonic goal of our lives here on this beautiful planet.

The moon draws the substance that flows towards it as it circulates around our planet, and is part of what enables Earth to be a place where life force can incarnate and express in physical, living form. No life exists without movement of nourishment. Without our moon, there would be no tides and very little effect from currents in our oceans, and Earth's life force would be severely impacted, for it is the movement of water on all levels that gives life – whether ocean currents and tides, the rain and rivers, ice and snow, or our own blood and lymph, or our spiritual nourishment through the light that flows.

In our human consciousness, it is our emotional self that is of a substance that can flow. When people speak of being in the flow, most usually it is an astral emotional experience: this substance of our beings moves in harmony, enabling all of our expression to be aligned with the flow, and thus it is much more energised. The next level of our human life stream that can move in a flow is the substance of our souls, for souls are born of and live in the Earth's Ocean of Love – her emotional body.

Our souls not only seek to awaken and develop wisdom such that they can nourish us as human beings, but they also have a role within Earth's livingness. They are part of Earth's ocean of feeling (the Ocean of Love), and as such they are moved and aligned by greater flows, at least that is the hope.

All souls, being of that Ocean of Love, are of a substance that flows. However, it is the development of the soul that enables it to be either a particle that needs to be carried by the sweep of the current around it, or it has developed sufficiently to have resonance with the cause of the flow, and thus its own resonance aids the flow. It becomes a particle in which the resonance sets up a harmonic wave, and thus harmonic movement. A younger, less-developed soul does not yet have the refinement of learning and wisdom in its substance, and so it cannot resonate and develop its own harmonic movement, and thus it needs to be carried by the effort of those around it.

The movement of Earth's Ocean of Love is essential for the nourishment and stimulation of her being, and thus our beings. The stimulus and movement of this ocean at full moon is stimulating to our souls, and spiritually sensitive people will feel this.

The great teachers Gautama Buddha and Jesus Maitreya incarnated to heal Earth, and also to awaken a pathway in her ethers that could continue to hold their resonance for millennia to come, so that others could follow; whether as teachers, to give more out to humanity; or as seekers who could be reminded of this experience of the light and re-awaken their yearning for soul, life after life.

The emphasis on these two great teachers is taking absolutely nothing from the validity of the many other spiritual teachers and traditions that exist. The factual difference is that the Christ impulse, and the Buddha impulse, gave us two major expressions of light for Earth's sake, and that is our focus here: the development of human consciousness in the context of the evolutionary path of Earth.

All spiritual and religious teachers and pathways that encourage, teach and enable human kindness, care and love on the path to better ourselves and our world, are of utmost beauty. But when it comes to

Earth's path, there are only these two great souls that have incarnated in our current era of evolution. Jesus Maitreya incarnated as the soul of love: love as a flow of consciousness, the flow from soul to soul, human to human, and to Earth and all in between. Gautama Buddha incarnated a great radiance of light, creating ripples of resonance throughout the substance of human and earthly life, as well as in the world of souls.

Thus, two stimuli were created: one, the direct flow of substance; and two, the ripples of resonance creating waves through the substance. These are the two major methods of stimulus in our world, and all spiritual teachings express one or both, otherwise they would not reach the human consciousness.

All awakening needs movement, or else we stay in the familiar, comfortable and static bubble of self. At full moon we have a greater opportunity to experience this stimulus: the Ocean of Love of Earth's emotional self is drawn to the gravitational pull of the moon, just as our ocean tides are, and so are our emotional bodies. This stimulus can help awaken us, to see things differently, to seek new insight, to open to new understanding. It can also be challenging, because if the substance of our being seeks to move and flow, but part of our being is locked into fixed patterns, or has become rigid to wall-in unresolved experiences, then movement is restricted, and we feel that. But that is what evolution of consciousness is all about: becoming aware of that which no longer serves the being we are becoming, and that needs healing, transformation and clearing. Then we can put our consciousness to the needed change, and step forward on our journey.

Thus the time of full moon is stimulating. The full moons energised around the incarnated lives of Buddha and Christ are not just energising because of the stimulus of flow and movement in our consciousness and soul selves, but they also hold extra stimulus through the resonant pathways and ethers left behind by these great souls. When their consciousness moves, they set up waves of flow and resonance through all the souls they have touched over the ages through their healing and teaching. They send ripples of awakening and loving light into humanity and Earth, through all the places, people and institutions where they have resonated in the conscious journeys of the millions they have touched over the last millennia. Thus, the full moons that have been energised by their presence remain energised. They are powerful points of stimulus in our earthly lives, and powerful times of healing for the Earth.

For example, the full moon energised by Buddha's life, known as the Wesak Festival, is not only a festival of the Buddha and the path he taught, but a call for compassionate action by all towards each other and the Earth. It is a call to seek and act from illumined insight, which itself is more accessible in the light at this time. All the illumined and conscious souls gather to help magnify this great moment, where the Buddha light is energised on a global scale for this purpose at this full moon – to help the ripples and currents of living, loving light illuminate life on Earth, and awaken our souls and personal selves to become more resonant with that light that nourishes and heals all life.

For those touched by Buddha's light (in this life or in past lives), it can be easier to experience this grace; but most have had a touch of it at some time on their path, and all can seek to resonate with the purpose with which this festival is energised: the awakening of consciousness to the path of choice and harmlessness, and to demand a planet of peace. Note that harmlessness is not passivity in the face of dark and destructive deeds.

The other full moons most energised by the great souls are Easter, and the full moon following Wesak known as Asala. Asala is the least known because it holds the promise of a future incarnation of the next great soul to stand upon Earth in 500 years, Maitreya; and because it is of significance in the blood flow of the Cosmic Christ through Earth as a living being of Cosmic Love and heart. It taps into a cosmic presence that is not so known in earthly journeys at this time, but it will become more so, and certainly as more open their awareness to this reality, it will strengthen its presence and blessings equally in our lives and within Earth.

The Easter full moon is well known as a time around which many Christian festivals are based, but it is not so well known as the festival of light and love that it is. As with Wesak, the great souls gather and lend their loving flow to support Christ, who magnifies that stimulus and flow as an awakening to souls in the Ocean of Love, as an awakening to hearts in the human family, and as a nourishing gift to all of the Earth – for Christ brings love into living flow to sustain Earth, like our blood sustains each of us.

Every touch of a great soul contains love, but the expression and purpose are different so as to draw different souls to them, and to develop different experiences and (thus) wisdom in souls and humans, and thus awaken consciousness.

Buddha and Christ work together – as they always have and always will upon Earth – because they represent the two elements needed for life, flow and light. Without flow we would not live, without light we would not live: flow of blood, of love, of relationship, of hope; light of the Sun, of our souls, of our teachers, of our Earth.

Both build and enable life and growth, so at these valuable times of full moon, when the ethers are energised, when the hearts of the great souls are focussed together for these events, open your mind and heart.

Add your heartfelt hope for Earth's healing to be magnified, and be part of the living light that enables the Great Change to awaken conscience and consciousness, so we can create the planet of peace we seek.

The Soul's Journey

In the world of souls, you exist in the Ocean of Love – the flowing milieu of loving intent that clothes every planet and star that has chosen conscious life as their path of evolution. Therefore, as a soul you can travel to any of these locations – according to cosmic karma, of course.

The karma we know here on Earth is the balancing of the Laws of Life as they express within her ring-pass-not, the bounds within which her consciousness develops. To journey outside that requires engagement with the loving entity that holds our universe, so that inappropriate journeys (that is, that are not concordant with the intention of spirit on all levels) are not undertaken. However, this is how many souls have journeyed to Earth, rather than coming into existence here on Earth herself.

Soul

A soul is born when an intentional spark of spirit enters into the Ocean of Love upon the planet or star to where that stream of consciousness has been called, and that spark draws soul matter around it according to the resonance held within that spark. Then what? This is but the start of the soul journey.

Soul is the primary vehicle of consciousness in our universe, because it bridges the world of intention, spirit, with the world of action, physical expression. By physical we mean those levels of vibration that hold coherence around planets and stars, and around humans and all life, where consciousness is to fulfil spirit's intent in matter. These vibrational levels, from a human point of view, include what may seem non-physical: those vibratory realms within which thoughts and feelings circulate and express. From a planetary point of view, these are part of her physical existence, and the Ocean of Love is her emotional body.

To bring spirit's intent into the body of any planet or star requires the birth of a soul in the loving embrace of that planet or star, as far as the conscious journeys we are exploring go. Spirit cannot enter matter directly, because its vibration is so fine that even in the most refined planetary consciousness, it will mostly simply pass straight through. You can think of the journey of consciousness as the building of a great vibratory net, refined and purified, so that these very fine vibrations of the higher realms may be caught and experienced, and then acted upon.

Everything in the universe is created with intent – that is life. Spirit does not extend a spark into matter without a reason. Usually, the impulse is in response to the Great Cosmic Plan to evolve certain expressions of life through a planet or star, and then the conscious call from that planet or star requesting that enlivening intention of spirit to come. Whether the resulting birth of the soul then goes on to incarnate that intentional expression deep into the matter of that planet or star is, again, a choice of the planet or star, in alignment with cosmic intent.

Whatever journey the soul takes, training and development are needed so that the soul can hold and express the fullness of its spirit's intent. Soul training occurs in two ways: either directly as a soul, or by sending out a further expression of spirit's life force into the physical planetary or star world, for example, the mental, emotional and physical worlds we perceive as humans on Earth.

This expression of soul is for all life: angels, humans, and all creatures. Even the smallest living entity has soul embrace, stepped down into a small physical life by being distributed through millions of creatures for the tiniest expression, then increasingly less and less in number as the journey proceeds upon the path of evolution.

On the soul level, training occurs through the embrace and direct infusion of consciousness from other illumined souls. This is only able to develop certain characteristics of soul, so that it can more consciously apprehend, and work with, the intent of spirit that created it, and express that more fully in the world of souls in which it is living. This is how the milieu of the Ocean of Love develops radiance and qualities that then help infuse the lower worlds.

To truly express those qualities in the lower worlds, the soul has to incarnate, that is, clothe itself in that denser matter – whether mental, astral, physical, or all three levels of vibration in the physical world. This incarnation requires different training; for just as on Earth in a human body, you can *know* everything about how to do something, but until you actually *do* it, you are not able to fully express that knowing, and say truthfully that you do know how. Soul training alone will not enable you to express the loving intent of your spirit's spark in this world without incarnating here.

Soul always incarnates with an intention, perhaps many; for all life is brought into beingness with that creative force of intention. The learning journey is then to find how to express that intent in this new medium.

For a human being, that is a long journey, taking many lives. In the initial stages, the human self has to learn how to engage with and act within the worlds of thought, feeling and physical matter, all the while trying also to understand the call and resonance of the drive and intent from the soul held within. This learning is returned to the evolving soul after each life, so that it can be held and built upon in future lives.

Gradually, the soul learns the ways of expressing in the physical world, and in each life the complex interaction of soul intention, and personal and global karma create a rich tapestry of experience through which to learn and express.

It is not just an open field of experience. All human evolution is guided by the enfolding embrace of Earth's intent and need, because humans have a particular role to fulfil in the conscious expression of cosmic intent and love's grace in her physical body.

Through her conscious intent, she has called and held to her the vibrational grace aligned with her choice to embody heart physically in our universe. She has called souls already evolved in the ways of physical expression in the mental and astral worlds from other planets and stars, and thus all humans who incarnate here are held within the embrace of one or more of those greater souls, to get a head start, if you like, on the journey.

These greater souls are embodiments of both their spirit's intent, and Earth's intent, for they have come here with the knowing and ability to engage in this partnership. The resonance of their combined intent manifests as a path on which young souls can journey, to learn both as a soul and as a human.

Because these great souls are here in concert with Earth's evolutionary journey, they all work together to fulfil the fullness of Earth's intent. They are the Greater Hearts who hold and guide into conscious expression that intention of Earth, to become a planet of heart. They have incarnated, and guided from the inner worlds, every major expression of loving light in our history: those times when great teachers have emerged and inspired, and continue to inspire, humanity. They have built and demonstrated pathways of knowing in our world; of consciousness in the inner worlds; and of loving partnership with each other, and with Earth.

Every human has incarnated in the auric nourishment of one of these Greater Hearts, whether in the far reaches of their presence, in the feint vibrations on the beginning of their journey, or more deeply engaged as both their soul and human self, learning to align with and express this loving intention more consciously.

Many humans move from one stream to another, learning the vibratory intention of more than one Greater Heart. It is all in accordance with their own soul's intent, aligned with the global milieu and need. We *only* incarnate to be, ultimately, of service to Earth's intention to be that planetary expression of heart in physical embodiment.

As a human, ultimately you will become the expression of your soul, the Greater Heart in whose stream you incarnate, and the Earth's intention that called you into existence in this world in the first place.

What a stupendous journey!

This is all to say that there is enormous meaning and intent within and around you, no matter where you are upon Earth, no matter where you are upon your path; and every life adds loving alignment into your being so that you can express this more and more.

Within this life, do those things that make your soul sing within you. You will know what they are, because they will feel right in your heart. You can check, to ensure they are of truthful and peaceful intent; you can evaluate and learn on your way, to witness your journey, and refine your actions and choices. You can seek and explore within your own consciousness, or in the embrace of a teacher you trust. There are so many options available to you! Life itself is a great teacher.

With every choice and action aligned with this intention, you can awaken more of your being to the resonance of your soul, and thus to the Greater Heart in whose embrace you learn, and ultimately to the call of the Earth that brought you here.

Then you become an active soul, helping the embodiment of heart in this beautiful world.

Find your heart's resonance, and shine in whatever small or great ways that are yours to express.

The Human Journey

Your Heart & Soul Consciousness

What is heart?

It is the deep home within you of your spark of spirit, clothed in soul, wherein lies all your vitality for life, all your purposeful intention, all your karma for your physical gifts and challenges.

Heart is pivotal in spiritual exploration because of this. You cannot become a soul-conscious being, without knowing your heart. To clarify: to be soul conscious means you have refined some part of your consciousness sufficiently to perceive the extremely fine vibrations of your soul; it does not mean you are a fully conscious soul in incarnation. Everything proceeds in stages.

Without opening the door to soul consciousness, you can never truly embody or embrace your spiritual destiny. In the most refined mind, you are still limited to how the mind perceives. Mind can never fully understand soul, for they are totally different media of existence. Soul consciousness is a medium like liquid: it flows, gently to soothe, or with strength, seeking to break up and dissolve barriers, depending on your journey and personal karma, which defines how your soul can act here in this world of personal expression on Earth. Karma gives the laws that enable action and reaction on this level, and that is defined by your soul, and by the Earth and humanity at large via the Board of Karma which weighs the opportunities and responsibilities of individual journeys with the journey of Earth and soul.

Always, it is a flow, which is why it is through your heart that you can most clearly resonate with your soul; for your heart is a vehicle of flow, and when we personally reflect on heart, we learn to work with the nuances and subtleties of the consciousness of flow.

Mind, however, is built of an element like air. It can easily move in any direction; it can blow gently or with strength; but you cannot rely on it to engage and align with one intent. Just like the flow of air on our planet: a gust of wind may meet a forest, a building, mountains or oceans, the presence of heat or cold – and everything it meets can redirect that air flow in many directions, or disperse and weaken it, or narrow and strengthen it. Mind is the explorer, yet it is also uncontained by soul's intent until you yield mind to soul.

In the lower mind – the mind we develop on the earlier part of our journey as a human being – we tend to build structures to organise and hold the vibration of different elements we have learned. This is an act of personal will, not an inherent property of mind itself. Most of these structures are rooted in the astral, emotional self, which does not like the free-flowing winds of thought disturbing its calm.

Our emotional self is also built of a substance that has liquid-like properties that can flow. Ultimately, we are emotional beings, for that is the most readily perceived substance of consciousness within our physical existence. Because they are able to flow, emotions can carry intent; or if restricted, their flow can be dammed into stagnant pools. Imagine you are standing in a flat and still lake or ocean, there is not much that impacts you. But, should there be currents, or waves, you are affected and moved. Our emotional bodies are the same in our personal consciousness.

Our physical (including etheric) body is focussed on presence, anchoring in physical place or activity. It does not make choices in and of itself, except via the complicated interaction between the body and old karma held in family or personal elemental coherences, which can structure physical reactions through health and wellbeing. Other than that, it is energised to act based on our personal motivations, and that comes down to the astral flows.

All motivation comes from flow, because our physical bodies here upon Earth have great inertia, just as all bodies of matter do, and it takes a moving force to shift that inertia. That is your emotional self, the substance of flow most near your personal consciousness. Even the strongest mind cannot force the physical into continued motivation if the emotional self is not involved. Mind is of the element like air, and although it can become concentrated and strengthened enough to apply force to the physical, it cannot sustain that without will. Will is an act of effort, and it costs every time you use it.

Everyone knows that if you continually force yourself to do something with mind, and thus will, but emotionally you are not in alignment with that effort, you will run out of will after a while. Reiterating this key point: to energise and guide your human existence, you must have flow in your being.

As it takes many ages to develop the ability to perceive and align with the flow of soul, then our emotional self is essential to how we can operate in this world, providing our motivations to either do things, or restrain from doing things, in accordance with what we perceive through our conscience.

To come back to why the mental body can never really be in charge: it is because to guide the physical alone, it needs to apply will. To guide the physical in alignment with the emotional self, will is no longer required, at least to the same extent. Thus, much of our so-called thinking is organised according to our emotional constructs: those areas where we easily flow and create action will invite thoughts and mental stimulus; those areas where we hold old, solidified patterns that do not flow will equally create rigidity in thought, or, as is often seen, no thought at all, and the human response is only triggered by these emotional constructs.

Our minds and emotions are in complex interaction throughout our lives, and we can change our emotional patterning by repeated mental effort; and likewise change mental perceptions by refining the emotional container through which our thoughts are conditioned and received into our conscious self. It is important overall to understand that to move and exist in this physical world, we are ultimately guided by the substance in our consciousness that flows. For most of our journey, that is our emotional self, but now, there is far greater access to that other flow, our soul self, and that occurs through our hearts.

It takes time to be able to perceive the fineness of vibration of soul, but in fact it is always there as the life force that sustains us – for we do not exist based on the food we eat and the activity we undertake in this physical world alone. You can eat well, exercise, be kind – all the things that we consider build a long life – yet when your soul calls you home, you will go. You need that inflow of loving light from your soul to stay alive, and that is given in accordance with your pre-agreed lessons and path to take in this life. However, this is not the same as a flow of consciousness: it is an expression of your soul's intent, which is a mix of will and love that holds you in life until you have walked your path and journeyed through your lessons.

Soul consciousness is totally other. Consciousness comes when the aggregate of learning and experience can be cohered together into a wholeness of expression. That is why soul consciousness is what you need to open to, to understand what can seem to be disparate experiences in life, and to truly find the purpose that aligns you to the path that threads through them with meaning.

To awaken soul consciousness needs your soul to have learned enough to have developed consciousness, in so far as your life is concerned; and for your personal consciousness to have refined enough to be able to perceive that very fine vibration of soul. That is where heart comes in. Heart is the anchor point for soul in our beings; the infusion of soul intent that keeps us alive enters our body here. Even without having developed much soul consciousness, inside our heart we do know this vibration.

The journey is to awaken what is inherently familiar, into a perception that can align us in consciousness with that soul intention that holds the promise and nourishment for our life, and then to enable the flow of soul consciousness to take over, or at least shape and guide, the emotional patterns we have developed.

This way we journey into a life of soul expression, where the wisdom of every lesson we have learned upon Earth can be the guide to our choices, rather than the emotional and mental patterning we have from this life alone.

Why does the soul not infuse our emotional and mental selves with this wisdom already? Well, for some it does, to varying degrees. But, for most, it is because to align with soul you need to have the consciousness in your personal self to do so, and that takes conscious development. Soul is equipped with the high-level vision and wisdom gained over your many lives, and its training in the inner schools of wisdom and love. Soul is not trained in the day-to-day functioning and expression of human life.

Your journey is to develop your consciousness so that you can align with soul, perceive the flow of soul, and be purified sufficiently in your personal self to be able to determine pathways of choice and action that enable that flow of soul to express and nourish what you do.

Start in your heart, because your heart already knows soul as that life force and flow that holds your life here. The path is to keep going to your heart until, through practice, you can differentiate the deep, fine resonance of your soul, from the familiar notes of your body, mind and feelings.

Then, gradually, take more of your consciousness there – take questions, reflections, insights, and weigh them up in this resonance of soul. Do they hold up in this space and place of heart and soul, or do they fall with too much weight? That shows whether they are built of too much of mind and emotions, without the refining resonance of soul.

The more you do this, the more you can align the wisdom and intent of your soul, with the day-to-day decisions and actions you make, to guide your life to be one of your heart's loving expressions, here upon Earth.

The Human Journey

As a soul, you are born from a spark of cosmic intention that is your spirit, clothing itself in Earth's Ocean of Love. As such, your soul has that cosmic intent within, and also the nuances afforded by the already-qualified substance of Earth's being – qualified both by her evolutionary journey and by the results of her choices. The co-resonance of your spirit's intent with Earth's need is what enables this alignment and creation of soul as a melding of these two vibrational media.

As a human, you are born of the karmic opportunity for your soul to express down into the deeper layers of existence. Soul's intent guides the inherent resonance within each seed expression on the levels of mind, emotion and body, so that the substance of Earth's body may be drawn into the form we call human. It is the same process for all creatures, with some variations where angels hold the resonance of the seed atoms, for conscious coherence.

In many ways, these creative processes to form soul, and to form the human self, are similar. However, there is one major and very significant difference: soul is always in resonance with its spark of spirit within, whereas the human self walks the path of conscious development, and to that end is given many choices in order to learn. Those choices can cloud over the intention of soul held deep within. In fact, in the many early millennia of the human journey, the soul offers very little guidance, usually because it is new to this journey and does not yet have the wisdom to impart; and because the human self simply has to go through many stages of learning and development to be even interested in, let alone capable of, seeking soul guidance.

The purpose of this differentiation is consciousness. Consciousness is, in one way of exploring it, a coherence that is built of many points of knowing, wisdom, experience and intention which enable a bigger picture view: where purpose is understood, at least in part; where meaning is perceived; where the patterns of cause and effect are understood; and thus, where choices are enriched by all these nuances, such that soul and thus spirit's intent can guide the human expression.

Because soul cannot guide the worlds of thought, emotion and the physical self directly, as its resonance is too fine and cannot be perceived by raw matter on these levels alone, the human journey is undertaken. This is how the human self becomes more than an aggregation of the matter on the physical, emotional and mental levels alone. Consciousness joins the dots, if you like, between experiences, expressions, intentions and results, and this creates an interlinked web of resonance – a bit like the webbed network of neurons in the brain. This web holds a resonance different to that of each of is contributing parts, for each part resonates on its own level, but creates something else when linked together. It is like the difference in sound created by plucking one string after another on a guitar, and then playing all strings together in a chord. The sound, the effect, the resonance are totally different!

It is on the journey of developing human consciousness that you sound the note of each level of your being (emotional, mental, physical), then you learn the sounds of cohered experiences that involve multiple levels of your being. Then you learn to purposefully and consciously sound the harmony that comes when your experiences are infused with knowing and wisdom, and thus meaning.

Here is where your soul can become more resonant within you! In the creation of the sound of a harmonious chord, the resonance goes beyond simply the sum of the individual notes. It is in this greater richness and fullness of sound that the soul may also be able to contribute harmonic tones, and enrich the sound further. I say 'may', because on this long journey of awakening consciousness, there are layers of that consciousness where soul may not resonate.

For example, one can develop a certain mental coherence, and sound a beautiful note of a radiant mind; but, without the supporting notes of the emotional self, giving the fullness of personal consciousness, soul is less able to be involved. Recall that the human self is created ultimately for the fullness of expression of soul and consciousness here in our physical world. Human mind developed without a relatively clear and harmoniously resonating emotional self is not able to fully perceive and respond to Earth's being, or soul intent, and thus the coherence is restricted mostly to mental substance alone.

To be able to respond, soul needs the full chord of human consciousness sounded on all levels. This does not mean the human self is, or becomes, fully soul conscious, but that enough purity and experience is contained in the personal self to be able to sound a chord involving all levels of personal vibration. Note that this is not the requirement when a soul has only clothed itself in mental matter, to learn, express and serve on that level alone, without becoming a fully physical human being. In this situation, the note sounded by the soul's intent only extends to the mental level, and thus soul and mental coherence can be achieved. It all comes down to the purpose and intention of an incarnation.

For a physically incarnated human, soul does not send forth its intent to develop mind, emotions, or body alone. Its purpose is to enable the evolution of a fully functioning being on all these levels, and therefore the note of creation and intention that it sounds can only resonate with the fullness of the chord sounded when all levels of the human self have contributed. Thus, as a physical being, you cannot find soul consciousness through mind alone, or emotions alone, or body alone; you have to develop the sound of all these together.

On the human journey there are many stages, both of the development of the note or notes of each level of your being, and in the development of a harmoniously-sounding chord integrating all of your being. This is evolution.

As soon as you, the human being, have enough consciousness to sound an integrated and harmonious sound within your being, your soul will respond! This explains some of the flashes of intuition that create that instant depth and irrefutable strength of knowing that can change who you are in an instant. You have resonated with your soul in that moment, and a greater consciousness is born within you, and once that resonance sounds in your being, you can never forget it.

This is the interplay of soul and human vibrations, to create that new vibration that sounds a finer note, and thus brings with it the wisdom of soul into living expression through you, the human self. This is how soul enables spirit's intent to be expressed right down into the human, and thus deeply physical world of Earth's being. This is why human development of consciousness and personal intention is so important, for without that, the consciousness of soul cannot infuse our human world. This is the path of the individual walking the path of self, and then soul, consciousness.

There are other pathways through which soul resonance may sound in harmony in these denser layers of Earth's physical body (the levels of our mental, emotional and physical selves), and these are also very important. The whole purpose of this conscious infusion is for Earth and all her life forms to hold and resonate with the orchestral fullness of the consciousness of Cosmic Heart. Humans are, of course, not the only life forms, and thus not the only holders of substance that must evolve.

For smaller creatures (for example, bees, or mice, or small fish, etc.), harmonic coherence is sought by the angelic family that holds and nurtures them, as these small creatures are not born of an individuated soul that can garner spirit's intent into that harmonic outreach as it does for individual humans. The angelic role in Earth's evolution is extremely important, and poorly understood by most humans who perceive angels, yet consider them to be here only to aid the human self.

The other pathway involves larger creatures (for example, many domesticated animals, eagles, elephants, tigers, dolphins, whales, etc.), and is the journey through a group soul. This is where the note sounded by the physical expression does not have to be from one being alone, but in the co-resonance of many to invite soul presence. Through evolution, each expression develops learning and consciousness that nourishes their shared soul, and that is then shared to all expressions of that life form. The soul richness is thus developed by the contribution of many beings, but not only that: it is able, in time, to cohere those resonances into the sound that can reach into each of its multiple life streams, whatever note in that resonance they may sound individually.

A form of group soul journey is now emerging for humanity as well, guided and supported by the Greater Hearts that are the guardians of human and planetary evolution. This is not about merging multiple human souls into a group soul, but of enabling certain groups of individual souls to collaborate in a new way. This creates a coherence of sound, and thus a coherence of wisdom, between those souls that can then reach out and infuse each human whose soul is involved.

What this means is that the collective wisdom of those humans and their souls can be brought together to speed up their human journeys. This is not just for their benefit, but primarily to benefit Earth in these rapidly changing times. As much soul infusion, conscience and consciousness as possible is needed to create positive change in harmony with evolution's journey on a global scale.

If this time of rapid change is not absorbed and resonated sufficiently in the consciousness of all life streams in incarnation, then cooperation with the Great Change is not enabled to the degree needed. Change through more pressure may thus occur, something we see in the chaotic expression of some people, and groups – but fortunately, not yet to the extent of global chaos, which must not be allowed to occur.

In your heart, you build the resonance of the coherent consciousness you need to contribute to positive global change, please work this way for the sake of the planet and all life.

The Conscious Journey

The uniqueness of the human journey is that you evolve in two spheres: the sphere of soul, and the sphere of physical human life.

Soul can evolve on its path of service without being an expression of love as a human life stream in the physical world of Earth. Such a soul does not have consciousness it can apply directly to a human expression, and must take the journey to develop it with other younger souls.

The development of consciousness always has a purpose, because it is the substance of evolutionary intent. We do not evolve consciousness to become illumined beings, just to sit there and be illumined. It takes will to express love into the physical world, it takes concentrated focus. Where does this will come from? It is energy that has to be expended, and, in the total harmony of energy and flows of life and force that make up our solar and cosmic existences, that expenditure of energy requires a return of energy to its source to keep the balance.

The drive to become conscious is the mechanism by which Cosmic Love enables engagement between that which has been created by the expenditure of will and the greater universe within which that life exists, so that the energy *can be returned!* Once that consciousness is achieved, and the incarnated being understands it only exists to be an expression of Cosmic Love through its own specialisations and gifts, then, in consciousness, will is no longer required to create and enable life, for the life can be created and sustained by the alignment created by consciousness: love flows in, and love flows back. Like a heart, sustained by the embrace of conscious intent. At this point, the being becomes a living cell within cosmic life, giving and receiving where its gifts and training are called for.

To reiterate, consciousness is the mechanism through which you may discover your purpose as a human, as a soul; and through which you can align with, absorb and express that purpose as the service of life.

It is this circular nature of life and consciousness that is least understood in the human experience.

By its very nature, the human being begins its journey learning to understand how to be within, and to build within the worlds of matter, emotion and thought. Humans are builders, and engage with the world in this way in order to build. That is the creative force that creates the human in the first place. Unlike the soul, where the spark of spirit's intent sounds a note and draws to it the substance of the Ocean of Love that resonates, a human has to be built with more conscious intention. The soul does send forth a note of resonance on the emotional, mental and physical levels, and that does enable similarly resonant substance to be attracted, but the human is a complex structure, not a resonant sphere of light as is the soul, and must be built with more intention. At first it is the parents, then it is angels, then after birth it is largely the human itself, as it journeys through life's lessons and opportunities.

Thus, the human self is built, and continues to build, because that is a core imprint within its very creation and existence. This is also the basic mechanism though which loving intent is expressed and evolved in matter, that is, in the body of this Earth.

For the same reasons as a human must be built, and not just cohered through energy resonance, the expression of light within Earth must be built. Matter cannot be easily moved by resonance alone, thus the role of humanity in creating light and love in our world is paramount.

This is why we walk the path to develop consciousness, for without that we would never be able to engage with, resonate with, understand and implement our purpose here in this world.

Consciousness builds a bridge of resonance through which the force of will can express: from spirit to soul, from soul to human, from human to the world, and then back.

Life is only possible within a circular system, where energy flows out, energy flows back; blood flows out, blood flows back. Without that, there is no life, just substance and matter, unmoved by will's intent, undeveloped by the purposeful engagement of service.

In a planetary sphere, the planetary being can hold together without much physical interaction with spirit. Spirit and cosmic intent infuse at the higher level, and the denser, physical substance just is. The exchange that enables planetary life circulates at the soul or higher levels. Not dissimilar to a human being: the soul is infused with spirit and circulates vitality back to spirit. The physical human self is not part of that energy circulation until sufficient consciousness develops. For many eons the human self more or less just exists in matter, learning along the way, but not connected as yet to the flow of spirit's intent.

When a planetary being chooses to become more conscious of its physical existence, it has committed to enabling conscious loving flow to circulate through its physical self. This is the choice Earth made long ago, and thus nature, humanity, and all life were brought into beingness through her intentional choice, in alignment with the will of Cosmos.

The reason Cosmos has interest in such an expression into physical matter is that this is cosmic intent: to create a universe that expresses and radiates loving light through all levels of its being.

The existence of consciousness at a soul level was not enough, and human evolution emerged. It is not that nature and all other creatures are not also of paramount importance to the life-giving expression of Earth's love, but their loving exchange with Earth is largely facilitated by the angelic family, which holds the streams of conscious intent that enables these flows of life to evolve and circulate. Here we are seeking to inspire your human journey, so on that we will stay focussed!

The Human Journey

When soul intent is expressed into the physical world of Earth, it is the beginning of a bridge of consciousness. Soul resonance always sounds deep within your heart, expressing that will to live that keeps you alive. To be able to engage with that intent, you have to build your human consciousness. This you do through the myriad of pathways you take in life after life, learning, experiencing and building the coherent resonances in your being that will eventually harmonise and become the melody of your consciousness.

With every step upon the way, you learn how to build in matter, inspired by your soul's intent that lives through you as your purpose. You build in emotional matter, in the substance of thought, in the dense physical matter, and learn how to sound that note of your purpose through these different media. You know this by experiencing the harmony of resonance it sets up within you. That is, something in you just knows you are doing what is right for you. This is why conscience is such an important component of developing consciousness, because it helps you align with and put energy into those activities and expressions that simply resonate as true in your being, that feel right, that energise you with a higher light, that fill you with hope.

When you build in this world, in alignment with your purpose – no matter if you build in thought, emotion, physical matter or all three – and you let that note of your soul's purpose sound through you, then more of your own personal self comes into resonance with that note, and that is the building of your consciousness. When more and more of your own being resonates in harmony with your soul's note, you become more and more conscious, and able to be a greater living expression of not only all that you are as a human, but also the intent and love you are as a soul. This resonates through what you do, and into Earth's physical body, and thus you become a beautiful being not only receiving the will of spirit through your soul, but expressing and magnifying that intent into our physical world. In that, you experience the sheer joy of purpose expressed, and thus the circulation of life force is completed.

The purpose of soul evolution is quite different from the human journey, but the alignment of soul purpose with a human journey is what builds the bridge of consciousness all the way from cosmic intent to physical earthly manifestation, and thus enables the circulation of life force through all those media, and love is expressed.

This is the ultimate purpose of the human journey. Start connecting with your heart, seek out that which resonates through your being so that you sound the note of your purpose, and make your difference here upon Earth, our world of love to be.

The Great Choice

The moment when a soul and its human expression begin co-mingling in their respective consciousness is momentous, for several reasons:

1. It marks a major turning point in the evolutionary journey of both human and soul;
2. It signifies a committed choice to serve in the Earth sphere as a vehicle of conscious change.

You may wonder how a soul and its human self can develop separately on the journey of consciousness. Remember, consciousness is an integration of learning, experience and insight that creates a fine web of coherence that enables a higher perspective of life's journey, providing meaning, understanding, hope and purposeful drive to fulfil that journey. For the soul, the perspective is largely on the journey from life to life. For the human self, consciousness is what aids the journey day-to-day, and year-to-year, in the unfoldment of purposeful learning and service (the expression of your highest goodness). These finely-woven webs of coherence develop in quite different media, and they do not resonate together automatically.

The process in which the wisdom of soul begins to touch the yearning and hopeful human consciousness occurs initially in small steps, usually by the release of soul intent in the hope that enough of the human self can pick up that fine vibratory input, and bring it into conscious attention. This begins the journey of exploration to seek understanding and greater wisdom, direction, and perspective in human choices and actions. This happens by holding that vibratory input of soul in the human consciousness long enough to review the human learning and experience against that soul input and see what resonates, and then translate that, through consciousness, into meaningful perspectives and insights.

To be able to hold the input of soul vibration takes effort and training, because all finer vibrations will either pass through or bounce off denser material if there is no vibratory resonance. This is the human journey: to awaken and refine the ability to perceive and validate finer and finer vibrations in the consciousness.

Remember also, consciousness develops at our edges; for example, at the edges of our awareness, between what is familiar and what is just beyond what we know; like the faint sound we can barely hear, until we focus upon it; or the visual clues life gives us that we ignore until we pause and allow our perceptions to focus and thus magnify their presence; or the subtle emotional or mental perceptions easily dismissed until again, we pause, notice, and more fully evaluate their message. It develops at that edge between our soul consciousness and our human consciousness, the significant focus of our evolutionary journey in this era of Great Change. There is great need for this, to bring more soul expression into our world, and enable a positive transition in this evolutionary moment.

When a human self has developed a fine-enough and coherent-enough consciousness to be able to resonate, at least in part, with soul, there is a massive acceleration in both the human and soul journeys. The human self can more readily evaluate human experience in the light of the soul's wisdom, and thus make more soul-aligned choices, which align the human self more and more fully to its ultimate purpose.

Remember, it is spirit that holds the ultimate intention that brings you, soul and human, into existence, and soul expresses that intention for you in each life as your purpose, not only in this life, but in the greater journey as a soul, life after life. Because your soul has chosen to serve spirit's intent in the earthly sphere, in conjunction with Earth's request, its major journey is to fulfil this purpose. Accordingly, your human self is here to learn and align with soul to fulfil that same intent in each life. It is true that soul learns and develops consciousness upon the soul level, but it cannot fully align with and express spirit's intent here in our physical world, and thus fulfil its reason for existing, until it can engage more fully with its human expression. Similarly, the human search for meaning and fulfilment can never be assuaged until soul wisdom resonates within the human consciousness.

When human and soul consciousness begin that co-mingling, soul can more fully express its purpose in the world, and the human self can more fully understand and align with its purpose. When alignment with purpose occurs, no matter what level, you create a pathway of coherent consciousness (at least to some degree) through which spirit's intent can flow – and as spirit's intent *is* evolutionary force, that is why evolution speeds up through this magnificent union! This is a major turning point for both human and soul.

It is clear to see why this is significant for Earth: a human expressing love's intention through spirit's force and soul's purpose, is bringing that loving, evolutionary flow into the physical body of Earth herself. However, there is another reason why the beginning of the journey of soul and human engagement in consciousness is such a profound moment, and that is because it signifies a momentous alignment of choice.

Spirit's intent is to share love in this world, or it would neither have sought expression in this world, nor been permitted to do so. Soul's purpose is to hold and resonate that love into the world of souls – into Earth's Ocean of Love – but then comes the choice: does it seek to express this into the depths of physical incarnation? Or does it remain as a holder of that love in the finer vibrating inner worlds? This choice is made in a complex interaction between soul and Earth, guided to some extent by spirit's intent, but largely it is a decision of love made in the Ocean of Love, where both soul and Earth presence are resonating together.

In some ways, the decision could be seen as simple: either there is enough shared intent to create a human expression, or there is not. In fact, it is complex because it is not a decision made at a single point in time, but one that is made through ongoing review and evaluation. Because the human self has to develop its own consciousness before soul can more fully engage and empower that human self to express that loving intent, both Earth and soul must await the possibilities that emerge when the first co-mingling of human and soul consciousness occurs.

However, the human journey is not bereft of soul input throughout its many lives. Soul provides the intent for each life, and this imbues the heart of every human with this purpose. In consultation with those who implement the Law of Karma, it imbues the seed atoms around which the mental, emotional and physical self are built with the patterns for this life's journey, and which best guide the developing human to find and fulfil their purpose within Earth's loving embrace.

The final choice as to the fullness of living expression as a soul, and thus with spirit's love, in this world of human existence can only be made when that human consciousness reaches into, and can receive, soul consciousness in whatever smaller or greater way this occurs.

Please note, this has absolutely nothing to do with how mentally-advanced and capable a person is, how emotionally pure, or how physically perfect; because these provide no measure at all of the presence of soul's grace. These are a product of karma's expression and human choice within that karmic embrace, and are simply manifestations to provide certain options for learning and expressing in this world. For example, plenty of people with great intellect demonstrate no resonance with soul, and make choices based on mind power alone. Personal and global conscience does not get a look in; thus, the catastrophic destruction of our planet proceeds through the actions of these greedy and heedless ones.

Because the human consciousness has to take the journey through many lives before it can co-mingle with soul, it develops its own perspective of life upon Earth. Soul does not take over the human self when this connection occurs, because soul cannot operate the fine-tuned interactions needed in human life to function in this world. The human consciousness is essential to the path forward on Earth, because it is the human consciousness that becomes the vehicle of soul input into this physical world.

At the point where there is co-mingling of human and soul consciousness, a momentous choice is made: shall the human self continue, in other words, choose the path of Earth service and commit to becoming a more fully expressed vehicle of soul love and purpose for the sake of the Earth ... or not?

If not, then the soul has a further choice to make in concert with Earth's loving embrace and spirit's purposeful intent: to stay and be of service upon the inner levels alone, or to withdraw and continue expression upon other worlds.

For those whose soul-human choice is to stay, it is only for one purpose: to be in alignment with, and in service of, the Great Change unfolding upon Earth, such that the embodiment of heart can proceed in her physical self. This is the evolutionary imperative of spirit, for each individual human, for nature and all creatures through their group souls or loving angelic guides, and for Earth herself.

This is why our current time is called the Great Change: spirit's call sounds more loudly, energised by the loving intent of cosmic heartflow. At every level of incarnation, that message calls every life to resonate, and choose to align.

Many young souls and humans young on the evolutionary journey, can still be part of this choice in two ways. Either their souls form into groups, where through shared learning they can speed up the journey such that choice can be made. Or they choose to surrender a certain amount of personal choice, and become a non-resistant expression in the human world, moving in concert with the increase of loving flow created by other conscious souls, angels, nature, and Earth herself. In this coming era, this is just as valid a path of conscious development, as the path of deliberate conscious choice through human life after human life.

Remember: the path of conscious development is for you to become consciously aligned with soul, and consciously contribute in Earth's journey to become a planet of heart. Conscious alignment is a vibrational activity. Whether you reach this by the long road of in-depth human experience, or upon the road of acquiescence to the loving flows of Mother Earth, is immaterial in the loving expression of spirit's intent. Some who have walked the long path are needed, in order to bring the wisdom and knowing of Earth's and spirit's intent into the milieu of human life; but in fact, relatively few are needed for this to be fulfilled.

What is most needed is for the mass of humanity to stop resisting the journey of evolution and of Earth's loving expression – by either path – and quickly! For Earth's moment of great conscious change is upon her. She has made her choice, and over these next decades in particular, and through some centuries to follow, the choices must be made by the human family.

Make your choice now. Become conscious, or acquiesce. Choose light and heart, or Earth and heart, and align yourself accordingly. Life's choices give you the richness of experience to nuance your choices day-to-day, so follow them to awaken your heart, and be part of the great positive evolution occurring in this wondrous world we know as Earth.

The Worlds of Souls & Humans

In the world of souls, the journey is about aligning between the Earth's Ocean of Love, her emotional self, and spirit's intent. In the world of humans, the journey is about aligning between the world of souls, and the physical world of Earth. The ultimate aim of bringing these two worlds together, of souls and humans, is to create a living, pulsing conduit of spirit's love between Cosmic Heart and earthly expression.

This love becomes love-will in effect, because Cosmic Love, which is what births spirit, is activated and directed by cosmic intent, which becomes purposeful will when embodied upon Earth, whether in the world of souls, or through the human embodiment. This is also why many humans shy away from deep and intentful dedication and devotion to a true spiritual path, because it is easy, in the human sphere, to misunderstand the presence of love-will as pressure, confinement, challenge, and shattering – yet it is not. These may be part of the journey, but that is your doing, and your path of learning through the complex lessons of your karma: to balance and refine your journeys past into wisdom for the future. What greater expression of love can there be!

In contrast, those who embrace this vibration of love-will, even if presented with challenges, feel the fullness of that intentful love as a driving spiritual and living purpose, that activates the heart and brings great joy in the fulfilment of each day.

Most people on a spiritual path are in between these two, for the human journey is nuanced by so many factors, including karmic patterns, the level of development of both soul and human (which determines how much spirit may express), the embrace of the Earth, and the embrace of Greater Hearts.

All souls are born into a pre-qualified medium within the Ocean of Love, because Earth has walked this path of conscious becoming for eons. She has developed nuances in her emotional consciousness, where human souls come into being, and these cohere as qualities and vibrational expressions of not only her being and conscious awakening, but of her spirit's intent as it embodies through her.

To help Earth on her journey of manifesting her spirit's intent, come the Greater Hearts: beings who have come from other planets or stars with much wisdom already gained on the expression of spirit. Some have also gone deeper through incarnating on Earth, to further evolve their understanding into wisdom imbued with Earth's reality and the world of humans.

There is a great cooperative, conscious merging between these Greater Hearts, and Earth's living, loving expression as a planetary being on the path of physical heart consciousness. Much of Earth's emotional self is organised thus, you could say, into nuanced vibrational qualities that hold not only her intent, but that are also magnified by a Greater Heart who imbues that vibration with further consciousness, and infuses more spirit into that expression.

In this way, the expression of spirit through Earth and the Greater Hearts is embodied in vibrational coherences, seen as magnificent colours moving and radiating around and through Earth herself. Humanity is held within this loving expression, such that each soul embodies within one of these vibrational coherences, held by a Greater Heart, in accordance with their spirit's intent.

For example, if a soul comes into embodiment with the intentful guidance to express through creativity, that soul will embody within the milieu of the Greater Heart and Earth's expression that nourish and guide creative expression in the human world. This could be any form of creativity, for we see this in not only artistic or musical fields, but in science, education, politics, religion – any field of human endeavour where the expansion of awareness is enabled by a creative approach. Or, a soul may embody with the directive intent to learn to wield power, to ultimately manifest spiritual will in human affairs; or to embody law and order as the spiritual truth it is, helping that concept be understood and expressed in our earthly world.

There are many journeys for the human soul, but each soul will always be embraced in this Ocean of Love by the Greater Heart where their spirit's intent holds vibrational resonance. This proceeds for many lives until such time as the soul has learned sufficiently on that path of expression, and it may then move to another sphere of resonance, and thus begin to learn within the embrace of another of the Greater Hearts. Or, a soul may stay in the one resonance until it can master that expression of spirit's intent, both as a soul, and as a human, and then either assist the Greater Heart in holding and guiding the souls in that embrace, or leave Earth to help embody that intent of spirit in other worlds.

Why this has deep and heartfelt relevance to you as a human being, is because ultimately you can only journey forward spiritually in this life when you find resonance in your consciousness with the heartfelt intent held in your heart. This is where your soul's resonance is held, and in your soul's resonance is the love-will of your spirit's intent, and where you can tap into the whole embodiment of that intent held by the Greater Heart in Earth's Ocean of Love (where your soul learns and dwells). Thus, you find your purpose, and the loving nourishment that holds you and guides you on your journey – and who does not want or need that?

In the early days of human embodiment, you could find the presence of your heart's love in the nuanced vibration, the colour, of the Greater Heart in whose embrace your soul dwelt. In later (much later) embodiments, when both soul and human have learned much, and developed much conscious resonance, you come into more direct guidance from the Greater Heart.

In the beginning of your journey, you will be influenced and guided by the shade of the vibration and colour which infuses your sense of purpose, then later when you become more conscious, you can be more directly engaged in the conscious expression of your spirit, of the Greater Heart who guides you, and of Earth's needs and love, all held in that collaboration of resonance in the world of souls.

Most of Earth's Ocean of Love is held by these Greater Hearts – but not all of it. This is for a combination of reasons: Earth has her own karma, some discordant elements within her own being that she is still resolving: vibrational elements to purify before they can be incorporated into the loving embrace of one of the Greater Hearts. Then there are the souls created by evolution upon Earth herself, guided by her spirit's intent and thus having less of an individual spirit's purpose, and who are not strongly enough of one vibrational expression to resonate with any one of the Greater Hearts. Usually, they form part of that earthly resonance still being worked out through Earth's karmic journey.

Lastly, there are those souls who have not been able to hold sufficient resonance with their human expression to enable their light to continue to flow. Even the youngest human expression has a flow of light from its soul, but if a human evolves such that it continually chooses human power over that of spirit, that resonance becomes less and less. Instead of being nourished by soul, the inner heart is closed, and life force is amassed by the lower magic of human greed – at its worst in the greed for, and expression of, human power. This is seen in the catastrophic destruction of civilisation and the deaths of many caused by such embodiments. Hitler was one, others are scattered through history, and unfortunately, in action to some degree today; nothing of light shines through them.

For these people, their souls become very challenged. Every soul is a vehicle of flow, from spirit and from Earth's Ocean of Love to its human self, and thus its ultimate expression as love upon Earth in the physical world. If that flow is disrupted by human choice, continuously made, then it becomes very difficult for that soul to remain in the Greater Heart's embrace, whatever the degree of vibrational coherence, because it cannot flow that intent down into the Earth. The pressure on that soul to enable that flow to Earth, and the disruption to the collective intent for that flow held by the Greater Heart (and all the other souls in their embrace), means that eventually, if the disruptive human choices continue, that soul will move out of the embrace of the Greater Heart, and reside in the yet-to-be-resolved part of Earth's astral consciousness. This does not happen very often, but it is a path taken by a few. They are the ones who manifest the life-less wielding of power upon Earth that we call evil, and thus cause so much disruption and destruction in our human world.

Do not fear you are upon this path if you see your imperfections, if you sometimes have hatred or too much anger, if you feel overwhelmed by and incapable of expressing what is in your heart. If you were on the path of repeated choice to close to the nourishing light of your soul and the Greater Heart's light that embraces your soul, you would not even notice these challenges. The only reason you feel all these conflicts and difficulties is because you are allowing the light in your heart to move in your being, and this is your conscience, and eventually consciousness. Without that, you would not be able to see the contrast between the lighter and darker shades of your being.

Experiencing light and dark is needed to enable choice, which enables conscious growth, which enables more soul light to resonate in your heart and flow through you. You will never be without the shades of light and dark until you become a Greater Heart. As a human you are a vehicle empowered to act with conscious choice; and unless you are directly in touch with spirit's intent (like the Greater Hearts are), then you will always experience the shades of human life so that you can enact that conscious choice, and fully manifest that loving flow from your soul into this world.

Let go of judgement of the parts of you that are as yet not infused with love and light, and instead see them as lessons, reminders and guides for your development of consciousness, and enactment of conscious choice to bring your shade of loving intent into this world.

In this way, you and the millions of other seekers in this world help the world receive more loving light, and empower more loving light with conscious intent so that Earth can use this to redeem her as-yet impurified elements. Darkness is decreased, light is increased, and the mis-guided humans who keep choosing human power over heart's loving intent will have less and less unqualified matter with which to work. Their mischief and evil will be curtailed, and their souls will be able to reinstate the loving flow every human heart needs.

This is our future, just remember that it can only come about through choice, whether consciously through the challenges and travails of a human life; or through the infusion of soul choice directly which can happen with younger human expressions and group souls, where the long path of human conscious development is not part of their journey.

Take heart: if you feel the light and shade of life, you are on the path. Just use your heart to guide your choices and actions as much as you can, and more light and love will flow to your heart, into your life, and into our beautiful Mother Earth.

Soul & Greater Hearts

In the early days of the human journey, the soul reverberates in a very gentle way, just enough to keep the human self alive; but also to sound the note, the colour vibration, of the Greater Heart's energy field in which that soul is embraced. This vibration is of utmost importance to evolution, for the sheer existence of life itself is not enough to awaken the evolutionary impulse within any living being. It is the note that sounds within, that comes from something higher in vibration, and yet that can also resonate in our human world.

When it does resonate with something in our human journey – we have that nudge from within, that tingling awareness, that jolt to the consciousness that makes us pay extra attention, not only to what it is in our human world that triggered this, but also to what it is within us that is rattling our conscious perception to look deeper.

Without this note sounding within, who we meet, and what we experience and choose in our human existence would have nothing to resonate with, apart from previous human experience, and that does not lift the consciousness out of the human journey, and draw the attention to soul. In this case, the human journey would remain in the human world alone, and little consciousness or evolution could occur.

This does occur in some planetary spheres, where the evolutionary journey is not of such import as it is here upon Earth. Here upon Earth, her choice to become a planetary embodiment of heart consciousness attracted the presence of those who embodied within her consciousness: to further qualify the matter of her being such that the evolution of humans and all life could be accelerated, to become co-creators of this evolutionary magnificence – to be that planet of heart.

Every soul upon Earth is either birthed within, or re-created within (if from another planet or star), the energy field of one of the Greater Hearts.

These Greater Hearts are beings who have achieved conscious integration between Cosmic Heart (Sirius) and Earth, and can hold the resonance of both spheres as a harmony within their beings. They can hear the note of Sirius, and resonate with the evolutionary guidance and loving intent Sirius gives; and they can hold the note that resonates deep into Earth's body, made possible by her choice.

Why couldn't Earth do this on her own? She could – but in a much, much longer time frame. Just as with a human, if she were to evolve without the higher resonance of evolutionary intent guiding her from within her heart, then her evolutionary journey would be indescribably slower.

All planets and stars are held and nourished by spheres of higher consciousness, and as they evolve, they have opportunities to take different pathways, just like we do as humans. Earth opened the door to becoming a planet of conscious heart, and thus we are all on that journey with her. Those who understand the opportunities and challenges of that momentous decision brought their consciousness here, to both represent the cosmic intent that supports and enables that journey, and to explore pathways to embody that intent in collaboration with Earth. In a simple way of exploring this, you could see these Greater Hearts as teachers, invited to a school wanting to excel in a certain discipline, and thus they bring their wisdom, and they bring about change in how that school operates to facilitate this.

Earth is a school for human and other conscious beings that wish to awaken and participate in the physical expression of Cosmic Heart. The various energy presences of the Greater Hearts are like different streams of learning in that school.

Everyone on Earth is within one of these streams, except those very few who have chosen a path of materially-centred greed to the degree that their soul influence is shut out. For the great majority, however, the path of evolution is awakened within one of these streams, by the presence of that nuanced and very fine vibration of the Greater Heart who holds that stream of learning.

As you develop as a soul, you will develop other notes and colours that represent the wisdom gained over many lives. But always, there is a core vibration to your soul, that is in resonance with that Greater Heart's energy and consciousness within which you dwell. It is always there, sounding as a deep note of truth and meaning within your own heart, because that is your soul's gift to you.

In deep meditation you may access soul wisdom as guidance, perhaps brought to your level of consciousness by a guide on the inner levels, but this is not the same as that deep, deep note that sounds the very vibration of your reason for being alive. That you can only find by accessing your heart, where that note sounds.

This is a note that does not waiver in intent or truth. In our search for meaning and answers, we can find many certainties on our way – certainties of mind, certainties of emotions. But unless imbued with the deep certainty in our heart, these can flip from absolute truth to shattered disbelief in a second – because they are built only of mind and/or feelings, and can thus be rebuilt or reshaped by other emotional or mental explorations and conscious awakenings.

What lies in your heart is that note of your soul that holds all the promise of your journey ahead – for that is the journey of soul, and of consciousness. As humans, we have a great propensity to build on and endlessly revisit what we have done and experienced in the past, this life and beyond. Valuable in part, for that is how we refine our insight and experience into meaningful learning that we can take forward. However, it is not always valuable, and too much human consciousness is bound up in this backward-looking exploration.

Consciousness does not develop out of this. Consciousness develops as part of the evolutionary stimulus, which shows us the way ahead. Consciousness develops so that we can build bridges between past experiences and future steps, and thus take positive and definite steps with wisdom and intent.

Those who inflict and perpetuate great evil in this world are not conscious beings at all. They may be highly intelligent, politically savvy, emotionally agile and emphatic, and thus manipulative. But without the note of soul integrating their human perspectives with the greater evolutionary plan (for their own individual journey and for all others they influence), they are not working for the light, or anything positive at all.

On Earth's journey, her evolutionary intent is merged with and expressed through the Greater Hearts who have brought their own consciousness to this process: to magnify the presence of their particular evolutionary expertise deep into her body, where we dwell as humans. They concentrate the key areas of evolutionary learning needed in order to assist Earth on her journey of heart.

There are many ways to evolve in consciousness, but here on Earth we are in the school of *heart* consciousness, and thus our lessons – that is, the pathways concentrated into our world by the Greater Hearts – are tailored for this. Once you understand this, that will help you resonate into the journey that is yours to take, based on what nudges you from within your own heart. Therein lies all the wisdom you have gained life after life, which is held in your soul; and the keynote of the classroom, the stream, in which you are evolving, held in resonance by the Greater Heart involved.

That Greater Heart's resonance helps your soul learn by providing the evolutionary wisdom and intent that they hold, so that your soul can review, discern and then absorb those lessons of life that are in resonance with that. Then as you evolve, you can learn to discern more about your own life choices, in accordance with what resonates with your soul, but also the Greater Heart's note within.

When you become aware of the Greater Heart's note within your being, no matter what you call it, then you become a human-soul alignment that draws more conscious instruction from that Greater Heart. In this way, you step onto a more accelerated path, which in the past has been called the path of initiation.

As you learn to hold more coherence of resonance in your human consciousness with both soul and Greater Heart, then that resonance may be sounded more loudly, and a greater flow of intent can flow. Thus you become of greater service, and on the path of more rapid awakening.

There are many factors involved. Suffice it to say, that this is the path to create major positive change upon Earth, and to vanquish those of evil intent. It is only when more channels are open that can let through Earth's great Ocean of Love into expression in our human world, that the collective resonance of human expression can be swept into greater harmony.

This we need. Start in your heart and learn to do yours with the loving light of your soul and of the Greater Heart in whose embrace you dwell shining through you.

Love & Will in Your Heart

Cosmic Love flows to all entities that live within Cosmos. As it descends further into the deeper realms of matter, it is received and stepped down by an act of consciousness. Consciousness is what bridges higher and lower, and enables that life-giving flow to reach all. For us on Earth, that bridging is provided by the consciousness of our Solar system, our Solar Logos; and the consciousness of Earth.

All evolution of consciousness comes about by the stimulation and organisation given from a higher realm to that of a lower vibration, so there must always be a conscious entity able to receive that evolutionary intent, and be the bridge for that into the world or being that is being stimulated to evolve.

For us as humans, that is our souls, and yet a new soul has little consciousness, other than embodying the evolutionary intent that creates the human expression. We are in the embrace of the Greater Hearts, who become the conscious bridge that nourishes our soul with their wisdom, to quicken the journey of spiritual evolution.

It is the same for Earth, who is embraced by the Planetary Logos, a great entity of consciousness who brings cosmic intent into a conscious presence that Earth can interpret and express.

This embrace, whether cosmic, solar, planetary or human, is always present. Even when you evolve your own consciousness to the level of the one who has embraced you upon your journey, then you begin the journey of awakening your consciousness to the next level, and the loving entity who embraces you from there.

At every level where evolutionary intent is expressed, it comes as love, but as it touches the denser vibrations it becomes love-will.

All spiritual love contains will, because it is an expression of utmost loving intent. It is an outward flow, whether of Cosmic Heart, Solar heart, Earth heart, or soul heart – and to create that flow that nourishes life, it has to be expressed with force. Just like your physical heart forces your life-giving blood around your body, which you feel as your pulse.

In the loving presence of that intent, you do not feel the force. As that intent enters into denser matter, it must exert a greater force in order to move that loving intent through that matter. Thus, as a human, you feel your heart beat; as a soul you are within the intentful pulse of the Greater Heart in whose embrace you live, and so on.

The heart is where force (that is, will) and love meet, mingle and create.

Most humans seek a spiritual journey based on what calls them, that is, what attracts them in their inner self. This is love. But no human can walk this path without will, without intent. It is the engine of creation, for love cannot create life, or spirituality, on its own. Love itself is the presence that comforts, illumines, inspires and gives vision to awaken consciousness, but consciousness cannot be developed without determination, effort, discipline – all of which are an expression of the will from within.

This is why the true spiritual path can seem paradoxical at times, for it draws you forward with such love, yet you cannot go forward without applying will – your will.

Similarly, the Greater Hearts expressing Cosmic Love into our sphere upon Earth bring that great love to our attention, yet it is also expressed with will. Thus, on the path you need to find and create with your own will, and you will also experience the force of the will of the Greater Heart in whose embrace your soul dwells. This is made manifest through your karma, to give you the constraints and opportunities to learn how to align your will with the loving intent of your path.

Such is the ever-present challenge of the spiritual journey. In the dense world we live within, it is hard to bring the radiance of love together with the intense, directional force of will. It is as if they belong to different worlds, and yet, it is in the bringing together of these creative expressions that our true spiritual consciousness awakens. It is only when we can work effectively with both, that we are able to embody love, and thus become the fullness of our soul's expression.

Heart is the key. In our physical heart we can know and feel love, and also feel the life-force that keeps us alive.

Because will is the driver of creative force, it has been expressed much through our minds and emotions, for these are the areas of human expression where it is easiest to express creativity in our world. This is what has helped to build the consciousness we have as human beings. However, it does not truly build the consciousness of spirit's intent through our souls, so we become spiritual beings creating positive change upon Earth.

The Human Journey

This is why the next great step on our evolutionary journey is to learn to work with will through our hearts, to create with love-will, and fully express our soul's love in this world. Not just experience it in a deep meditation, but to do something with it, in this needy time of challenge and change upon Earth. In your physical heart's rhythm and structure, you will find something to work with in your consciousness to develop this. First there is the drawing in of that which holds nourishment (love), this takes force. Then there is stillness and silence, gathering and holding that vitality in poise and radiance, allowing the intent of love to infuse all. Then will is applied to direct that love and nourishment out into the physical body.

Do the same on your spiritual journey. Use your will to open to, and draw in that nourishing, loving intent. Sit with it, to infuse it with your knowing, and let it infuse you, until the alignment of conscious love occurs within you. Then you apply effort and intention to direct that consciousness in an outflow to create with love in our world.

To complete the flow, we need to understand that we are not here as isolated human beings on our own individual journeys. We are here for our respective journeys of consciousness, certainly, but we are primarily here at the invitation of, and in relationship with, Mother Earth.

Our flow of intention is guided by the loving intent of our souls. Our souls are guided by the wisdom and loving intent of the Greater Heart in whose embrace we dwell. The Greater Hearts are here in total conscious cooperation with Earth, and express cosmic intent merged with her loving consciousness.

When you express your loving intent, what flows through you is the loving intent of Cosmos sent for Earth, and stepped down through all these levels of consciousness until it reaches Earth herself. This is one of the ways she receives the nourishing intent of Cosmos and her soul, deeply into her physical self; and this is our dharma as human beings. The other ways are through the angels and nature, and some comes directly through the Greater Hearts, through their physical retreats, and occasional earthly incarnations and interventions.

Because this flow of loving intent is intended for Earth, it is in creating this flow to Earth that you will be more and more nourished. What she receives into her heart is circulated and reinvigorated in her being, and becomes part of the nourishment that flows to you from your soul; and the cycle of heartbeats and heart flow can continue, creating loving nourishment and evolution for all.

Therefore, on your journey, do not look for spiritual returns, look instead for how you can enter and more consciously engage with the intent and flow of what is in your own heart, and how to give that to the Earth. That shall then invite inflow from your soul, and start that wondrous cycle of loving heart flow between you and Earth, and all shall benefit.

Earth service, whether to other humans, to animals and nature, to Earth directly in meditation and spiritual effort; any or all of these will awaken your heart to more and more loving flow, and thus consciousness, and thus you become a greater change agent here upon Earth. You become a living cell in her heart, and life cannot get better than that.

Christ, Buddha, Greater Hearts & Your Path

As the light of the Sun reaches us here in our physical world, we see it as a bright light, but also know it is made up of many colours. It is no different to the nourishing light of Cosmos. As it comes down through the layers of vibratory resonance from higher to lower, it refracts into its different constituent vibrations. These we perceive as qualities, because the light of Cosmos is what nourishes consciousness, that life-awakening network of wisdom, experience and the yearning to evolve, that make up the qualities of our being.

The light of Cosmos stimulates different pathways according to the quality held in each resonance, and these are the key notes of evolution: the key journeys to undertake to realise the fullness of conscious beingness. Just as you undertake different subjects at school, which you then need to integrate as an adult to enable your exploration and effectiveness in your day and your life – it is the same on the evolutionary journey of a soul, a spirit, a planet, a star. You start within the embrace of one of the qualities of consciousness, then progress to others, and then eventually, depending upon your pathway, you may learn the full spectrum of the qualities in the nourishing light of Cosmos.

On Earth, we have two beings who are the primary holders of all the vibrations of Cosmic Love: Buddha, and the Bodhisattva (also known as Christ). These are names that might bring up memories of past experiences, or of what you have learned in lives past about the physical incarnations of these beings. Realise that Gautama, who incarnated 2500 years ago in order to attain, and then bring the Buddha consciousness into his human consciousness and into the world, is a very different being in his role of Buddha of Earth. Just as it is for Christ. Maitreya overshadowed Jesus during his years of ministry, to bring the Christ consciousness into the world, but has a very different role as Bodhisattva of Earth.

Gautama, Maitreya and Jesus are great Masters of consciousness – but Gautama and Maitreya also hold the role of being Buddha and Bodhisattva of Earth respectively, and as such they radiate much more than we have known through their personal incarnations of consciousness. They hold the multi-vibrational inflow from Cosmic Heart, and distribute it around our world through nature; into Earth directly at certain times of the year in collaboration with Earth herself; and into the vibrational qualities held by each of the Greater Hearts. In this way, the great inflow nourishes all life on its evolutionary path.

The role of Buddha of Earth is vast, and has little to do with the teachings created through his incarnation as Gautama. Those teachings, and subsequent teachers of Buddhism, have helped awaken many millions over the millennia since he was present upon Earth, and continue to stimulate and nourish those who strive for a conscious life. His role as Buddha of Earth, however, involves the evolution of the whole Earth and all her forms of life, not just some millions of humans, nor with Buddhism in its many humanised forms.

Buddha stands at the edge of the ring-pass-not of Earth, the auric boundary of her presence and conscious reach, and bridges that boundary to receive the inflow from Cosmic Heart. Many other beings assist, including Great Angels, both within and outside Earth's ring-pass-not, and the cosmic Mothers who nurture all life in the universe. The Earth herself is involved, through the one who has embodied within her consciousness, the Last Kumara. She will become known and named in the coming era, for she will become the next Buddha in the not too distant future.

However, it is the one who is the current Buddha of Earth upon whom rests the responsibility of guiding, deciding and metering the flow of Cosmic Love into Earth's being.

All conscious development needs guidance, for should you simply be taken in barely conscious form and held in the fullness of light, vibration, intention of a much greater consciousness, you would dissolve. If the consciousness you have developed does not have the clarity, the ability to expand to hold the greater light, and the ability to guide and direct that light, then you do not have the vibrational strength to be able to remain a conscious vehicle in the presence of that greater light, and you will simply become merged with it, and dissolve into it. This means that you would no longer grow in consciousness.

As the journey upon Earth for her (and all her life streams) is to enable conscious engagement with the greater light and love of Cosmos, and thus become a planet of heart, a great inflow of Cosmic Love cannot be allowed until there are enough conscious pathways for that light to flow and merge into the body of the Earth. Therefore, the role of Buddha is immense, for the inflow and thus intent of Cosmic Love must be tempered to balance all that is unfolding in the conscious realms of earthly life, such that evolution can proceed with the right nourishment. Buddha looks largely out from the ring-pass-not of Earth, to perceive the incoming loving intent from Cosmic Heart, and then in consultation with all the Greater Hearts and the Bodhisattva, determines how much flow may come in.

The role of the Bodhisattva, or Christ, is similarly of little resemblance to the life we know of through Jesus. That was a life to bring about the incarnation of a certain light of Cosmic Love, to stimulate particular teachings for humanity (continued by other teachers since then), and to attain a certain alignment in deep physical consciousness for future work. In the role as Bodhisattva, Maitreya works closely with Buddha on this profound inflow of Cosmic Love to Earth, but with the focus being upon its expression through all the Greater Hearts, and thus into Earth and humanity, for the sake of aiding the evolution of consciousness. Thus, this role is often seen as that of the Great Teacher.

Maitreya works closely with all Greater Hearts to manifest this loving inflow in accordance with cosmic intent and Earth's karma, and present all evolving life with opportunity and choice to learn and grow in consciousness. Thus, Maitreya looks more to the Earth, and is the guiding light for the evolution of love, which is the result of consciousness.

As this great cosmic inflow passes through the ring-pass-not of Earth, into Earth's denser realm, its singular brilliance refracts into multiple colours just as the sunlight does. Each of these constituent vibrations holds a core quality, and becomes a path of conscious learning. Each is held by a Greater Heart, who has developed the consciousness to be able to receive this great inflow from Cosmos, hold that intent within, and filter that intensity down into our earthly world of human consciousness such that we may apprehend and learn, and thus evolve. In our inner worlds, Earth looks like a wondrous sphere of many colours, as each of the Greater Hearts holds their resonance in the worlds of higher consciousness.

There are many more beings involved at every step in this descent of Cosmic Love, but the primary flow is as described, and it is important to understand it because it gives depth to your conscious apprehension of the Great Change we are in.

Earth's choice to become a planet of heart has been made, and the cosmic inflow has increased accordingly. This unavoidably creates pressure in the earthly realms, as that energy seeks inflow and expression in our world. The pressure gives opportunities for rapid spiritual growth, if you are open to that. It also creates fractures in those conscious enough to know there is choice, but who say 'no' – such as certain leaders who choose death and destruction through war, climate change denial, or other forms of materially-focussed greed and self-centredness.

For many, the extra pressure is felt as change in the outer world, with not so much pressure for inner conscious change; and many will simply flow along in the aura of others who guide in one way or another. However, if you perceive the change, if you feel nudged to learn and awaken something else inside yourself, or if you perceive a need for something more, then you are one of those being called to respond.

Even though the Buddha, the Christ and the Greater Hearts, with all their helpers, hold and bring this flow of Cosmic Heart into Earth so that all may grow in that light, it is not their role to incarnate it into the physical world we inhabit as humans. That is our role, those of us who hear the call, feel the pressure of the Great Change, and know there is more to be done for love and light to become manifest in our world.

There are enough of humanity with enough consciousness to be able to align with, and let through this greater inflow of Cosmic Love, but it takes awareness, choice, and action.

Do what you are called to do with more love, knowing you are in this greater stream of consciousness-changing life force. Choose what you do, with Earth and our collective future in mind. You do not need to think intensely about which Greater Heart's embrace you are in; or the deeper inner truths of your journey, to be a conscious and cooperative vehicle for Cosmic Love, filtered down to your level of consciousness through all these great hearts, so that it may live through you and give the gift of loving light to Earth and all.

Call of the Heart

Wake to the Call of Your Heart

When you have woken up and realised there is more you can understand, and more you can do – rather than more you can gain for your personal self, and more you can control for your empire (whether that is personal, family, corporate, national or identity) – then you have heard the call of your heart.

Heart is the centre of life. It gives life physically, and no life ends until the heart stops, even if all other functions have failed. It gives life spiritually, regardless of whether that is energised and nourished by extant religions and spiritual practices, or your own inner search and fulfilment. But when you hear the call of your heart, it is not, and can never be, just about you and your life, because every heart is embraced by the grace of a Greater Heart that gives life and meaning.

Reflect on your physical heart. You may consider it to function in complete independence. But that spark that ignites and energises your heart to give life, that physiologically and scientifically indefinable spark that keeps your heart beating, or allows it to cease when your time has come – that spark is from your soul. Your soul holds the intention for your physical, living expression, and energises or withdraws that intention in the embrace of the flow of life within and around you and the world as a whole.

Soul is of the Earth, within the great Ocean of Love that is Earth's emotional self. Your human self is part of the Earth in physical and human emotional and mental levels of vibratory substance.

Everything is of life, and is part of a loving, intentful expression! And the life force that energises all levels of this expression flows through the heart.

Your soul heart flows intention to your physical self through your physical heart. Hence the common language expression of 'follow your heart,' because that is where your ultimate life-guide is held. Where does the life force come from to energise and ignite your soul heart? Two sources: the intention of Earth herself, through her emotional embodiment of her own life plan, thus imbuing the Ocean of Love, and all souls within that, with that energised intention. Plus, the intentful embrace of one of the Greater Hearts (from near or from further away according to your journey), who embody a particular intention within Earth to help her align with Cosmic Heart.

The Greater Hearts work together with the Planetary Logos, the soul consciousness of Earth, who receives the inflow and intent of Cosmic Love from Cosmic Heart, and with Buddha and Bodhisattva in their planetary roles. Together they create a presence of that great cosmic intent in conscious streams that can more rapidly qualify the vibrational substance of Earth herself, through humans, nature and all her life streams.

The intent of Cosmic Heart manifests upon Earth, through Greater Hearts, through Earth's embracing heart, through your soul heart, to your physical heart. The flow of life force and intention steps down from the finest vibrational nuance, progressing through each level of increasing density until it reaches the great depths of physicality, where we live and function as humans, and where nature and all her creatures express upon Earth.

The flow of heart's intent to nature and all her life streams is guided and manifested through the hierarchy of the greatest to the tiniest of angels. Angels are beings of flow, and never hinder this loving nourishment. However, their intentful expression relies on receptive energy spaces so that their fine attunement can create and express the blueprint of life in the ethers, and build the worlds of nature in harmony and balance. These places of receptive energy can be disrupted by humans, who do not heed this vibrational intent and need for balance.

An evolving human can heed this in two ways: as a direct impression through their oneness and attunement with nature; or as a conscious understanding from within their own heart, or both. This is the edge of human development, where impression becomes consciousness, and where judgement of right and wrong becomes aligned with the life-giving flow of intention all the way from Cosmic Heart to your heart.

This is where you wake up, and see in the illumined daylight of conscious revelation that choices need to be made in a greater context, and actions need to be taken to enable the loving expression of positive change – aka evolution – to progress.

Humanity is waking up through both these stimuli. Nature is grieving and screaming her despair at our collective greed and ignorance. Cosmic heartflow is increasing because Earth has sought that greater alignment, thus the flow of intent increases through all the Greater Hearts, to our souls, and to our personal spiritual and physical hearts.

Challenge and change! You cannot evolve consciousness without challenge, or else you would not become conscious.

There is a certain element of humanity that does not need to evolve consciously at this time, and therefore is not on this path. They are the souls who are in the gentle flow, and whose human expressions are guided more by the milieu of the surrounding consciousness in which they exist than by their own individual soul intention. However, many of humanity are in the intentful and thus more direct flow of conscious intent – and must wake up! Because when you do wake up, you become part of the Great Change. Just by your realisation of the need to seek more understanding, and more intentfulness in your actions, you become a vehicle of more heart.

Heart does not require your personal certainty to flow. In fact, certainty can be the very thing that destroys the light-flow of heart. Certainty as a human being comes from our mind, when we construct a rigid framework within which we understand life; or from our emotions, when we codify our feelings into familiar, repeatable expressions. Both of these tend to be inflexible when the nuance of life's unfoldment and the evolutionary path energise change.

When you wake up to the nuance of life's understanding and expression through your heart, you can find a different kind of certainty: the certainty of alignment and resonance. Alignment with the intention of your soul (and all that flows through it), which gives you life and purpose. And energetic resonance with nature and Earth, so that you feel one with beautiful Mother Earth, and resonate in your place and purpose here in the greater sphere of planetary life.

Through alignment with your soul's intention, you come to understand what resonates with your truth as a being of life and light, and certainty radiates through you in that alignment. Your choices can be made in that alignment, your actions can be energised in that alignment, and both can be adjusted in that living flow of intention that nourishes your heart and consciousness, to manifest in your life here upon and within Earth. You are no longer captured and bound by rigid thoughts, contained feelings, and structured expectations and plans.

It is a major shift, because it seems you have to let go of much that you may have thought as true, planned for your future, and held as emotional comforts. Yet, when these truths, plans and comforts are no longer nourished by your own inflowing life force and intent, and no longer resonate with the world in which you live, there comes a time where the effort to sustain them requires so much personal will and effort that the relief of letting them go is magnificent; and the shining light of the new day fills you from within and without.

This is the wake-up call. Start the journey. Consider your certainties fallible, and realise how essential it is to find that harmonic resonance in your relationship with, and presence here on Earth.

You need that nourishment, and when you open your consciousness to that – then upon every step, facing every challenge, awakening to every new opportunity, realising every loving resonance with Earth your home, you will be gifted light and insight to see, know and act in alignment with your soul and the loving flow of every heart in this loving expression of life.

Then you are doing yours. No need for grand roles of leadership, unless that is your personal path. No need for amassed intention to carry you, nice though that may be – because the flow of heart will give you every support you need when you search for it, choose it, and let it fill you.

No need for full realisation and certainty, for this is a living journey, and all that is certain is the destination, where the consciousness of the heart shall be fully expressed through the human family, and resonant in both humanity and nature as living expressions of the heart of Earth.

This, then, is the call of the heart: wake up!

The new world beckons, and needs you.

The Call of Evolution

When you wake up to the call of the heart, when you pay heed to the tiny, almost inaudible voice in your mind, when you acknowledge the gentle yet persistent pressure in your feelings that something needs to change in your life – you open to the flow of heart, the flow that nourishes who you are.

Yet heart cannot nourish without choice. Heart energises life, no matter on what level of physicality or consciousness it is centred, and life is never a static, motionless expression. Always there is movement, whether to grow, to forage, to awaken in consciousness, to create in the world. On every level of existence, life is an expression of choice. Even if that choice could be seen as somewhat, or even entirely, preprogramed or instinctual, somewhere, on some level, in every expression of life there has been a choice to enable that expression to flourish in this world.

Choice enables movement. No choice means you are swept along in the choices of other beings around you, or that you stagnate.

If you hear or feel the call of your heart, you are gifted the great opportunity to awaken and make a conscious choice.

Does that matter? Yes, profoundly.

Consciousness is the force of evolution in our universe, because it is pure intention, intermingled with the milieu in which it is resonating to manifest that intention from the highest source. Thus, consciousness is the vehicle we need in order to create positive change – whether we seek that for personal transformation, or to evolve global peace, they are the same.

Consciousness arises from choice, when the reflections on that choice are infused with higher intent. Thus we come back to the inflow of heart, also a choice. As soon as you begin to hear or feel the presence of your heart's awareness, you have already opened to that consciousness. Even if you need time to fully register these inner impressions, unless you absolutely and forcefully shut down these inputs, you have said 'yes' to your higher self infusing your perceptions, and thus your choices, through your heart. In this way, you open the door to consciousness, where you bring that intention of your higher self into the milieu of your personal self, there to begin a resonance that allows you to increase your ability to perceive higher intent, and interpret how to respond and take action in the physical world in alignment with this higher intention.

Every time you do this, you awaken more consciousness in your being, and every choice enables the flow of your heart to increase, flowing from your soul to you, from you into the Earth.

You cannot awaken in consciousness without becoming a conduit for the greater evolutionary plan to awaken and manifest more greatly in the world. There are few pathways for the flow of heart to reach into the physical world in which we live. We, humanity, have a major role in enabling this, and thus enabling the expression of evolutionary intention, and the unfoldment of positive change, because we can become conscious and make these choices that matter.

Other conduits are through the angels that hold conscious intent into the substance of Earth in specific locations, and who nourish the life-flows and expressions in nature; and through the Greater Hearts who anchor their key resonance and the evolutionary intent that is theirs to guide, in certain locations within the Earth sphere. Neither of these can work in independence from the expression of heart flow and conscious choice within humanity. Humanity's choices enable or disrupt the expression of the Earth's life force and evolution through nature – this is obvious and visible in our physical world, and even more impactful in the overall expression and awakening of evolutionary development in our Earth as a whole.

Every significant location that holds presence and energy (created by a great angelic presence in resonance with Earth and nature) is a conduit of loving light into Earth. When we acknowledge and protect it, we empower that expression to not only flow freely into the Earth, but into us as well. When we see and feel these sacred places, we have created a resonance in our being with that sacred inflow, and that will never leave you. You know this already: when something in your day reminds you of a place where you have experienced this presence, you are not only transported by the memory of that place, but your whole being resonates with it too. This is real, and every time you do this that resonance increases not only in you, but in the world, and the inflow of that intention is magnified to aid consciousness and evolution on Earth. Unfortunately, the contrary is true too, and there is only so much destruction of these sacred places of consciousness and intentful inflow that Earth can sustain.

This is an important, so very important, response needed from the awakening humanity, to protect and strengthen these places of resonance that hold evolutionary intention in the body of Earth.

It is similar concerning the evolutionary inflow held and nourished by the Greater Hearts. While they do not need humanity to enable their presence in the locations of their foci – their own past journeys in the human world have achieved this – the Earth needs more of this loving light, and here we, humanity, must choose. It is just as we have described about your resonance with the presence of Great Angels holding a sacred place upon Earth, except that for the most part, your ability to resonate with the keynote of a Greater Heart starts within your heart, rather than in a sacred place upon Earth, although the two may overlap.

Every soul is born within the energetic embrace of one of the Greater Hearts, because all conscious life is nourished this way in the body of Earth. As you awaken, you will awaken the resonance already within you that is imbued with the evolutionary intent of the Greater Heart's embrace wherein your soul dwells.

Many people, traditions and teachings see the awakening to the resonant presence of a Greater Heart (including, but not limited to, Jesus and Buddha, and the religious expressions and traditions built around them), as part of their journey upwards in consciousness, as part of their personal growth and self-development. Your personal and spiritual development may occur, but it is not the purpose of that contact.

The Greater Hearts are here to support the awakening journey of the Earth, to become a planet of heart and a radiating beacon of that magnificence as a physical expression in our universe.

They hold evolutionary intent as received from the greater cosmic flow of loving, intentful force, that is, consciousness. They enable that force to become consciousness within the Earth sphere, while she develops that consciousness within herself.

When you feel the call of spiritual awakening, it will have resonance with the evolutionary intention held by a Greater Heart; and this is a call to align and contribute to the expression of this intent in this world.

This is service, and the reason why no spiritual journey can ever unfold without it. It is the giving to Earth of that evolutionary intention with which your heart resonates, and thus can energise and consciously express and magnify into the physical world in our care. No matter if this expression is small and seemingly personal, for example, tending a garden, cleaning a shared space, cooking for others in need, donating time or funds to important causes. There is only one measure of how effective your service is: how much heart you put into it, with the conscious intention to create positive change in our world, for the Earth and all life.

You are not here on Earth to find ways to escape all the challenge and confrontation of our changing world. You are here to find the resonance you have with the greater inflows of evolutionary intent within your heart, and bring that into the world, through whatever gifts you have.

This is the call of the heart, of our heart, of our soul heart, of the Greater Heart in whose embrace our soul dwells. Ultimately, it is the call of Earth's heart that we are responding to. Earth's heart has called this evolutionary journey into her being, to become a planet of heart. All souls, including us, the angels, nature and Greater Hearts, are here in alignment with this evolutionary inflow, and thus we can only evolve if we align with that flow.

Heart to heart the intention manifests from the highest vibration down to the densest here upon our Earth. This is the stream of consciousness. This is the flow of life. This is the nourishment for all we are and do. And we find it and live it through our hearts.

When your heart calls – wake up! Accept this loving inflow, and do yours for the shared world we live in.

Your Evolutionary Role

In the loving flow of the evolutionary impulse that lives in your heart, and that awakens as you awaken your consciousness, you touch your life's purpose. Most importantly, you touch the qualifying vibration of love that tells you what quality is yours to embody upon Earth.

This makes it sound very singular – and in the broader picture of Earth's evolution it is, and that is key to you finding and enacting your purpose for living here upon this beautiful planet. How it manifests in your physical, emotional and mental life is, of course, full of the nuances created by your strengths and experiences from this life and past lives. Always, however, the keynote sounding and reverberating through your actions and choices will hold this quality that fills and nourishes your heart.

Evolution is not random; it is a carefully guided journey to enable the outcomes to be achieved that are held in the initiating spark that creates each expression of life.

This spark comes from the loving intent of those who hold understanding of the worlds into which that life will be born; who hold a picture of the whole; who work in positive and intentful collaboration with the greater light of life, the heart of our universe itself, for that is the source of all life as we know it.

Upon our Earth, that spark comes first via the Kumaras, great beings of cosmic life force who hold that intentful electrical charge that enables life to emerge – that is, that brings matter and spirit together.

Matter and spirit would not mix otherwise, for they are at such different vibrational levels. In the spectacular process of evolution in our universe, heart has been created as the vehicle within which spirit and matter can co-mingle. This applies to every level – whether cosmic spirit infusing cosmic matter, as happens in the Cosmic Heart, Sirius; Solar spirit infusing our Solar system via the heart in our Sun; earthly spirit infusing our physical world via our Earth's heart; human spirit infusing our physical human self via our heart.

Yet this co-mingling and infusion, while enabling life force to flow and life to exist, does not in and of itself facilitate a conscious journey, whereby the being so infused becomes a conscious collaborator in the great plan of evolution's intention.

If the intent of our universe were to enable infusion of all matter only, then very few beings would be needed; just those needed to hold each level of creation such that spirit's love could simply permeate all matter in their embrace. This was the keynote and evolutionary intent of previous incarnations of our living universe, hence why all matter does at least have the memory and resonance of spirit's love held within.

However, the intent held in the creative force of our Cosmic Heart is of consciousness. Therefore, not only is the evolutionary path one of infusing all levels of matter with spirit to create life, but of enabling all those levels of matter to become consciously cooperative and active in alignment with that will of spirit.

Coming back to our earthly sphere, the Earth is alive because of the spark of spirit in her heart, but she evolves because of the higher beings that hold the intent consciously, and thus enable her to evolve in consciousness. Eventually she will hold her own full consciousness within our universe. That is a long way along the evolutionary path – not least because, for her consciousness to become fully present and spirit-infused,

Call of the Heart

all beings in her planetary sphere also need to become fully conscious and cooperative with spirit.

As we have covered before, nature and all her creatures are held, loved and guided by angelic beings, and consciousness is enabled through their fully cooperative alignment from higher to lower. The choice as to how quickly full consciousness infuses the earthly matter held by all these life streams is up to the Earth, and how quickly she can enable those finer vibrations to sound through her being.

This is where we, humanity, come in, for we are here at Earth's request, as beings able to bring consciousness, and thus spirit's intent, flowing from highest to lowest, into conscious expression into matter itself. The angels of nature are never physically embodied, and neither is it the role of nature and all her creatures to bring spirit's intent into physical materialisation. They collaborate together to enable the natural world to be nourished by that conscious intent, but humans are the chosen vehicle to enable conscious intent to become conscious action, right down into the densest matter of our physical world.

Earth's journey of conscious unfoldment requires us to take that journey too.

The Kumaras came to assist Earth on her journey, but who is there to assist humans on their journey? The Greater Hearts. In the presence and conscious guidance of the Kumara holding the intent of the present era, the Greater Hearts are those trained in other planetary or stellar journeys and able to resonate with the task at hand; or, as is now possible, those who have taken their own conscious journey upon Earth. Each Greater Heart holds one of the keynotes of the evolutionary intent of Earth's heart, and thus between them all, they fully infuse all journeys of consciousness upon Earth.

Every human soul comes into being within the resonance of one of the Greater Hearts; that is the only way to embody here upon Earth. Your soul is bathed in this loving resonance, and as you awaken your consciousness, more of that loving intent can infuse your human self.

Some of the Greater Hearts have become known through spiritual texts and teachings of the last millennia; many are not known. Some humans who present themselves as an embodied Greater Heart are definitely not one, for to do so is the path of glamour and self-aggrandisement, not the path of love and consciousness.

You do not need to know the Greater Heart within whose resonance your journey of consciousness evolves, but if you find resonance with certain teachings, or teachers, that inspire growth and goodness in you, be open to that. There are many people who strive to aid their fellow human beings in many ways, and any of these ways may be yours for the next steps on your journey.

Consciousness is not the result of spiritual training alone. The evolutionary imperative is for consciousness to develop such that the body of Earth herself can become fully and consciously an actor in the expression of Cosmic Love throughout our universe. Love can express in every nuance and action of human life.

What was categorised as a 'spiritual' path through many traditions in the past millennia, is not the path energised for our current and unfolding journey of consciousness. Hence why many religious and spiritual traditions are faltering and failing, for they have become more obsessed with their own influence and power in the world, cemented in their past and traditions, rather than enabling the positive change that is needed in all spheres. This is okay, all vehicles of conscious development come and go. Do not feel sad or abandoned, but find your own heart's keynote. You know what is right for you personally, and what is right for you to do and be in this world, in your heart. Give it a chance to nourish your insight and understanding, and forego any rigid dismissal based on dogma no longer resonant with the love that all evolutionary intent gives, freely, and fully.

Wean yourself off the pervasive perception that we are waiting for a saviour. We, humanity, are the saviours of this world, this beautiful planet that we call Earth.

Should any of the Greater Hearts incarnate and become known in the future – such as the coming incarnation of Maitreya and others around him – this is *for the Earth*, not for you. Of course, every human and all of nature are beautifully blessed whenever a Greater Heart embodies. We are part of the Earth, and every time a Greater Heart incarnates the Earth takes a great step forward, and thus we can all do the same. But these incarnational embodiments of Greater Hearts are few. Instead, they work tirelessly upon the inner levels, to inspire and infuse every human heart in their care, so that humanity can embody and put into action the loving intent held by Greater Hearts for the Earth.

This is your awakening, your service, your ultimate realisation of consciousness: you are a beautiful, radiant, living cell within the body of Earth, and your cooperation with Earth's heart flow of cosmic intent, and with the other cells with whom you resonate, will enable perfection in a way you can barely conceive. Yet the utter fullness of love and pure joy that will follow calls your heart, for in your heart you know the plan, and that is your journey to follow.

The Greater Hearts are there to infuse your heart with that loving evolutionary intent, and even in times of great challenge and darkness, seek to go there so that you can endure, and with loving grace be part of the positive change we so need in our world.

The Resonance of Your Heart

In the heart of one we call a Greater Heart, lies the seed atom created by the spark of cosmic intent they have embodied, and that holds all the intention for conscious evolution that is theirs to guide in this sphere.

Conscious evolution is guided by vibrational resonance, for consciousness is not in and of itself inherent in matter. It is created by the co-resonance of the guiding light, where the bigger picture of life's journey is seen, with the inner substance and physical matter of the life form itself.

Conscious evolution upon Earth has been established for many millions of years, through Earth's choice. When she made her choice, the Kumaras came to hold that resonance of cosmic intent that aligned with the Earth's call. As evolution proceeded, and the resonance of Earth's choice with cosmic intent deepened into her being, it qualified into more and more unique yet harmonious expressions, just as the light of the Sun expresses in all the colours of the rainbow here in our physical world. One source of light, yet full of many different vibrations.

As the expression of conscious evolution deepened through Earth's body, the Greater Hearts were called to hold, energise and guide each of these different vibrational notes.

Angels were also called, to embody and guide these vibrational qualities through nature and all her living forms.

For human evolution, it is the relationship with the Greater Hearts that is paramount, for we are on the vibrational continuum that extends from Cosmic Heart through to the Earth's Kumara, to the Greater Hearts, and to the body and physical heart of Earth herself. We are the vehicles-to-be of conscious expression that will enable cosmic heartflow to bring the consciousness of life into living harmony in our physical world.

This is why every soul is born into the vibrational embrace of one of the Greater Hearts, and will energise its human self to discover, learn and resonate with that vibrational embrace. At its simplest and highest level, this is your purpose for existence. Then, of course, come the many millennia of lives through which your soul comes to understand how to resonate consciously with the vibration of the Greater Heart (in contrast to simply being infused with that vibration, as happens in the early journey), and learns, with your human self, how to infuse that vibration down into the physical worlds and create consciousness at the human level.

In truth, you do not ever become fully conscious, because as you develop the ability to harmonise and resonate with more and more of your soul's consciousness, you realise the subtlety of vibrational resonance goes deeper and deeper through the Greater Hearts and eventually to the Cosmic Heart, from where the intent for Earth's conscious evolution arises.

Consciousness is not a state of being to attain, it is a vibrational harmony that can be perceived, and thus acted upon in any circumstance.

Neither is consciousness your pathway out of human life, into some sanctuary of light in the inner worlds. Nor is it the purview of a spiritual path alone, for Earth is not evolving on one trajectory of spiritual perception alone. She is evolving as a planet of heart, and heart nourishes every expression of life – and every expression of life is needed to enable livingness to exist.

Thus, we have Greater Hearts holding the nourishing resonance that enables consciousness to develop in every sphere, and enables the fullness of life to express. All are themselves nourished by the single intent arising from the co-resonance of Cosmic Heart's love, and Earth's choice to evolve this way. Yet each holds an individual keynote, to give home to that unique impulse created as it differentiates into the human and earthly worlds.

Within the vibrational intent of each Greater Heart, there is also further differentiation into what we can call qualities or attributes. These are what are more closely aligned with the vibrational purpose held in our own souls and hearts.

These qualities are not about human life, they are about a conscious life. Thus, we have, for example, the vibrational quality of knowledge. In the early human journey, it may manifest as knowledge for knowledge's sake, or for power, or for the many other reasons humans seek knowledge. Eventually it becomes co-resonant with the guiding impulse from your soul in your heart, and it becomes a vehicle of knowing and aligning with the knowledge of your purpose and responsibility to contribute to positive change here on Earth.

Another example is the quality of devotion. It may manifest as a narrow-minded, blinkered, one-pointed dedication to an individual, a teaching, a cause, a belief, not always with positive outcomes; just as is the case with those obsessed with knowledge in the early stages of conscious development. But as soul and human evolve and learn to refine and resonate with the conscious quality of devotion (not the human attachment to its stimulus), then you become infused with the graciousness and one-pointed love that enables higher consciousness to be celebrated and drawn down into the human and earthly worlds – again, as ever, to empower positive and conscious change.

There are many such examples.

In your heart is the key vibrational resonance that is yours to align with, and that can guide you in all you do, because it is the part of the conscious evolution of Earth that you hold.

When you tap into that beautiful resonance, learn how to utilise that vibration to energise your actions, to help you discern your choices, and enable you to become a being of greater consciousness.

In every what-may-seem small choice and action you take, if you seek to bring consciousness to it, you bring the resonance of your heart into the world, and through that, the love of the Greater Hearts, of the Kumara, of Cosmos, and of Earth herself will be present.

This is how we change the world: when we each do ours to be conscious.

Aligning Our Conscious Evolutionary Flow

In the great flow of loving intent from Cosmic Heart to nourish and guide Earth's evolution, the role of the Greater Hearts has been, and still is, to be the great guiding embrace that nourishes every human soul (and thus heart) with the resonance that enables wise choices and aligned actions, to further every human on their path, and thus the Earth as a whole. Similarly, the angels have their role with nature, where they embody and flow cosmic intent into all living forms within nature's embrace.

These two great infusions of spiritual guidance and cosmic intent have always had interaction, because they work collaboratively for the sake of achieving the evolutionary outcome upon Earth. However, their fields of expression and action have remained largely separate, with Greater Hearts focussed on humanity as a vehicle of the evolution of consciousness, and the angelic family focussed on the Earth and her physical well-being and expression through nature and all its creatures.

This has worked well while humanity was developing astral and mental consciousness, which are largely personal and thus contained within the human sphere. This is not to say human beings have not interacted with, and related deeply to nature; we know that is not the case, but by and large, humans have been under the evolutionary imperative to develop individual consciousness, because that is the nature of the type of energy beings they are: beings of form, and builders of form. This is a simple truth based on the way consciousness interacts with the dense physical matter of Earth. It needs a form in which to build resonance, such that knowing and eventually wisdom can be held within that form, and thus create that higher resonance with the Earth herself.

If consciousness were to develop in the fullness of the body of the Earth all at the same time, it would take enormous effort (that is, Cosmic Will), and that is not the chosen journey.

We, humanity, are the cells within which consciousness can develop, one by one, and we become more and more light, and the Earth becomes filled with the light of consciousness cell by cell in her, and our, journey, until eventually all cells are light.

Let us now look at nature and all her life forms and expressions: are they not vehicles of consciousness too? Yes, they are, but in a different way. Nature and all her creatures are infused with cosmic intent via the angels, who step it down through their beings, from huge to tiny, to bring that energy and resonance into the etheric level at its deepest. That resonance is the nourishing blueprint in which nature lives, and evolves.

This is a form of consciousness, but not in an individuated way. The consciousness is created by the intent held by angelic focus, within the milieu of matter that is theirs to hold. In a way, it is like a direct one-to-one type of consciousness, where its direct infusion does not require personal choice, it simply is. Much of nature is like this: it holds and resonates with the level of light it is given, and lives in that resonance within the body of Earth. For example, majestic trees hold a particular resonance, and many humans feel this. They have not chosen to become this resonance of conscious expression, they simply are that, and bring great wisdom into the ethers of Earth through their presence. This is another reason it is so important to let the great trees be, for their impact on our world is far greater than their physical beautify and ecological value alone.

Much of nature is filled with small creatures and plants which play their role collectively, enabling a multiplicity of energy infusions to flow directly into the Earth, and the world we live in and interact with.

Some humans who evolved upon this Earth started as beings held within the angelic flow of nature, then evolved to a point where they could develop an individual soul and start upon the path of choice and individuated consciousness on the human journey. There are many animals who progressed upon this path, but many millions of years ago the pathway to transfer from a nature-infused being to an individual soul-infused being was closed. This was done to enable the overall vibration of humanity to be raised more quickly, in order to bring that particular consciousness of a higher vibration into the body of Earth, to meet the needs of her evolutionary path. The many highly evolved animals continued to evolve, and although still largely under the guidance of the angelic streams of consciousness flowing into nature, many of the Greater Hearts also have special relationships with certain animal species, and share their love with them. Many of these animals share their love and wisdom with us, when we let ourselves hear and respect them.

This has been the journey of evolution for many millennia. But now, the evolutionary imperative is moving into a different phase, the phase of heart consciousness. Heart consciousness is radically different from the consciousness of mind and feelings, because it cannot be contained to the human form. Heart creates flow. Heart consciousness creates flow. Your physical heart enables flow throughout your physical body. Your spiritual heart creates flow through you to the Earth: from your soul to you, to Earth, and back through the Ocean of Love (Earth's emotional self), wherein your soul dwells. Hence why we also come to such a fascinating time in Earth's and humanity's evolutionary journey, for now the angelic beings are becoming integrally involved in human evolution, not just in nature.

There have always been points of contact between angels and humans in time and place, but these have been within the evolutionary choice and development of the individuals concerned. Many great composers, for example, have been able to align with and infuse angelic resonance directly into their music, and this is one reason why many have struggled to keep balanced, for the intensity of that flow is very difficult for the nervous system to absorb. However, these interactions were for a particular purpose, and not generally part of the infusion of consciousness of the heart.

That is what we come to now, in our human and earthly journeys: the awakening of heart consciousness. The consciousness of mind and feelings are still built of form, and contained, even though they are our vehicle for interacting with, and creating in our world.

In the awakening heart consciousness, you feel yourself as not only a being of form, but as part of the living flow that nourishes you, Earth, nature and all. Earth consciousness arises, and we certainly need this, so that we care for her properly.

As more and more of Earth's human cells open to this flow, then the great evolutionary angels are able to pour more of their loving, intentful flow into the Earth, and more light infuses all life. Of course, it is also that Earth has called for this journey, and thus these angels are seeking those human hearts that open to this flow, and this creates pressure for humanity to choose and take this next step on the evolutionary journey.

In this evolution of heart consciousness, both the Greater Hearts and the Great Angels are involved in this way. The Greater Hearts hold their resonance of consciousness in the earthly and human worlds of being, to stimulate awakening, conscience and growth on the evolutionary path. Then as soon as there is co-resonance all the way from soul to human heart, whatever the qualities or wavelengths, the Great Angels enable their loving light to flow, bringing a livingness and force to those qualities that can magnify their effect in our human world.

In this time of Great Change, evolutionary opportunity, need and choice are highlighted. The Earth's heart is seeking and seeing greater inflow, to bring more living light to her being and all in her care, and to energise her whole being with more radiance and love. We, humans, are the conscious link between the worlds of light and her physical self, and become those channels of greater light every time we open our hearts to her care, through whatever calling is ours to give to.

Embrace the Earth with love in your consciousness, connect to your heart with choice, and you can step into this flow to help this positive change awaken through peace and realisation, not calamity and destruction. The flow is coming, and cannot be held back because of the few remaining who have conscious choice but continue to say no, dragging their nations, their races, their organisations and followers into obstruction and repression of evolution's great grace of life itself.

Angelic Flow & Divine Mother

For the flow of Cosmic Love to move through Earth, which is her choice and dharma, the substances of flow within her conscious ring-pass-not need to resonate and move.

Just as with a human, and all life capable of consciousness, flow can occur through emotional substance, and physical liquid. Both have the ability to flow, given direction and impulse. The substance of mind does not flow, it is like air in the physical world: able to vibrate with light, but not coherent enough within itself to become a flow. Gusts and breezes, yes, but not a singly-directed, coherent flow, which is what is needed to enable the expression of the living force of Cosmic Love, earthly love, human love.

This is anathema to what the human mind has created as the path to selfdom, self-realisation, power and greatness – which is the light of mind. This is surely needed, for it enables a coherence and resonance to be contained in the human self. The mind, when illumined to a certain degree, and cleared of rigid defences and limitations, can become a reference for conscious choice. It can hold sufficient reflections and vibrations of human and soul light that it aids conscience. But it cannot be the vehicle of flow that the human consciousness needs to become in this next stage of our, and Earth's, evolutionary journey to enable the flow of heart.

This idea of mind as the saviour and path forward for humanity needs to change, so that we see mind as a tool not a destination, as an aid, not our spiritual destiny.

The activation of angels in relation to humanity is part of this evolutionary shift, for they are beings of flow. They aid in the expression and movement of Earth's flow in her physical self, through her ethers and nature, and work collaboratively with the Greater Hearts to enable the flow of love and consciousness in her astral self, the Ocean of Love wherein our souls dwell and evolve.

As the need for the expression of Cosmic Heart grows (an evolutionary fact), the need for humanity to fulfil its role in flowing with and expressing this movement of conscious love and intention also grows. Thus, the pressure on humanity today. The inflow of Cosmic Love is happening. Earth is absorbing some directly into her body through angelic actions, and through her own heart consciousness held and guided by the Lady Kumara responsible in this Age of Heart unfoldment. But for heart consciousness to evolve in Earth's physical consciousness – not just in her body – we, humanity, must engage and create it. We are the vehicles of her fullness of physical consciousness. It is just like our own conscious journey: we become human with the impulse of the divine spark engaging in, and creating flow through, our physical hearts, and thus we are alive. Yet we are not conscious within the realms in which we live – the astral, mental and physical levels embodied by our physical consciousness – until we learn and develop this capacity to blend and express our spiritual intent with this medium.

This creates the powerful conjunction of human and earthly evolution of the heart: we must immerse in the expression and creative intent of this life force of heart, the heart of the Earth, and our inner heart aligned with our soul, here in the physical world. We are a conscious expression of Earth's physical life force, and we are the destination of love's flow from our souls into our physical embodiment. This is the brilliant design of the heart's unfoldment, created at the beginning of time in our universe, and here upon Earth it is coming to the fullness of its expression.

Why the angelic flows in and through the ethers of the Earth and all her worlds of nature cannot fulfil this is because this consciousness is not actually physical. Humans are the beings capable of self-consciousness in the physical world, who can align individually with, and express, their soul's intent, and thus the Earth's loving intent from her Ocean of Love.

Thus we have this conjunction of evolutionary need, and the pressure is created within humanity to enable the flow of heart. Angels are here to assist, but every step relies upon human choice to enable, and to flow with, that love of the heart's flow.

This pressure is most manifest in the emotional self, for this is our vehicle of flow of higher consciousness. It has ripple effects through our minds, and through our physical bodies, because we are one being, but it is in the emotions where the choice must manifest – but gently.

As with any flow, if you let it build to a torrent, it will destroy much of what it flows through, and this creates great challenge. Yet to stop it flowing altogether is to stop the flow of life, for we live to evolve, and this is our evolutionary path. These can both be seen in the challenge upon Earth today.

The angels assist by holding and guiding some of that flow for and with us. Our task is to purify our emotional selves such that the flow can move through us, and be consciously imbued with our intent, and thus manifest our little bit of cosmic heartflow all the way down into Earth's physical body and consciousness.

On our path of evolution, we learn the flow of astral matter through the expression of feelings, mostly through interacting with the world we live in, and striving to understand the influences around us. We learn to express and receive astral flows in relationship with each other. We also learn to express these flows through creativity, whether artistic, scientific, or everything in between. Many indigenous peoples have understood and worked with loving flows to Earth, but the majority of humanity does not hold this knowledge or capacity, even though it has long been the focus of the angels to help us bring loving flow through to the Earth.

The energy embrace of the Divine Mother is a beneficial way to learn how to let this flow through. We all have, somewhere in our being, an ability to relate to mother's love, for even in the most unconscious of human mothers, the creative unfoldment that enables a baby to grow is infused with love, and many angels are involved. And Earth is our mother, the physical nourisher of our human lives.

However you connect to the Divine Mother, find your way to this alignment, whether through deities we have come to know through the past – Lady Mary, Quan Yin, White Tara as a few examples – or directly through your love for Earth. In this connection and alignment, seek to purify yourself, so that you can become a being of greater loving flows. As you align your choices and actions, then more and more flow will move through you, nourishing you and the Earth. The many angels that work with the great Mother deities, and with Earth herself, will flock to you and infuse you with the knowing and guidance you need.

At this time upon Earth, we see much expression of hatred, separatism, and desire to destroy – whether expressed individually, racially, politically or nationally. This is exacerbated by the pressure to enable more flow of love, for if you do not purify, then the pressure creates dams and torrents, which express as unregulated and destructive forces.

Ours is the path of choice, to align with and enable loving flow to purify, not destroy, and it starts with our own conscious acceptance of, and alignment with, the greater path and flow of heart that is ours upon which to step forward.

The Great Change: Form to Flow

In the loving embrace that is evolution's guidance for all life on Earth, we are in one of the greatest transitions upon that journey: from form, to flow.

As human beings (along with many other creatures and expressions of life), we have been held and guided by the impulse to build form: to build bodies, to build homes, to build societies, to build knowledge, etc. Consciousness needed a form in which to anchor, and through which to interact in this dense, physical world. But let us not forget that the expression of life on this planet is upon the singular path of becoming conscious, so that the resonance of spirit's love can reverberate within this physical sphere we call Earth. This was Earth's choice long ago, for consciousness is the path of becoming a planet of heart; this was her commitment to Cosmic Heart, and her response to the universal need for the physical heart's expression in the greater cosmic life.

Why consciousness is needed to enable the evolution of heart is because heart is neither just a presence in form, nor just a flow – but a unique merging of the two. The form is not only the vehicle of the flow, but it holds the intention that creates and guides that flow. The flow is not just an expression of substance in movement, but an expression of that intention, imbued with both purpose and the life force that nourishes it.

We have many elements of beingness involved. You cannot create life with a pump alone. You cannot nourish life with flow alone. And these two primary elements need consciousness to weave their various elements together, because consciousness is a spiritually magnetic substance that enables coherence, whether that be of intention, of form, of flow, of life force, or of all elements together.

In the early stages of the human journey, coherence, and thus consciousness, is held by the soul, which infuses light and intention into the human heart. That soul is in turn held and guided by the resonance, and thus inherent wholeness and purpose, of the part of Earth's Ocean of Love wherein it exists, in the embrace of one of the Greater Hearts. Thus, the coherence of life purpose and life force is imbued into the spiritual vitality of the human heart, and the bridge of consciousness is awakened between soul and human expression. As evolution proceeds, both the human self and the soul learn to cohere and co-resonate more and more, in knowledge, experience, love and care, and consciousness becomes more present not only spiritually, but emerging into the human personality itself.

We have walked a long path of building on many levels. The flow has always been there to enable and sustain life, but it has not been the focus of evolution's intention. We have received flow from Earth's Ocean of Love via our soul to incarnate, and that flow is then withdrawn when we are called back to soul.

Now, we move to an era where the flow is the primary focus of evolution's intention. Collectively, as humanity, we have built all the form that is needed, of human and societal expression, to enable heart's flow to now express as a creative force of consciousness.

Thus, the major shift, from the evolutionary emphasis on building, to the intentful push to work with flow. The conscious work with flow is essential in order for the heart of the Earth to become that vehicle of conscious intention it is to be, enabling Cosmic Love to circulate through her, to infuse and radiate from her being, and be that extraordinary grace of Cosmic Heart in living expression in the physical level of our universe. This is her dharma, our dharma, and the path we are on.

As we shift from the intentful guidance of building, to that of flow, another major shift is occurring: that from what we call 'masculine', to the feminine expression of cosmic intent. The Greater Hearts holding the primary evolutionary intent through the last eons of the building phase of human and earthly conscious development have guided with a masculine expression. As we move into this new phase, it will be held and guided by the feminine.

The masculine element, in terms of consciousness and intent, has little to do with the manifestation as man or woman or in-between in our human world. Rather, this masculine element expresses as a piercing, one-pointed force, needed to bring spirit's love all the way down into the dense physical levels of our world, there to build the form in which that love can reside. Truthfully, you can look at our world today and wonder where that love is. But it is there, despite all the hatred, anger, separatism, violence and ignorant destruction going on. It is there, built into the form of who we are collectively as humanity.

This must always be remembered, that although we walk an individual evolutionary path as human beings, our efforts are not just measured individually, but collectively, and it is the collective expression and reverberation of consciousness and conscious choice upon which the great transition of evolutionary expression is based. It is only the few who transgress, and yes, they cause great harm, but that can change quickly – for they are but a few. The intention of the many is gaining global coherence, and through that, the great infusion of cosmic intention can build more and more loving presence. This is not based on the number in humanity who resonate with this global coherence – but the amount of consciousness applied. Some have developed much consciousness, many have some consciousness, even more have only glimmers of consciousness, just as it is in any family with younger and older siblings. The younger are guided by the older, and thus the overall consciousness of humanity can enable the expression of divine intention.

Now we move to the expression of cosmic intent through flow. Now the feminine expression of love shall become a greater and greater influence in the unfoldment and creation of consciousness – so that we individually, humanity collectively, and Earth herself, can become that conscious coherence of intentful, building force combined with loving flow, that is heart.

Thus, the major shift. Thus, the Great Change.

Again, this spiritual expression has no concrete alignment with whether you are a man, a woman, or do not identify in a binary way. This is about how you work with your conscious intent. How you create with the love that infuses your heart, what you envision as the future Earth and what you choose to enact with your conscious choice.

There has already been a transition among the Greater Hearts, and there will be more, as those more trained in the wielding of flow as an evolutionary guide take on more responsibilities. They have always been there, just less prominent to our spiritual gaze, for evolution's intentful force has not called upon them. There is also a transition in process to the newly emerging Kumara, who embodies and expresses the feminine principle of flow into the whole body of the Earth.

Within humanity there will be many more leaders emerging who understand the embracing, intentful purpose of flow. Many more women, but also men and others who uphold this conscious expression, will step forward as guides and mentors of people and of nations. This is already seen, even though the conscious understanding of how to work with flow is only beginning to emerge.

If you want to aid this transition, find your flow. This you can experience and understand within your own heart, where your own soul guides and infuses you, and naturally enables this greater infusion of the feminine principle unfolding within Earth's sphere, within the embrace of the Greater Hearts, and within the guiding love of Cosmos herself.

This is the emerging era of flow – find your certainty in that.

Become Living Light

In the crushing cascade of love, I come. The force of good, will to good, heart awakening, materialism denying, force of nature.

For my force flows with life, I am life force, that which gives and takes life, that which gives and nurtures the karmic journey; that which gives, tones, refines the note of my presence in physical Earth life.

Life. I am that.

The force that brooks no defiance, else lifeless you become. Like the many, as good as zombies, death-like aggregations of matter, held in shape by desires and forces of lower emotions, bound into the life's blood of Earth by the force of personal will, driven by need, fear or ignorance.

But, I am life. The force that cascades into those who seek. The force that enlivens those with bright eyes. The love that embraces those who stand steady with hope.

No matter if you waiver, in the onslaught of earthly challenges, if you seek, I am there.

Love. Hope. Life force. The promise of future enlightenment. For all flows of life lead to the light, for they all come from the light, born of the light, evolved in the light, then called back to the light.

Yet ever the journey brings you into the fullness of the matter within which you incarnate. When you come from the light, you are that.

When you return to the light, you are light of a million colours and shades, nuanced, evolved, developed through experience and learning, to become not just light – but living light!

That is evolution. Otherwise, why move from light just to return to being light? No, as you evolve upon Earth, you enrich the light that you are, so that you become one who brings the benevolence, grace and blessing of what light becomes when expressed in our human and earthly world.

Become that, choose light, then my cascade shall enrich you, fill you, nourish you.

(please note, this was written as a direct communique, and 'I' does not refer to the author)

Responding to the Call of the Heart

Practices

Heart consciousness has a very different feeling and presence to the consciousness of mind and emotion with which we are familiar. Because of this, to find heart, to strengthen it in your life, you need to take your consciousness there regularly, to experience it and build it into the fabric of your knowing and being, and awaken it right down into your cells.

The following guided attunements will give you this experience, by taking you into your heart, while also engaging your mind and emotions to deepen and anchor this consciousness in your daily life and awareness.

These practices can help you bring the wisdom and healing of heart into your life, and help you find your way of responding to the call of the heart to create positive change in yourself and our world.

All practices are available as free audio downloads from
www.CalloftheHeart.net/practices

Meditations for Heart

Start in Your Heart

Awaken and develop your heart consciousness with this 6-minute practice that guides you into your deep inner heart, to experience your heart light, and centre your consciousness in a peaceful place.

Deep Heart Attunement

Go deeper into your heart, into your inner sanctuary of living light, to rest in that loving presence, seek insight into your life's questions and challenges, and open to the deep heart within you for contemplation and nourishment.

Meditations to Balance and Clear

Just as with your physical health, your inner self is impacted by your day-to-day life and choices. Taking an active path of spiritual development can also create stresses and strains, in the same way a new physical exercise program will for your physical body. For physical health we need a good physical diet and exercise, for our inner health we need good inner nourishment and exercise too.

These guided meditations bring a variety of qualities of light to balance and nourish your inner self, and clear and purify your inner bodies, to help you develop greater inner fitness and flexibility.

Flame Meditation

Sit within each of the eight flames of light to revitalise, clear and balance your inner being.

A great daily practice to bring greater harmony to your heart path. Regular practice helps you actively engage with your journey of consciousness and evolution of heart, and supports your balance and focus on the way.

Heart Flame Healing

Activate and immerse in the 3-fold flame of your heart, the flames of soul light deep within, and strengthen and balance their qualities of hope, purpose and love in your being.

These flames nourish our journey in the three dimensions of our human world. Purpose anchors us with meaning to the Earth, hope lifts our consciousness to seek the higher light, and love connects us to all other living beings around us. By sitting and absorbing the purity of these flames, you build their strength and clarity, giving healing, balance and wholeness to your consciousness.

Earth Healing Meditation

Bring your heart into the flow of living, loving light from the Master of Love Maitreya, to heal and nourish our living Earth. Earth healing is an essential practice on the path of heart.

We have a vital role within the loving embrace of our Earth, to choose the path of heart, and to help awaken and strengthen spiritual consciousness to empower peace and care for all, and dissipate harmful energies. This is our service on the journey of heart consciousness. Participate with friends to magnify the healing.

Deep Healing

Healing and care is needed when undertaking any program of exercise and transformation, whether physical or spiritual. Spiritual healing occurs through applying the right energy vibration to the patterns built within our inner self, helping them to loosen and transform, and become more free-flowing in our personal consciousness. At the same time, all deep healing can open doors to another layer of our being, and bring deeper challenges into our awareness. It is up to you to measure and balance all inner work, so that you can maintain balance in your day.

Hope Healing Meditation

Revitalise in the living light of hope in your whole being, to uplift and inspire your wellbeing and wholeness from deep within. This healing brings you deeply into the source of hope in your heart, increasing this quality throughout your consciousness and into every cell.

The golden light of hope is vital on life's journey, especially in times of challenge and change. It is the essential fire of consciousness that uplifts us, giving vision for the future and positivity in our day.

Yasodhara's Healing Embrace

Sink into Yasodhara's peace and grace and let the loving golden light of this great female Buddha nourish, comfort and heal you. Yasodhara is one of the great Mothers of the World, who works tirelessly to nourish and lift our consciousness, and give love to all who seek a path of heart. She is deeply connected to Earth's heart and is very actively involved in the evolution of our world. Her radiance is of beautiful rose and golden hues.

Renewal Guided Healing

Immerse in the healing, renewing flow of living light, to revitalise your cells and inner self, and gently strengthen that loving flow within.

This healing takes you to the inner Temple of Renewal, where you can immerse in the flowing living light, to heal and cleanse, and renew your inner resonance with soul and heart. Renewal is the journey of clearing, growing and evolving into your most radiant self. After immersing in the living light, experience the radiant grace of the Rainbow Tara who brings renewal into our world, and who blesses and heals all who take this journey.

Continue Your Journey

If you would like to explore what is offered in this book in greater breadth and depth, or read the latest teachings, you can browse and search the complete library on the website, and listen to the podcasts.

Any questions you have about these teachings or practices are welcome, please send them through the contact page on the website, or message through the Call of the Heart Now facebook page.

www.facebook.com/CalloftheHeartNow

www.CalloftheHeart.net

Glossary

Age of the Heart

The evolutionary period we have now entered that will see great unfoldment of heart consciousness in humanity and the Earth. Also known as the Age of Aquarius, which is defined astrologically as the next period of approximately 2150 years. There are various opinions about when it is beginning exactly, but its influence has been acknowledged since late last century.

Akashic record

An inner record of deeds and actions for all beings on Earth; the balance sheet that guides our karmic patterns so that we heal our past, and learn for our future.

Angel

Angels are beings of light and flow, and an integral part of the heart flow from Cosmos to Earth, bringing that living light to nourish our planet. They are especially involved in building and nourishing nature. They range from great cosmic beings, to the smallest angel guiding the growth and development of flowers. They radiate streams of light which can look like wings. Angels are quite different in energy structure to human beings. While they may come to guide humans from the inner levels, they should not be confused with most inner guides who are usually human beings not currently incarnating. Angels are sometimes called devas, a Sanskrit name for shining one, due to their deep radiance of living light.

Asala

A significant spiritual festival held on the full moon of Gemini, where humanity's call for light and love brings forth the blessing of Maitreya, the current Bodhisattva of Earth, to infuse Earth and all life with greater healing, consciousness and alignment with the unfolding plan of evolution.

Asala is the third in a sequence of three very important spiritual festivals held every year, commencing with the festival of the Rising Light at the full moon of Aries, followed by the festival of Buddha at Wesak, on the full moon of Taurus.
See also Wesak

Glossary

Astral

The vibrational level where our emotions move, flow and express. It is finer than the physical level, yet it permeates our physical body, enabling us to feel and interpret emotional energy into expression in our day-to-day lives. An evolved and finely-vibrating astral body can be very radiant and beautiful, but it should not be confused with the soul, which is of a much finer vibration.

Atlantis

A continent that was home to the Atlantean civilisation, where the focus of human attainment was development of the consciousness of emotion. Due to misuse of power and selfish abuse of the astral (emotional) forces, the continent sank through a series of floods many millennia ago. Many of the souls who incarnated on Atlantis continue to incarnate on Earth to evolve their consciousness further.

Aura

The energy field made up of the finer vibrations of our human self: our etheric vitality, astral (emotional) self, and mental body. These vibrations extend through and beyond the physical body, and often appear as an egg-shaped radiance of various colours. The colours indicate qualities learned, and their clarity and brightness indicate their strength and whether they need cleansing and refinement. All living beings have an aura, including animals, plants and our planet.

Board of Karma

A group of Greater Hearts and assistants on the inner levels, who review and guide the implementation of lessons, opportunities and limitations (that is, karma) in any one life for individuals, as well as for nations, races and other groups of consciousness.

Bodhisattva

A Bodhisattva is a highly evolved Greater Heart who has taken on the role of nourishing and guiding the spiritual evolution of Earth and all life. The Bodhisattva is a great teacher. He or she radiates through every spiritual, religious or life pathway that brings you to the light.

Currently, the Master Maitreya fulfils the role of Bodhisattva within the Earth's ring-pass-not, and seeks to inspire every heart to align with the evolutionary journey of heart, in collaboration with all other Greater Hearts, Buddhas and Kumaras. Maitreya worked specifically with the Greater Heart

Jesus, to infuse his work and bring the path of love into humanity's consciousness in this physical world.

The Bodhisattva is also known as the Christ, but should not be confused with Jesus and his role 2000 years ago, nor limited to the religion of Christianity that evolved from the inspiration of that life.

The Bodhisattva, or Christ, is an inspirational, teaching role for all life on Earth. While the role has been held by a masculine expression these last 2000 years, it will be held by a female expression in the coming era, to support the next phase of conscious evolution.

See also Maitreya

Buddha

A Buddha is a Greater Heart who has evolved to the very high consciousness where he or she holds the whole Earth in light, and guides and energises that light to nourish the consciousness of every being on every level, whatever evolutionary and spiritual path they follow.

The current Buddha of Earth is Gautama, who incarnated 2500 years ago to become the Buddha in his physical self, and thus incarnate that light into the physical body of the Earth. Through this incarnation, Buddhism evolved and continues to express the Buddha light in many ways. However, the role of the Buddha of Earth should not be limited to that physical life of Gautama Buddha and the pathway of Buddhism that followed.

The emerging female Buddha of our current age is Lady Yasodhara, who will incarnate with Maitreya in 500 years. Together they will bring the next vibration of light into Earth's body.

See also Yasodhara

Chakra

Chakra is Sanskrit for wheel, and refers to the vortices of energy in our inner bodies (etheric, astral, mental) that connect our inner perceptions and our physical senses. When purified in an evolved being, they can enable fine vibrational inputs from higher realms. However, when undeveloped or not purified, they can be unfiltered doorways to the worlds of lower energy amalgamations and the illogical contortions of reason and belief created by mischievous spirits or even by dark entities who work against evolution's grace. This is why not all intuitive perceptions are true and of a higher light. Note that the heart chakra is not the same as the heart spoken of in this book.

Glossary

Chela
A student of a spiritual teacher.

Christ
See Bodhisattva

Cosmic Heart
The heart of our living Cosmos, pulsing love, living light and evolutionary intent out into the realms within which our Solar System and Earth are evolving. In many traditions new and ancient, Sirius is known as the Cosmic Heart.

Cosmos
The living body of vitality and evolutionary intent embracing a number of star systems and planets, within which our Solar system and Earth are evolving.

Dharma
Dharma is the path of service that aligns you with your evolutionary journey, and holds the lessons and blessings you accepted before incarnating. It is your deep, inner life-purpose. Fulfilling your dharma enables you to balance your karma, to free you from limitations and awaken your gifts to evolve further on your evolutionary path.

Elemental
Elementals are entities on the involutionary arc of life, that is, on the path descending into physical incarnation. They are focussed downward into matter and help us to incarnate, but then they may hold us back when we seek to evolve into more light. Family elementals anchor the patterns of the family tree, enabling inheritance of family traits both good and challenging.

Etheric
The etheric is a level of our inner being that is a finer in vibration than our physical self, but more dense in vibration than the emotional body. It is the primary conduit through which our prana / vitality / chi is absorbed and circulated through our physical body. It can be replenished by the vitality that comes from the Sun, or certain trees (mainly eucalyptus and pine trees) and certain energised places in nature. The etheric body holds the blueprint upon which the physical body is built, and is important in healing.

Evolution

The journey of life to become and express higher purpose within the stream of the conscious intent of Cosmos. All life is evolving, whether plant, animal, human, angelic, planetary, solar or cosmic.

Great Angels

Highly evolved angelic beings who have a conscious role in distributing the evolutionary flows of living light to guide nature, Earth and humanity.

Great Change

The period we are in now, where the intent of evolution is guiding the change from the consciousness of mind and emotion, anchored in the personal self, to the consciousness of heart, opening to the wisdom of soul.

Greater Hearts

Beings of great consciousness who embody and guide the evolutionary flows of light and love to Earth, angels and humanity. Collectively, they embody and guide the higher consciousness of Earth and humanity, and bring that light into human perception through the many pathways of teaching and life experience that they nourish. They hold all human souls in their embrace, and infuse them with love and purpose. Many have walked the path of human life on Earth and have become known, for example, Jesus, Lady Mary, Quan Yin, Gautama, Yasodhara, the Count of Saint Germain. Often referred to as 'Masters', they work together for the good of Earth and all life.

Group Soul

A group soul is one that expresses through a number of incarnations at the same time. The collective experience is gathered into one soul and shared with all future incarnations. Animals have group souls, created by Earth's intent to support the diversity of her expression. More developed animals have less incarnations for each soul, thus you see greater light and wisdom in their eyes and through their engagement with the world.

In this time of great change, a form of group soul is emerging for humanity. Individual souls will come together and blend their energies into a collective wisdom, built upon all the lessons learned individually. Each soul still maintains its individual evolutionary journey through its own human incarnation; however, each soul now has access to the collective wisdom of the soul group. This will speed up the conscious development in humanity, because it enables each individual soul to develop greater wisdom without having to take the longer journey of learning only through their own experience. This will become more and more common as the evolutionary push to increase human consciousness gathers pace.

Heart

Heart is where the soul's intent resonates within a being.

In humans, it is a place within your being and consciousness, near your physical heart. It is not the chakra, but the deep anchor point of your soul within you, a place of deep stillness and energised presence. It is your source of life-force, love and true intuition, where you align with and become part of the global change of consciousness that is happening in our world. Through your heart your soul intent stimulates your personal purpose, igniting the spark of life that sustains and nourishes you throughout life. Heart holds the keynotes for your evolutionary journey of consciousness.

Using meditation practices that help you get in touch with your heart resonance can help you open to that wisdom and purpose. For example, the *Deep Heart Attunement* (a free guided meditation available to download, see page 265), or see all meditations in *Responding to the Call of the Heart* (page 264).

Incarnation

When a higher intent, such as from spirit or soul, enters into a lower level of vibration, and gathers and energises matter and substance to create an embodiment on that level. For example, a human being is an incarnation of soul in our physical world to take the human journey; an angelic being embodies on the inner levels of Earth to take their journey and manifest their intent there.

Inner bodies

The inner bodies are the more finely-vibrating elements of our physical embodiment, and include our etheric body, the body of vitality; the astral body, the vibrations of emotion; and the mental body, which infuses our thinking. Our inner bodies and physical self form our personality, the vehicle of conscious evolution in our physical world. Our inner bodies form the aura, which appears most commonly as an egg-shaped form of various colours around the physical self.

See also Personality

Involution

The path of descent from spirit into matter, as part of the journey of conscious becoming. Humanity has mostly finished this phase, but it still exerts a pull to the material in many people's consciousness.

Jesus

One of the most well-known of the Greater Hearts, from his incarnation 2000 years ago when he worked closely with the Bodhisattva Maitreya to embody the path of love upon Earth, and bring humanity into greater contact with that light. He continues to work for Earth and all life, beyond the paradigms and structures of the human religion of Christianity. Jesus worked closely with Muhammad, to infuse his teachings with the same light of love.
See also Bodhisattva

Karma

Karma balances our past with our future by giving the grace and opportunities to awaken new realisations and skills so that we can become greater beings of light and love; and/or by giving the limitations that pressure us to change and heal patterns from the past that have stopped our conscious journey or caused harm.

Kumara

A Kumara is a spiritual being with cosmic connection and intent. A Kumara helps bring evolutionary force to the whole being of the Earth, embracing all life with that intent, aiding the evolution of consciousness.

The Last Kumara refers to the last of the Kumaras who came to Earth from other planetary spheres, and who is becoming one with the Earth for this next major evolutionary step into the consciousness of heart. Embodying the major inflow of feminine energy for this coming evolutionary change, she is also called the Lady Kumara.

Law of Attraction

The characteristic of our universe that is the embodiment of love. It is the attraction between elements, whether particles of matter, or beings of consciousness, and all in between. Without the Law of Attraction, we would have no force of gravity pulling us to Earth, no pull of light calling us to spirit, and no magnetism of love drawing us to each other.

Glossary

Logos

Logos is the name given to the being embodying greater planetary and cosmic life; for example, the Planetary Logos embodies in our Earth; the Solar Logos is embodied in the Sun and our Solar system.

Maitreya

Maitreya is a being of enormous consciousness, a Greater Heart who currently holds the role of Bodhisattva, the great teacher of all. He radiates love and light into the world and into every heart.

He has been actively involved in stimulating conscious awakening through the many spiritual pathways available on Earth, bringing love and wisdom to all who seek. He works with all the Greater Hearts to awaken souls and consciousness, irrespective of religion or spirituality. He overshadowed Jesus when he walked on Earth as Jesus Christ, and it is prophesied he will incarnate in around 500 years to become the next Buddha of Earth, stimulating another great awakening of light and heart in our world. The preparation for his incarnation has already commenced, and many feel his presence as his heart flow descends through the Mother of Light all over the world. He has a physical presence in the Himalayas, from where he sends out blessings to the Earth every sunrise and sunset.

Mental level

The mental level of vibration of mind. Note that thoughts are often expressions of emotions and hence have an emotional vibration, and are not of the mental level.
See also Inner bodies

Mineral family

The level of evolutionary life that is at the beginning of the ascending arc back to spirit, where the focus is on development of consciousness in dense physical matter. Higher forms of the mineral family are the gems, in which purified crystalline structures are created, and precious minerals that hold a higher resonance and form through the Law of Attraction.

Ocean of Love

A place of loving light that is the astral level of Earth's consciousness, and the soul level of humanity's consciousness. Greater Hearts and human souls reside in this Ocean, creating the light of Earth and stimulating the evolution of consciousness in our world.

Personality

The vehicle of our conscious journey in this physical world, made up of our physical-etheric, astral, and mental bodies. After many lives of development, the bodies of the personality become more and more integrated, giving the personality strength of character and many skills. The personality is our vehicle on Earth through which our soul can resonate.
See also Inner bodies

Planetary Logos

The Planetary Logos is the great being who embraces and holds our planet as she takes her own journey of conscious unfoldment, bringing higher consciousness and wisdom to help her on her journey. The Planetary Logos receives the inflow and intent of Cosmic Love from Cosmic Heart, and works with the Buddha and Bodhisattva in their planetary roles to infuse Earth and all life with that evolutionary intent and wisdom.

Ring-pass-not

The ring-pass-not of Earth is the edge of her conscious envelope, within which her life evolves. It is held and protected by the Planetary Logos and other Greater Hearts. The ring-pass-not ensures that forces not interested in the evolution of light and love do not enter, and that the flow of loving light from Cosmic Heart is allowed in at the right pace for the evolutionary journey to take place. Too much light would create change too rapidly and conscious evolution would not occur, matter would simply be infused with light rather than creating and knowing light.

Sanat Kumara

The current Kumara holding Earth in Cosmic Love and conscious intent.
See also Kumara

Seed atom

The atom which contains the blueprint for our personality incarnation; the pattern from which our physical and inner bodies are built and develop during gestation and throughout life. There are seed atoms for the physical, astral and mental levels; they contain the essence of patterns to be realised in each life, according to our karma.

Sirius

Sirius is the central Sun of our Cosmos. It is a great centre of Cosmic Heart that pours love into our Solar System and especially into Earth in this period of transition to the Age of the Heart. The Greater Hearts on Earth absorb the intention and loving light from Sirius, to aid the unfoldment of life and consciousness in alignment with cosmic purpose.

Solar Logos

The Solar Logos is the being of consciousness that embraces our entire solar system and its evolving life, absorbing and infusing all with cosmic intent.

Soul

The soul is the part of our human existence that lives from life to life, gathering the wisdom and lessons of each life, and sending forth the spark of light for each new incarnation. The soul resides in Earth's Ocean of Love, and is within the embrace of one of the Greater Hearts who aid us on our journey of consciousness. Soul is of a very fine vibration and not easily perceived in our human consciousness, until we gain enough wisdom and refine our inner bodies sufficiently for that very fine resonance to be picked up. However, the light of soul is always radiant in our hearts, for that is what keeps us alive. Using meditation practices that help you get in touch with your heart resonance builds your capacity to sense the light of heart and soul. For example, the *Deep Heart Attunement* (a free guided meditation available to download, see page 265), or see all meditations in *Responding to the Call of the Heart* (page 264).

Spirit

Spirit is the spark of intent that initiates and gives direction to the conscious journey through soul and human incarnation. It is of a higher vibration than soul.

Sun

The Sun is not only a great physical entity at the centre of our solar system, but also a living consciousness infusing our world with living light and vitality, and energising all life with the vision, love and will to evolve.

Venus

Venus is a planetary being that has evolved further on the path of consciousness than Earth. Many Kumaras and Greater Hearts on Earth have come from Venus, bringing their wisdom and experience to aid Earth's journey.

Wesak

Wesak is a festival celebrating the life and ongoing blessings of the male and female Buddhas who continue to aid life and consciousness on Earth. It is an opportunity for humanity to sound a collective call of the heart for light and love to heal our world, as the Buddhas open the pathways of resonance that enable more light to be given and received. This festival occurs every year on the full moon of Taurus, with many rituals and celebrations held the world over in the Buddhist tradition. There is also a significant ceremony held with Greater Hearts and other beings of light in a hidden location in the Himalayas, to enable the major down-flow of golden light and consciousness that the Buddhas bring to humanity to touch our physical world each year.

Wesak is the second in a sequence of three very important spiritual festivals held every year, commencing with the festival of the Rising Light at the full moon of Aries, and concluding with the festival of Asala on the full moon of Gemini.
See also Asala

Yasodhara

One of the Mothers of Light nourishing conscious change in our current era. She has a deep presence in the Earth's heart, and a significant role in helping Cosmic Love to express consciously through the Earth and radiate out into the universe. She is very close to humanity and Earth, and her rose and golden radiance infuses all who seek her healing. She was Gautama Buddha's partner 2500 years ago, helping incarnate the Buddha light into the Earth.
See also Buddha

Index

Entries in **bold** indicate a note title; in ***bold italic*** indicate a description.

A

Age of the Heart 38, 87, 117, 148, 180
Akashic records 157
angelic family 12, 26, 207, 210, 250
angelic flow 13, 48, ***254–255***
    of nature 252
angelic guides 76, 216
angelic intent ***63–65***
angels 5–6, 8–9, 13–14, 16–18, 27–29, 32–34, 38–42, 47, 53, 59, 64–65, 75, 77, 122, 155, 170, 196, 204, 207, 209, 216, 229, 236, 240, 243, 248, 250–252, 254, 256
    bridge 27
    Earth angels 34
    evolutionary angels 253
    Great Angels 3, 232, 241, 253
    guardian angels 59, 75
    human angel 107
    of nature 245
    work with 41
animals 5, 10, 75, 108, 116, 122, 170, 230, 252
    and angels 33, 59, 252
    and Greater Hearts 252
    eating 60
    evolution 58
    group soul 5, 34, 207
    relationship with humans 60
ascension 96, 118
ascension process 117
astral 16, 41, 44, 63, 67, 99, 101–102, 109, 112–115, 123, 139–140, 142, 148, 163, 190, 196–197, 200, 221, 255–256. See Also emotion
astral body 143
    of Earth 6, 139
astral consciousness 250, 255
astral manipulation 124
astral self 141
Atlantis 11, 157, 159

B

Board of Karma 148, 199
Buddha 54, 153, 165, 191–192, 194, 230–232, 234, 236, 242
    Buddha light 193
    Buddha of Earth 231
    Gautama Buddha 190–192

C

call of your heart **235**, 239
chakras 100
    [description] 177
    & higher consciousness 177
Christ 153, 190–192, 194, 230–232, 234
    Cosmic Christ 193
conscience 68, 121, 124, 132–133, 143, 180, 183, 194, 201, 207, 221, 253
    & consciousness 211
    & discernment 104
    & guilt 150
    emotional 21, 178
    framework for 180
    global 184, 215
    soul 104
    voice of 69–70, 77
    without 37, 105
conscience of heart 38, 178
conscience of mind 68, 105, 254
conscious choice 178, 221, 260
    & Cosmic Heart 64
    & evolution **12**, 14, 139, 259
    & flow 77, 254
    & mind 254
    & nature 240
    & positive change 158
    & soul 83, 167

& the call of your heart 239
& the Great Change 166
& young souls 216
of plants and animals 122
consciousness [description] 67, 155
consciousness of heart 68, 175
consciousness, bridge of 210–212, 226, 258
consciousness, higher 21, 43, 48, 85–86, 118, 133, 177, 223, 233, 249, 256
Cosmic Heart 1–2, 14, 64–65, 75, 122, 155, 174, 179, 207, 217, 236, 244, 250, 255
  & angels 27, 65
  & Buddha 231–232
  & Earth 65, 258–259
  & Greater Hearts 224, 234, 236, 248–249
  & Planetary Logos 236
  call of 64
  pulse of 1, 12, 75, 78, 118
cosmic heartbeat 17–18
cosmic heartflow 13, 63, 187, 216, 227, 231, 234, 237, 248, 256
cosmic intent 15–16, 18–19, 43–44, 47–48, 57–58, 110–111, 139, 156, 172, 175, 195, 212, 224, 227, 247
  & angels 34, 47, 250–251
  & Cosmic Love 217
  & Earth 1, 47, 75, 85, 247
  & Greater Hearts 11, 223, 229, 233, 236, 247
  & humans 109, 197
  & Kumaras 247
  & planetary evolution 139, 210
  feminine expression of 259
  flow of 46
  in soul 58, 203
  is love 52
  perception of 46
  through flow 260
Cosmos 5, 9, 16–17, 19, 24, 46, 138, 153, 156, 172
  & consciousness 9, 155
  & Cosmic Heart 1, 64
  & Earth 10, 15, 110, 121, 140, 155, 210, 232

& evolution 12
& Greater Hearts 233
& Ocean of Love 10–11
blood of 119
flow & angels 13, 16
flow of 12, 32, 229
heartbeat of 10
light of 230
love of 22, 26, 80, 95, 112, 119, 122, 226, 250, 261

D

devotion 123
  higher intent 68
  path 100, 217
  types 91, 249
devotional practices & heart 177
dharma 126, 130, 160, 229
  of Earth 1, 254, 259
  of nature 171
  of planets 12
  of Sirius 9
  spiritual 179
  wheel of 161
discernment
  & belief 128
  & consciousness 183
  & emotion, feelings 82, 86, **89**, 125
  & evolution 22, 59
  & evolution with angels 42
  & facts 104
  & groups 147
  & harmlessness 124
  & heart 70, 78, 87–89, 93, 100, 126, 129, 182, 250
  & heart intuition **85**
  & higher truth **126**
  & intuition 89, 91, 127–128, 143
  & karma 57
  & knowledge 181, 183
  & soul 58
  & spiritual contact 182
  & spiritual practice 84, 93
  & wisdom 105
  between inner & outer 7
  between matter & love 22, 50, 96
  for peace 82
  how 7, 30, 44, 52, 70, 81, 83–84
  in flow 32, 41

Index

of justice & guilt 150
of mind 55, 57, 101, 104
with soul & Greater Heart 226
Divine Mother 254, 256

E

Earth health & trees 170
Earth heart 65, 122, 227
Earth school 224
Easter 193
elemental 200
emotion 73, 79, 187. *See Also* astral
  & conscience 21, 104, 178, 180
  & consciousness 68, 70, 90, 109, 183, 200, 213, 228
  & devotion 100
  & discernment 7, 86, 89, 91, 93
  & Earth 36, 38, 108, 171
  & evil 142, 144, 147, 225
  & heart 100, 114
  & intuition 30, 86, 92, 182
  & involution 132, 143, 149, 157
  & karma 57, 81
  & light 28
  & love 52, 54, 67, 93
  & materialism 124
  & mind 99, 102–104, 123, 146, 181, 201, 205
  & music 48
  & nature 119, 169
  & path 72, **98**, 129, 151
  & political power 113
  & soul 69, 99, 135, 137, 140, 155, 166, 186–187, 196, 201, 203–205, 209
  & truth 127
  & will 201
  & wisdom 104
  alignment 68
  building with 23, 128, 211
  changing 115
  colour of 141
  lower 22, 113
  mass of 112–113
  negative 41
  of humanity 98, 189
  purify 45
  structure of 99
  substance of 23, 90
  to awaken heart 67
emotional body of Earth 6, 139, 190, 192, 195, 218
emotional certainty 50, 93–94
emotional cults 126
emotional demands 98
emotional flow 41, 72–73, 82, 90, 92, 119, 188–190, 200–202, 254, 256
emotional language of vibration 91
emotional manipulation 113–114, 126. *See Also* astral manipulation
emotional motivation 37, 200
etheric
  body 119, 141–142, 152, 200
  body of Earth 170
  level 139–140, 171, 251
  seed 140
  self 151, 165
etheric vitality from trees 168
evil 144, 147, 150, 221–222, 225–226
  & greed 144
  & involution 143
  & knowledge 105
  & love 10
  differentiate from darkness 142
  of today 126, 159
evolutionary intent 12–13, 19, 48–49, 76, 78, 107, 109–110, 115, 242
  & angels 5, 33–34, 49
  & consciousness 208, 227
  & Greater Hearts 240, 242, 245, 247, 259
  & Kumaras 108, 157
  & love 52, 55, 227, 246
  & soul 63, 65, 162
  of Earth 85, 108, 119, 223, 225

F

flow of heart 114, 239–240
  & angels 236
  & choice 237, 256–257
  & mind 254
forgiveness 4, 129, 143

G

gravity 109, 124, 155

& soul 130
is love 53
of spirit 175
Great Change 12, 26, 60, 62, 70, 75, 77, 101, 105, 109–111, 119, 137, 146, 158, 162, 166–167, 194, 208, 213, 216, 234, 237, 253, 257, 260
Greater Hearts 11, 30, 40, 47, 58, 76, 80, 153, 158, 218, 220–225, 227–232, 234, 236–237, 240–241, 243, 245–246, 248, 250, 252–253, 258–261
   angels and 41
   family of 23–24, 26–28
Greater Hearts, bridge 11, 227
greed 10, 59, 61, 75, 95, 124, 131–132, 137, 149, 162, 173, 181, 188–189, 215, 220, 237
   & angelic flow 6, 8
   & choice 8, 78, 146, 159, 162, 233
   & civilisation 157
   & Earth 8, 75, 137–138, 178
   & involution 149, 157–158, 162
   & religion 145, 162
   & soul 157, 160, 224
   & spiritual journey 71, 137, 146
   driver of evil 144
   political 149
group soul 5, 207, 216, 222
   [description] 172
   for humanity 207
guidance from heart 133, 159, 222, 236, 250
guides 34, 80, 169, 201, 260
   angelic 42, 59, 75–76, 216, 245, 248
   Greater Hearts 48, 197, 220, 229, 247–248, 258–259
   healing 164
   inner 86–87, 151, 224
guilt 99
   & forgiveness 4
   & justice 147, 149–150
   collective 121

H

healing 34, 93, 111, 123, 127, 151, 164, 192
& angels 38
& Greater Hearts 29, 219
& karma 20
& soul 152, 154
Earth 171, 190, 193–194
spiritual awakening 190
heart centre 177
heart chakra (not heart centre) 177
heart consciousness 36–37, 64, 121, 149, 171, 177, 180, 183, 218
   & conscience 180
   & flow 171, 179, 252
   & soul 184
   difference to mind and feelings 252
   of Earth 163, 223, 255
   school of 225
   to awaken 62, 65–66, 88, 184, 253
heart energy 114–115
heart flow 66, 119, 178, 230, 240
   cosmic 216, 237, 248, 256
   of Earth 63, 247
   of soul 236
   with Earth 230
heart resonance 64, 115, 133
human angel 107
human choice 64, 75–76, 97, 114, 135, 212
   & flow 221, 256
   & karma 215
   & soul 84, 158, 216
human consciousness 8, 23, 28, 33, 40–41, 50–51, 56, 70, 73, 82, 84, 94, 98, 104, 125, 135, 174, 192
   & angels 6
   & change 133, 164
   & Earth 63, 174, 215
   & flow 190, 254
   & Greater Hearts 233
   & matter 21, 109
   & mind 58
   & Ocean of Love 76
   & soul 26, 34, 68, 84, 162, 205, 211–212, 214–215, 226
   & the past 225
   & young souls 76
   bypassing 85

Index

evolution 137
Jesus & Gautama 190, 231
human consciousness, development of 25, 191, 205
human world 127, 129, 184, 259
  & Earth 176
  & evil 221, 226
  & flow 13, 78, 124, 253
  & Greater Hearts 241, 253
  & light 26
  & love 188
  & soul 57, 152, 162, 206, 216, 219, 222
  strong leaders 63

I

illumination 4, 43, 52, 58, 74, 100, 123, 139, 142, 153, 161
  Buddha light of 190
  of astral matter 113
  of matter 108
incarnation
  & moon 190
  Cosmic Heart 174
  Cosmic Love 208
  great teachers 11, 191
  Greater Hearts 197, 234, 246
  greater souls 156
  heart 177
  Jesus, Gautama 190-191
  Law of Attraction 155
  love-will 122
  pull of matter 124
  soul 26, 94-95, 130, 138-139, 153-154, 156, 160, 165-166, 171, 195-196, 198, 206, 258
  spiritual intent 100
  upon Earth 1, 28, 30, 34, 39, 53, 121, 125, 131, 141, 161, 173, 178, 197
indigenous people, culture & Earth 36, 38, 136, 169, 256
intuition 30, 44, 46, 69-70, 85, 87, 89, 91, 101, 125, 127-128, 180, 182-183, 185, 206
  heart intuition 85, 88
  language of 89, 92
involution 130-133, 143, 145, 149, 155-158, 161-162, 186

Involution to Evolution 154

J

Jesus 54, 153, 165-166, 190, 231-232, 242
Jesus Maitreya 190-192
justice 147-148, 189
  & guilt 150
  of soul 149
  true 148-149

K

karma 5, 20, 41, 57, 61, 80, 82, 84, 90-91, 95, 119-120, 132, 135, 141, 143, 147, 149-150, 164-165, 194, 197, 199, 215, 217, 228
  Board of 148, 199
  cosmic 194
  family 200
  grace of 93, 117, 143
  guidance of 20, 84, 95, 120, 161
  Law of 20, 135, 148, 153, 156-157, 161, 167, 173, 215
  of Earth 220, 233
karma release 4, 122-123
knowledge
  & evil 105
knowledge, crystalline structure 102
Kumara 108, 140, 157, 159, 244-245, 247-248, 250, 255, 260
  first, of Earth 110
  Last Kumara 107, 110, 232
  Sanat Kumara 157

L

language of the heart 85
law 147-149, 154, 160-161, 219
  and karma 199
  of Attraction 155, 159, 163, 175-176
  of Karma 20, 135, 148-149, 153, 156-157, 161, 167, 173, 215
  of life 194
  of soul 149
living light 8, 16-17, **49**, 50, 58, 93, 114, 152, 194
  [description] **49**
  of Cosmic Heart 75, 78, 122
  of Earth 51, 118, 122, 253

of heart 51, 71, 74, 122, 126
  walking in 73
Logos
  Planetary 227, 236
  Solar 227
love-will 122, 218, 227, 229
  & cosmic intent 217
  & spirit's intent 219
love, guide and teacher 20, 62, 76, 81, 97, 107, 177

M

Maitreya 153, 190–193, 231, 233, 246

meditation 115–116, 133, 137, 171, 182–183, 189, 229
  & service 230
  & soul 224
mental
  analysis 38, 56, 81
  awareness 38
  breakdown 77
  capacity of humanity 102, 170
  coherence 205
  colour 141
  consciousness 250, 255
  constructs 8, 72
  discernment 7, 56–57, 89, 101
  expression 197
  manipulation 126
  motivations 37
  obtuseness 30
  path of detachment 100
  resonance 151, 209
  rigidity 50, 94, 103
  structures 72, 128, 160
mental body 100–102, 143, 186, 201
  & knowledge 102–103
  crystalline 103, 105
  difference from mind 100, 102
mind
  & change 79
  & choice 108, 254
  & consciousness 109, 183, 252–253
  & conspiracy 146
  & discernment 7
  & doubt 55
  & Earth 129, 131, 171

& Earth care 119, 188
& emotion 99, 102, 104, 115, 123, 157, 181, 201, 205
& flow 14, 188, 254
& heart 100
& intuition 87, 182
& law 148
& love 188
& mental body 177
& path 72, 100
& soul 58, 69, 161, 199–200, 203, 206, 215
& wisdom 101
alignment 68
builder 23
certainty 224, 237
crystalline 103
development 37, 169
difference from mental body 100, 102
element 200–201
illumined 115
knowledge 104
relationship with Earth 38, 169
without conscience 37, 105, 178, 181

moon 190, 192
  full moon 189, 191–194

Mother Earth 16, 38, 45, 53, 120, 141, 161, 174, 216, 222, 229, 238

motivation 48, 84, 130–131
  & spiritual path 72
  from flow 200
  from heart 131
  higher 82
  self-interested 37

O

Ocean of Love 9–11, 75–77, 118, 130, 136, 139–141, 155–156, 172–173, 185–186, 189–192, 195–196, 203, 209, 214, 217, 219–220, 226, 236, 252, 255, 258
  & soul 58, 135, 148, 185, 194
  vibration of 57, 163
  within 2, 22, 26, 63, 122, 218–219, 235

Index

P

path of heart 38, 45, 70, 72-74, 99-100, 175
personal consciousness 71, 89, 129
 & emotion 200-201, 205
 & soul 202
 of Buddha & Bodhisattva 231
Planetary Logos 227, 236
plants 59, 75, 116, 122, 168, 172, 251
 & angels 5, 33, 122, 170
 evolution 58
 intelligence 59
 soul development 5
prayer 17, 116, 133, 182, 189
purification 113, 117, 182, 187
 & Earth 140, 220, 257
 choice 143
 greed 157
 mind, emotion 45, 104, 256
purpose 85, 130, 202, 204, 206, 208, 212-214, 219, 238, 242, 249, 258, 260
 & Cosmic Heart 1, 207
 & soul 2, 152, 159, 163, 173, 175, 184, 206, 211, 214-216, 258
 & Wesak 193
 human 170-171, 173, 184, 209, 212, 215-216, 243, 248
 of Earth 174
 of Last Kumara 110
 of plants 170
 on Earth 39
 will & love 1, 218

R

relationships
 & flow 35-36, 194, 256
 & Greater Hearts 248, 252
 & karma 20, 80, 120
 & love 1, 120, 163, 170
 & soul 166, 171
 between mind & emotion 181
 between nature & angels 33, 75
 harmonic 29, 238
 human 161, 176
 in minerals 59
 of indigenous people with Earth 36
 of trees & Earth 35
 residual vibration 86
 with animals 60
 with Earth **36**, 38, 59, 95, 119, 121-122, 170-171, 173, 176, 184, 229, 238
 with inner guides 87
 with nature 169, 171-172, 176
religion 23-25, 68, 73, 160-161, 174, 177, 180, 184, 188, 219, 235
 & intolerance 43
 & separatism 162
ring-pass-not
 [description] 194, 231
 & Buddha 231-232
 & cosmic inflow 233
 of Earth 5, 156, 194, 232, 254

S

school of Earth 203, 224, 230
 & heart consciousness 225
seed atom 140-142, 186, 204, 215, 247
seed of evolutionary intent 162
seed of soul 140, 187, 204
self-awareness 68, 114, 137, 151
service 43, 137, 159, 161, 189, 208-210, 212, 216, 226
 to Earth 160, 198, 216, 230, 242
 your 126, 242, 247
Sirius 5, 9-10, 16, 155, 223, 244
Solar 8, 24, 43, 46, 208
 being & Earth 1, 5, 16, 47
 deity 19
 heart 2, 122, 179, 227, 244
 intent 80, 118
 will & love 118
Solar Logos 227
Solar system 10-11, 19, 227
soul
 [description] 5, 138
 & choice 58, 121
 & conscience 69, 254
 & cosmic intent 47, 203
 & Earth 4, 63, 136, 155, 174, 191, 197, 214, 217, 220, 229
 & emotion 79, 99, 187
 & evolution 7, 26, 107
 & full moon 191

& Greater Hearts 26, 219, 221–224, 226–227, 229, 241, 245, 248, 250, 258
& heart 31, 65, 67, 70–71, 73, 88, 117, 136, 160, 167, 184, 199, 202–203, 224–225, 229, 260
& justice 148
& karma 80, 120, 148
& Last Kumara 108
& mind 58, 69, 199
& nature 167, 171–172
& Ocean of Love 1, 63, 118, 122, 135, 139, 191, 194–196, 217–218, 235–236, 258
& true consciousness 68
& Venus family 109
& will 227
& world of causes 107
human & angel streams 5
song of 30–31
spark of 235

soul bridge 3, 175, 195

soul certainty 57

soul choice 84, 94–95, 153, 222

soul colours 141

soul consciousness 63, 85, 151, 153, 195, **199**, 202, 206, 210, 213–215
& emotions 69
& plants 170
flow of 156, 199, 202
of Earth 236

soul flow 190, 201, 203, 220–221, 236–237, 240, 255
to Earth 171
to Earth through trees 170

soul group 5, 34, 170, 172, 207, 216, 222

soul guidance 83, 85, 89, 202–204, 215, 229, 260

soul incarnation 23, 139, 149, 151, 153–154, 158, 172, 174, 196

soul intent 45, 119, 130, 160, 169, 177, 198, 202, 204, 206, 211–212, 215, 229, 255, 258

soul journey 2–3, 194, 225, 230

soul justice 149–150

soul life 159

soul love 39, 52, 70, 152, 158, 163, 167

soul mates & relationships 20, 171

soul note 46, 173, 211

soul of angels 5

soul of Earth 18, 75

soul of humanity 63

soul of Solar system 19

soul purpose 175, 214

soul resonance 67–68, 99, 152, 164, 167, 174, 192, 198, 203, 205–206, 211, 215, 219

soul responsibility 120, 137

soul stimulus 32, 34, 80, 186–187

soul teacher 179

soul training 195–196

soul travel 194

soul wisdom 54, 226

soul, Earth's intent 118

soul, new 140, 163, 227. See Also soul, young

soul, older 2, 144

soul, resonate with 154, 159, 166, 173–174, 206, 248

soul, role of angels 40

soul, search for 174

soul, spirit & matter 163, 166

soul, young 2, 26, 63, 76, 109, 144, 155, 160, 191, 197, 216. See Also soul, new

souls, great/greater 108, 135, 153, 156, 192, 197
& full moon 193–194

spark
of cosmic intent 19, 173, 203, 247
of Earth heart 18, 244
of joy 49
of life 88, 139
of love 64
of soul 170, 186, 235
of spirit 140, 172, 195–196, 199, 204, 209
via Kumaras 244

spirit 135, 145, 160

Index

& choice 25
& consciousness 173, 210
& cosmic intent 19, 140, 172, 210
& Cosmic Love 217
& cosmic matter 9
& gravity 175
& Great Change 216
& heart 199
& matter 244
& soul 138, 140–141, 163, 166, 175, 195–196, 203–204, 206, 210–211
contact 127
flame 138
flow 36, 220
intent 62, 138, 140, 163, 195, 213–214, 216, 218–219, 221, 228, 245, 255
love 45, 217, 244, 257, 259
of Earth 18, 218, 220, 244
spirits, mischievous 177
spiritual
  by-passing 161
  dogma 123
  glamours 98
  growth 151, 233
  healing 164
  journeys 137
  life 162
  maturity 81
  path 48, 63, 71, 74, 85, 100, 123–124, 183, 217, 246
  practice 31, 73, 84, 93, 97, 161, 177, 182, 235
  realisations 127
  teacher 165, 191
  traditions 184, 246
  training & development 47, 123, 242, 246
  vitality 178, 258
  will 219, 227
spiritual flow 179, 190, 252
  & angels 33
spiritual intent 100
  of soul 45
Sun 194
  colour vibrations 230, 233, 247
  evolution of heart 5
  pure love 55
  Solar spirit 244
  vitality 168

T

trees 10, 35, 59, 117, 121, 170
  & angels 35
  & Earth 170, 251
  hug 172
  presence of 34–35
  vitality 168

V

Venus 5, 16, 109, 158

W

way of the heart 126. *See Also* path of heart
Wesak 193
wisdom *104*, 183

www.ingramcontent.com/pod-product-compliance
Lightning Source LLC
Chambersburg PA
CBHW071857290426
44110CB00013B/1180